D1871112

Sex Trafficking in South Asia with a Special Focus on India

Sex Trafficking in South Asia with a Special Focus on India

Rekha Pande

KALPAZ

©Author

All rights reserved. No part of this work may be reproduced, stored, adapted, or transmitted in any form or by any means, electronic, mechanical, photocopying, micro-filming recording or otherwise, or translated in any language, without the prior written permission of the copyright owner and the publisher. The book is sold subject to the condition that it shall not, by way of trade or otherwise, be lent, resold, hired out, or otherwise circulated without the prior publisher's written consent in any form of binding or cover other than that in which it is published.

The views and opinions expressed in this book are author(s) own and the facts reported by them have been verified to the extent possible, and the publishers are not in any way liable for the same.

ISBN: 978-93-5128-215-0

Price: ₹ 900

First Published, 2016

Published by

Kalpaz Publications
C-30, Satyawati Nagar,
Delhi – 110052
E-mail: kalpaz@hotmail.com
Ph.: 9212142040

Printed at: G. Print Process, Delhi

Cataloging in Publication Data—DK
Courtesy: D.K. Agencies (P) Ltd. <docinfo@dkagencies.com>

Pande, Rekha, 1955- **author.**
Sex trafficking of women and girls in South Asia with a special focus on India / Rekha Pande.
pages cm
Includes bibliographical references.
ISBN 9789351282150

1. Human trafficking—South Asia. 2. Human trafficking—India. 3. Human trafficking—Law and legislation—South Asia. 4. Human trafficking—Law and legislation—India. 5. Women—Crimes against—South Asia. 6. Women—Crimes against—India. 7. Girls—Crimes against—South Asia. 8. Girls—Crimes against—India. I. Title.

HQ281.P36 2016 DDC 306.3620954 23

Contents

Foreword

Swamy Vivekananda's Quote: "All power is within you, you can do anything and everything" is apt in our fight against trafficking of persons across the world. In India, we have the best of legal mandates with new sections of law like Section 370, 370A IPC, Protection of Children from Sexual Offences Act, 2012, Juvenile Justice (Care & Protection) Act, 2015 and the Criminal Law (Amendment) Act, 2013 (called Nirbhaya Act as the enactment was made after a nation-wide public out-cry for safety of women).

The author Dr Rekha Pande who has been associated with the Centre for Women's Studies, at the University of Hyderabad, has given a wide angle view of the entire trafficking problem in India and institutional response on trafficking. Having worked as Anti-Human Trafficking Nodal Officer for the combined state of AP from 2005 to 2011 and having had the opportunity of bringing all the stakeholders like law enforcement agencies, Prosecutor Dept., Nodal Non-Govt. Organisations, Women & Child Dept., Sarva Siksha Abhyan together we understood the missing links, commitment quotient, pursuing behaviour and finally the political 'will' to fight. In AP and Telangana States several institutionalised processes have been put in place like–

(i) Role of District officials specially, the District Magistrate, the District Supdt of Police, the Project Director of Women & Child Welfare Officer and others have been defined.

(ii) The concept of rescue, raid, rehabilitation and reintegration have been streamlined.

(iii) The designation of Anti-Human trafficking Nodal Police officers in each District/Commissionerate have been ensured.

(iv) The Creation of Victim Support Fund u/s 357 A Cr.PC through a Govt. Order.

(v) Establishing Anti-Human Trafficking Units (AHTUs) in some target districts.

(vi) Designating Senior Officers of and above the rank of Dy. Supdt of Police in the Districts/Commissionerates as Special Juvenile Police Unit Officers.

(vii) Designating Addl. Dist. and Sessions Judge Court as Special Court in Protection of Children from Sexual Offences Act, 2012.

(viii) Designating Addl. Public Prosecutors as Special PPs to present cases before the Spl. Court under POCSO Act, 2012.

(ix) The investigation friendly measures of audio-video trial (u/s 275 Cr.PC).

(x) Taking down witnesses statement in Courts in the same language as spoken. (Sec 277 Cr.PC)

(xi) Completion of rape cases trial by trial court within two months from the date of filing change sheet (u/s 309 Cr.PC) regarding speedy trial.

(xii) In-camera trial in rape cases (u/s 327 Cr.PC) and for offences under POCSO Act, 2012 (Sec 37).

(xiii) Victim's right to engage her own legal counsel to argue his/her case under POCSO Act.

(xiv) Victims right to prefer appeal in higher courts (u/s 372 Cr.PC) than leaving it to the Police/prosecution Dept.

(xv) Audio-video recording of statements of victims u/s 161 (3) Cr.PC and by the Court u/s 164 Cr.PC and several other legal amendments have been made since 2006 onwards.

With plethora of investigation-friendly amendments in the procedural law of our country, all that what we need is to take up a massive 'capacity-building programmes' for both the Police and prosecuting officers who are the key stake-holders in setting law into motion in Criminal Justice System and bringing the offenders to Justice.

We must have sufficient 'budget allocation' for victim-witness support fund on lines of UK/Germany to enable victims/ witnesses come forward to give evidence without fear of consequence. Unfortunately budget for victim-witness support is not created and if special allocation is made by some States it does not commensurate with the quantum of offences, number of victims/witnesses, NGO support mechanism and 'will' to come and depose evidence in courts.

Finally, Professor Rekha Pande's work deserves encomiums as she has dealt with all aspects of this multi-dimensional problem which can only be tackled by various stake-holders joining hands together. The recent judgement of the Supreme Court of India in Prajwala Vs U.o.I, has ordered State Govts. to create a separate investigating wing called "Organised Crime Investigating Agency" (OCIA). Proper and sensitive personnel, coupled with budget, requisite 'Political Will' alone can mitigate the problem. More conviction of traffickers will result in less induction. A massive drive to ensure that the traffickers are punished in a short time would alone create 'fear' in the minds of traffickers. Prolonged justice delivery system enables traffickers going out on bail and never apprehended again as they have pan-India network while Police is unable to go out of State quite often due to variety of reasons.

In wish that ever law enforcement officer and prosecution should read the book of Professor Rekha Pande, to gain more insight and arrive at possible remedies. Networking with various departments is the key success. No ego please. No Superior. Subordinate complex please only compassion and empathy should be the driving force. The book may be kept in all libraries, more particularly with Police/Prosecutor/Judiciary training institutes across the country.

"**Be a partner in Anti-Human Trafficking drive**".

S. Umpathi
IPS (Retd)
IGP, I/c APPM Revision Cell,
DGP Office, AP.

Acknowledgements

It was my research on Devadasis that made me interested in looking at the issue of trafficking. The institution of Devadasis was an important institution that continued to play a very important role in the religious and cultural life of India, especially the Deccan from the medieval times to the present times. Devadasi was a woman who was dedicated and attached to a temple. They were unmarried temple servants who had been dedicated to temple deities when young through the rites which resembled 'Hindu' marriage ceremonies. The married temple girls were eternally free from the so called inauspicious widowhood. All these girls were regarded as "*Nityasumangali*" – the ever auspicious women — because these women were married to the immortal God, there was no chance of their ever becoming a widow and being deprived of their marital status and the toe ring, which was a symbol of this status. These were very rich women with a lot of wealth in medieval times but with the loss of patronage to the temples with the coming of Colonialism, many of these girls found an easy entry into sex work. We came across hundreds of these women who worked as Jogins when we were out on field work during a project on the Girl child, in Varni during the 1990's. These were very beautiful women and I had interacted with a large number of them during my lengthy stay at Varni. These women always stayed with me as I started looking into the various dimensions of prostitution and trafficking and I need to first and foremost thanks them.

Any work of this kind is not possible without the support and ideas from different quarters. I owe a lot to many of my students in Women's studied especially Barnali Das, Pooja Chetri and Sarmishta Sahoo who are looking at the issue of trafficking in different regions of India and a lot of debates and experience sharing of the field work with them at various points of time has enriched me. I would also like to thank Ajailiu Niumai for her support and Mayuri Chaturvedi, who has assisted in data collection for this Project. I would also acknowledge the financial help received from UGC in carrying out this Project. There are many individuals and institutions who need to be acknowledged regarding this project. Many of my friends are responsible for making this book a reality. I gratefully acknowledge the help received from Mr S. Umapati. Inspector General of Police (Crime Branch-Andhra Pradesh) who has always been a great help. When I was working as the Director of the Centre for Women's Studies in Maulana Azad National Urdu University we had a series of meetings and formed an Anti-trafficking Network and I have benefited a lot through his insights into the issue. I acknowledge many of my friends working in the NGO sector, especially, Jameela, Mahajabeen, Padma, Prashanti and Mumtaz Fatima. This book could not have reached its final stage without their encouragement.

I would like to acknowledge and extend my heartfelt gratitude to my husband Dr Suresh Pande who has always been a great support for all my academic endeavours. He has also read pages of the manuscript to provide an insight. My elder son, Sankalp, and my twins Tarun and Varun have always been my major pillars of emotional strength and support. Words alone cannot express what I owe them for their warmth and love and providing all the technical support from long distance.

Preface

Trafficking in women is a reflection of the complex social issues facing the global society today. Trafficking in persons is a serious crime and a grave violation of human rights. Every year, thousands of men, women and children fall into the hands of traffickers, in their own countries and abroad. Almost every country in the world is affected by trafficking, whether as a country of origin, transit or destination for victims. Trafficking of humans is done for various reasons. They are trafficked for labour, organ trade, begging and commercial sexual exploitation. A major issue facing our society today is the trafficking of women and girls for sex work. Sex Trafficking, the use of women in prostitution and trafficking networks is becoming a major focus of international organised crime. Today more than a million citizens are at an increased risk of further violence, as well as unwanted pregnancy, sexually transmitted infections like HIV/AIDS due to trafficking.

When examining the problem of trafficking from a gender-perspective, we note a similar pattern of prominence of the underprivileged and marginalised gender (women) as major victims of trafficking. Women and young children, particularly young girls are the most vulnerable targets of and often at the receiving end of such atrocities. Subsequently, the magnitude and impact of trafficking is manifold in case of women and young girls. Various academic and media studies point to the invariable link between prostitution and trafficking. In general, trafficking is often linked with sexual exploitation of the victims. Prostitution as a profession and as an agency is mostly linked with the demand and supply chain of trafficking for sexual purposes, which is commercial sex work. Till date, the terms trafficking and prostitution are interchangeably used to describe the plight of the victims. Often, the victims of trafficking are employed in commercial sex work. In other words, a significant number of commercial sex workers are sourced through the process of trafficking.

Trafficking is a multi-dimensional problem encompassing a whole range of economic, social and cultural issues which are varied and highly complex. Most of the victims are trafficked with the promise of better jobs, better career prospects and marriage. Some are inducted forcibly through abduction. Putting together the poor socio-economic indicators, poverty levels and the subjugation of women in the forms of derogatory traditional practices of bonded labour, Devadasi, and prostitution establishes links with frequency and magnitude of women trafficking in different regions.

The liberalisation of the economy in the wake of globalisation in the third world has vastly diminished traditional means of livelihood for the poor. Poverty and deprivation, secondary status accorded to women in society, prejudice against the girl child, weakening of the family structure, changing public attitude towards sex and morality, the caste structure, urbanisation, migration and the growing consumerism are some of the factors that have contributed to trafficking. Most of the women trafficked come from drought prone areas or from agricultural background and their farm lands have not been able to sustain the livelihood of their families. The conversion of large tracts of agricultural land for commercial aqua production, the diminishing viability of traditional livelihood skills, lack of education and skills for alternative means of income all reduce such victims to a situation of no other option but to enter into the sex trade.

Women trafficking increased in South Asia after the 1990's. This period witnessed new structural changes in many of these countries with rapid acceptance of free market economy and the government loosened its restrictions. Countries opened markets for free economy and the government withdrew from developmental functions for the poor and rural areas. This increased the number of people below poverty line. Human smuggling and trafficking is a thriving activity for organised criminal groups, and it is gradually replacing the illicit drug trade as the largest illegal business in the world. It is already the most lucrative illicit business after the smuggling of narcotics and arms. Human smugglers and traffickers make high profits with low capital investment and face a low risk of detection and if caught and tried, encounter relatively short prison sentences in comparison with drug traffickers. A majority of these illegal immigrants are women who often end up in the sex industry and fall into the hands of traffickers.

A close examination of the source-transit-destination patterns in different Indian states reveals that poverty and illiteracy are the biggest markers of the source points. On the other hand, the destinations pointed are marked with high migrant population, industrial and commercial infrastructure and transport hubs. For example, states of Telangana, Andhra Pradesh, Assam and Odisha serve as source places whereas states of Delhi, Kolkata and Goa are the major destination points within India. The present book examines this issue from a gender perspective and analyses three agents in this issue namely, the victims, the police, the Non-Government Organisations (NGO's) and Community Based Organisations (CBO's) involved.

Chapter 1

Introduction

Trafficking in women for sex work is a reflection of the complex social issues facing the global society today. However, this is part of the larger issue of trafficking in persons, which is a serious crime and a grave violation of human rights. Every year, thousands of men, women and children fall into the hands of traffickers, in their own countries and abroad. Almost every country in the world is affected by trafficking, whether as a country of origin, transit or destination for victims. Human trafficking poses serious threats to human life and dignity all over the world. Particularly speaking of a globalised world, the shameful act of human trafficking not only points to the loopholes in the existing socio-legal measures that claim to attain an equal and dignified life to all individuals, but it also questions the continuous practice of mal-treating human beings who are trapped easily because of their ignorance and poverty and are trafficked for different purposes such as sexual exploitation, slavery, bonded and forced labour in domestic as well as commercial fronts.

In geographic terms, trafficking emerges as a global issue since it is not confined to a particular country, region or community, but it is widespread all over the globe. However, the magnitude and consequences of human trafficking are far more evident in developing nations and underprivileged communities. It has been pointed out that despite the fact that all human beings are born free and equal in human dignity, every day thousands of women and children are sold so that their bodies and their labour can be exploited. Despite international labour standards and a UN Protocol against human trafficking, millions of victims, particularly children - made vulnerable by poverty and exploited by criminals - are working in mines, sweatshops, brothels and plantations - trapped by debt and violence. In a perverse commercialisation of humanity, they are used like products and then thrown away (Kofi Annan, 2007). Trafficking is globally seen as an atrocity against human-kind as a whole and denial of basic human rights to life, independence and dignity. According to international data, human trafficking is reported to be the third largest international crime, following illegal drugs and arms trafficking. It is estimated to generate an annual global profit of 31.6 billion US Dollars, mainly employed in criminal operations and illegal circuits worldwide (Basler, Patrick, 2005).

The trafficking of women and children for sexual exploitation, which has emerged as a new security threat, is one of the most gross and outrageous violations of human rights in the world today and is unacceptable (Pande, 2014, 277). Human trafficking can affect the security of a country through either its citizens being taken and sold into this modern form of slavery, or people being brought into a country as low or underpaid workers, against their will and then sold into sexual slavery. It is thus a human security, and a national security, issue. Today, the need to widen the concept of security and distinguish between "hard" and "soft" security threats has been increasingly accepted. Yet the separation between hard (traditional) and soft (non-traditional) security threats has been almost total, and in many ways artificial. It has been a positive trend to elevate the so-called new security threats, but there has been a failure to understand in what way old and new security threats overlap and in fact reinforce each other. Traditional approaches to preventing trafficking, to protect and assist trafficked persons and bring criminals to justice have had only limited impact. This issue threatens the very fabric of societies through crime and disease. It exacerbates corruption in already weak states, impairing their economic and political functioning and prevents the states in the region from developing in a positive direction. In fact, there is a close association between trafficking, globalisation, migration and security and we have to recognise trafficking as an organised crime and a violation of human rights and of women's rights in particular that compromises the security of individuals (Pande, Rekha, 2014, 277-278).

When examining the problem of trafficking from a gender-perspective, we note a similar pattern of prominence of the underprivileged and marginalised gender (women) as major victims of trafficking. Women and young children, particularly young girls are the most vulnerable targets of and often at the receiving end of such atrocities. Subsequently, the magnitude and impact of trafficking is manifold in case of women and young girls. Globally, the reports show that children and women, especially young girls, constantly fall victim to human trafficking and continuously abused for sexual and economic exploitation. It is believed that every year, nearly 600,000 to 800,000 people are trafficked for the purpose of sexual and industrial exploitation and of these approximately 80 per cent are women and girls and upto 50 per cent are minors. The data also illustrate that the majority of transnational victims are trafficked into commercial sexual exploitation (Report, Trafficking in Persons, 2005). A considerable population of these people is from developing countries, particularly in South and South-East Asia, including India and Indian sub-continent (Samarasinghe and Burton, 2007, 52). According to a report of the International Labour Organisation (ILO), nearly 56 per cent of trafficked persons are in Asia and Pacific regions. (International Organisation of Migration, 2007)

Background of Trafficking

Human trafficking is a complex phenomenon owing to the variation in its causes and impacts and it can only be examined and addressed with a multi-dimensional approach. To begin with, the roots and historic origin of trafficking may be traced in the old-age practices of prostitution and servitude, including forced/ bonder labour and many of these are found in India also.

The most common term in ancient Indian texts for servitude is Dasatava and for the slaves it is Dasa. Manu has given seven categories of Dasa (salves) in Indian social system. They are– (i) dasa who are captured in war, (ii) those enslaved in return for food, (iii) those born (as next generations) in the house of the master (who is the master of the parents of dasas), (iv) those who are bought, (v) those who are inherited as a part of patrimony, (vi) those who are given away by their parents, and (vii) those who are enslaved for not paying a fine or an execution of a judicial decree (Chakravrthy, 1985, 38) Kautilya's Arthshastra also provides nine different types of dasas, who are: (i) those who are captured in a war, (ii) dasas born in the house of the master, (iii) those reduced to the status of dasas for food, (iv) those who were purchased, (v) dasas who were received as gifts, (vi) dasas who were inherited, (vii) those who were reduced to the status of dasas by a judicial decree, (viii) dasas who were mortgaged, and (ix) those who sold themselves as dasas (Chakravarti, 1985, 39).

Uma Chakravarti argues that both in classifications of Manu and Kautilya, the dasas who are enslaved in return of food indicates poor socio-economic condition and lack of adequate means with those who were forced to employ themselves to servitude in lieu of daily food. This situation can be analysed in terms of modern day global poverty and food-deprivation. The facts that (a) many men, women and children are deceived into trafficking on the basis of false promises of a good earning and a better life, and (b) that a majority of the victims of trafficking are from poor sections, only reinforce the old-age tricks of deceiving poor and underprivileged persons and further trapping them into modern-day enslavement through trafficking. Similarly, Manu and Kautilya's category of dasas who were bought/ purchased can also be roughly translated in the modern day methods of trafficking, particularly in the situations where the victims are bought for a lump-sum amount from their own parents or other acquaintances and they are further sold and re-sold through different traffickers. The fact that many victims of trafficking continue to survive on mere food, clothing and inadequate economic gains reflect their status as modern day dasas.

In India, the ancient references of dasas, in case of women, the equivalent term was dasi and they were procured in mostly the same manner as in the case of male dasa. These dasis were largely employed in domestic services, as agricultural labourers and also for sexual pleasure of their masters (Chakravarti, 1985, 58). Sexual exploitation was particularly evident in case of young dasis, whereas the older ones were put to serve in domestic households. On the other hand, young virgin girls were considered to be an honourable "gift" from one king to another, or from a king to his priest (Chakravarti, 1985, 57). This pattern of employing dasis to sexual as well as economic purposes in ancient societies draws similarities with modern patterns of same kinds of sexual and economic use and abuse of women victims of trafficking. Another practice for exploitation of women, which we see in the past is the Devadasi system. They were employed in the temples as dancers, singers, musicians and for offering certain services to the deities. Often they were not allowed to marry a mortal man. Some of them were responsible for the smooth functioning of the temple administration (Pande, 2004, 25). This was a brutal form of enslavement of young girls who were given to the service of God much before they attained puberty, and later were subject to sexual exploitation. In most of the cases, the consent of these young girls was insignificant. The women thus gifted were employed to the domestic chores at the king's palace and/or the temples and were subject to sexual as well as economic exploitation. The kings, noblemen, vassals and generals donated these girls to the temples and we have a large number of inscriptions proving these details (Pande, Rekha,1, 2006, 496). In the context of trafficking, the practice of Devadasi underlines the trends of sexual- commodification of women, their marginalisation, and their constant exploitation. Some recent studies also show the link between the practice Devadasi and trafficking of women. According to one such study of Anti-slavery International, the young Devadasi are easy victims of trafficking because of their pre-established sexual openness and lack of familial ties whereas the older Devadasi may end up serving as perpetrators of trafficking (Maggie Black, 2007). Given the fact that that practice of Devadasi is more evident in the Indian states of Maharashtra, Andhra Pradesh and Karnataka, and mostly in under-developed pro-poverty regions, the links to trafficking are more likely to occur. Most of the girls who enter as Devadasi end up in prostitution. This became very clear to us when we interacted with the Jogins (a folk variation of the devdasis) from Andhra Pradesh, during our work in a Project and had stayed at Samskar a Non Government Organisation founded by Mrs. Hemlata and Mr Lavanam Gora who through Challi Nilayam were working for the emancipation and rehabilitation of the Jogins and their children (Pande, Rekha, 2008, 101).

The practices of women slavery and Devadasi draw our attention to prostitution which is yet another form of exploitation of women. Various academic and media studies point to the invariable link between prostitution and trafficking. In general, trafficking is often linked with sexual exploitation of the victims. Prostitution as a profession and as an agency is mostly linked with the demand and supply chain of the trafficking for sexual purposes, which is commercial sex work. Till date, the terms trafficking and prostitution are interchangeably used to describe the plight of the victims. Often, the victims of trafficking are employed in commercial sex work. In other words, a significant number of commercial sex workers are sourced through the process of trafficking. Over three-fourth of brothel-owners all over the country (India) admitted to have "direct dealings with traffickers." (Sen and Nair, 2005, 105). These dealings include sale, purchase, hire and transfer of girls for the purpose of commercial sex work. The frequency of such "dealings" between brothel-owners and traffickers ranged from one to five times in a month, which indicates a high incidence of trafficking of women for sexual exploitation. Moreover, the data shows that the maximum number of victims were trafficked (sourced) from Andhra Pradesh (18.9 per cent), followed by neighbouring states of Karnataka (10.2 per cent) and Tamil Nadu (8.7 per cent) (Sen and Nair, 2005, 106).

Trafficking is a multi-dimensional problem encompassing a whole range of economic, social and cultural issues which are varied and highly complex. Most of the victims are trafficked with the promise of better jobs, better career prospects and marriage. Some are inducted forcibly through abduction. Poverty and deprivation, secondary status accorded to women in society, prejudice against the girl child, weakening of the family structure, changing public attitude towards sex and morality, the caste structure, urbanisation, migration and the growing consumerism are some of the factors that have contributed to trafficking. (Pande, Rekha, 2006, 35). Putting together the poor socio-economic indicators, poverty levels and the subjugation of women in the forms of derogatory practices of bonded labour, Devadasi, and prostitution establishes links with frequency and magnitude of women trafficking in different regions.

Definition of Trafficking

Historically, the term, 'traffic' was used to refer to "movement of persons for immoral purposes and prostitution. (George *et.al.*, 2010, 65). Traditional meaning of the term 'trafficking' referred to kidnapping and enslavement of workers- especially women and children for commercial sexual exploitation (CSE) (Huda, 2006: 375). It has been argued that until 1970 the term 'trafficking' was understood solely within the limits of prostitution and sexual exploitation. However, present literatures have broadened the definition of 'trafficking' by describing it as modern slavery, rape for profit, and other similar practices that includes forced labour of various kinds (George *et.al.*, 2010: 65). Sex trafficking is a practice that involves moving of person within local or national for exploitation in the sex market and it is a business venture, in which traffickers trade the sexualised bodies of others for money, i.e. the commodity is a person, objectified in its sale by one party to another. (Farr, 2005: 2). Trafficking in women is thus an illicit transport of women for sexual and economic exploitation, and other personal gains (Okonofua *et.al.*, 2004: 1315).

The act of trafficking refers to the mobilisation and displacement of persons from one place to another through deception or coercion, leading into their physical as well as economic exploitation. The United Nations Palermo Protocol defines Human Trafficking as: "Trafficking in persons" shall mean the recruitment, transportation, transfer, harbouring or receipt of persons by means of the threat or use of force or other forms of coercion, of abduction, of fraud, of deception, of the abuse of power or of a position of vulnerability or of the giving and receiving of payments or benefits to achieve the consent of a person having control over another person, for the purpose of exploitation. Exploitation shall include, at a minimum, the exploitation of the prostitution of others or other forms of sexual exploitation, forced labour or service, slavery or practices similar to slavery, servitude or the removal of organs (U.N. Palermo Protocol, 2000).

The consent of a victim of trafficking in persons to the intended exploitation set forth in sub-paragraph (a)...shall be irrelevant where any of the means set forth in the sub-paragraph (a) have been used; The recruitment, transportation, transfer, harbouring or receipt of a child for the purpose of the exploitation shall be considered "trafficking in persons," even if this does not involve any of the means set forth in the sub-paragraph (a) of this article; "Child" shall mean any person under 18 years of age. (U.N. Palermo Protocol, 2000, Article 3). Hence, this protocol gives the various ways and circumstances in which a person can be trafficked and this includes children who are less than 18 years of age.

Trafficking is thus the buying and selling or coercive capture of human beings for purpose of exploitation (especially commercial sexual work), forced labour or enslavement of any sort. It circumscribes 'the recruitment, transport, purchase, sale, transfer, harbouring, or receipt of persons: by threat, force, coercion, or deception, for commercial sexual exploitation or other allied slavery like practices '. Human trafficking therefore includes "...the lack of consent, brokering of human beings, transport, and the servile conditions of the work or the relationship with traffickers." (George *et.al.,* 2010: 65). Hence, it is described as a modern form of slavery where women are bought and sold for forced labour such as commercial sexual exploitation (CSE) and other similar slavery like practices. Some scholars argue that it is indeed the most lucrative business and earns revenue that exceeds 'drug trafficking'. (Kara, 2010), (Sen and Nair, 2005).

Women Trafficking under Globalisation

Scholars argue that trade in women and children for sexual exploitation took new dimensions with the global market (Farr, 2005, 139). The business of sex trade has become organised and more co-ordinate with the advent of globalisation of market economies which can be traced back to the period of fifteenth and sixteenth century (Sengupta, 2001, 3137). (This period laid a strong and effective underpinning to the criminal groups to take the business across the national and international borders). The root of emerging forces of globalisation is traced back to the end of cold war, dismantling of state socialism in the USSR and the collapse of Berlin Wall (Sengupta, 2001, 3137). In the last few years, globalisation had transformed the economic scenario of the world. It had altered the economic, political, societal, and cultural composition of the world, as it created greater interdependence amongst countries by increasing amount of cross-border trade in goods and services, international financial flows, and labour (Wang, 2005, 1). The easy movement of liquidity across countries led global GDP increase drastically, which consequently led to the upsurge of world development.

In fact, Globalisation, is presented as a great boon for all people. (Hawthrone, 2004, 245). Globalisation connotes the deepening relationship and penetration in the economy and development of an interconnected economic system. Globalisation encompasses many aspects including expanded international trade, telecommunications, monetary coordination, multinational corporations, technical and scientific cooperation, cultural exchanges of new types and scales, migration and refugee flows, and relations between the world's rich and poor countries. Globalisation has affected the third world in more than one way. Though defined in myriad ways, all definitions of globalisation share one of its chief characteristics i.e. the flow of global capital and its thrust towards the creation of a global economy. Today, it is the economic changes that are altering structures and cultures. Most of the economies of the developing world are now in the process of restructuring in the direction of free market and liberalisation with an overall aim at developing outward looking internationally competitive economies, with negative social consequences. The ideology and the guiding dialogues in the global world is the movement towards capitalism. (Pande, 2001, 1)

The free play of markets, liberalisation, privatisation and competition has become the key words in the path towards globalisation. The three pillars of neo liberalism i.e. Privatisation, liberalisation and restructuring have impact on the daily lives of women. Women have been pushed into free trade zones to work under exploitative conditions. Thousands of families have been displaced and forced to migrate in search of better livelihood. In this rapidly shifting paradigm, the state, instead of helping the poor, marginalised and socially disadvantaged people, has gradually withdrawn from essential sectors like healthcare, education, power and water (Pande, 2001, 1).

This is followed by the withdrawal of the state from more and more welfare oriented activities and south Asia is no exception. However, the response of different countries has varied substantially with reference to the length of adjustment period, intensity of adjustment and the component of the adjustment package. Since there was already a disparity existing in the world, the reduction in the social sectors undermined the quality of human resources thereby jeopardising the countries prospects for achieving sustained economic development in the future. Complementing the forces of global capital is technology, which has given a new meaning to the speedy exchange of information. Simultaneously, we see is a flow of ideas, culture, people and images across borders. This 'borderlessness' has an amazing grasp on our lives and notions. Chandra Mohanty speaks of feminism without borders, one that acknowledges the fault lines, conflicts, differences, fears, and containment that borders represent (Mohanty, 2003). Amongst the various issues such as growing fundamentalism, major gaps in the organised and unorganised sectors, the issue of trafficking, the exponential growth of the global sex trade is one of the major threats in the world today.

Women trafficking increased in South Asia after the 1990's. This period witnessed new structural changes in many of these countries with rapid acceptance of free market economy and the government loosened its restrictions. Countries opened markets for free economy and the government withdrew from developmental functions for the poor and rural areas. This increased the number of people below poverty line. Globalisation accompanied by population increase, urbanisation, international migration, colonisation and political change contribute importantly to the growth of prostitution and the trafficking in women and girls around the world (Gail and Stephanie, 2005, 119). Bars, dance clubs, massage parlors the pornographic industry, international hotel chains, brothels and tourist industry have all intensified the commodification process of women sexuality.

It has been pointed out that as long as countries in the region maintain their policies of restrictive immigration, trafficking can be expected to continue and almost certainly increase (Skeldon, 2000, 52). Human smuggling and trafficking is a thriving activity for organised criminal groups, and it is gradually replacing the illicit drug trade as the largest illegal business in the world. It is already the most lucrative illicit business after the smuggling of narcotics and arms. Human smugglers and traffickers make high profits with low capital investment and face a low risk of detection and, if caught and tried, encounter relatively short prison sentences in comparison with drug traffickers. A majority of these illegal immigrants are women who often end up in the sex industry and fall into the hands of traffickers. The growing presence of women in trafficking and related activities like sexual tourism have become a source of livelihood, profit making and the accrual of foreign currency for the economy of a country (Penttinen, 2008). These dynamics generate a shadow economy which includes informal, criminal services and the sale of women for sex. Globalisation hence reinforces the preexisting structure on a global scale through the commodification and selling of women sexuality (Ritzer, 2010).

Globalisation therefore brought a drastic revolution to the world economy, thus resulting in various constructive changes across the world. The debates of benefit from globalisation is immense- great wealth, increased freedom to buy, freedom to communicate across borders and a choice of foodstuffs from every part of the globe. Further, globalisation is breaking the traditional norms, opened new avenues for women. Because of which more and more women were seeking new economic and livelihood opportunities (Jana *et.al.,* 2002, 70). Similarly, globalisation heralds dependency on transnational companies, theft of indigenous knowledge and plant stocks, exploitation of women for the benefit of mobile men, further appropriation of cultural resources and flattening of culture through the domination of American cultural products, from McDonalds and South Park to Coca Cola and Microsoft. (Hawthrone, 2004, 245). Hence, globalisation creates neo-colonisation of developing countries by the more developed one.

Yet, there is another side to globalisation also and as evident from the discourse it has massive and devastating consequences. Poverty and inequality is increasing across the globe, i.e. 'richer are becoming richer, while poorer are becoming poorer'. The negative outcome of globalisation is exerting an adverse impact on the world subjecting poor people to a disadvantageous position. Critics argue that globalisation brought with it immense modernisation; however it placed rural population in a subverted position by limiting their livelihood choices. This led to their migration to urban centres, which thus rendered them to an awkward position since they knew little technical expertise to sustain and survive in an urban set up (George *et.al.,* 2010, 69 and Vindhya and Dev, 2011, 130). As long as the current economic globalisation process privileges movement of finance capital while restricting the movement of labour or human capital across national borders, trafficking of people continues. (Jana *et.al.,* 2002, 70).

Therefore, one can argue that globalisation has brought in many benefits but it also has another side to it. In countries like South Asia it has led to marginalisation and victimisation of rural people seeking to migrate for livelihood choices and more so in the case of women further laying down a fertile ground for traffickers to use their vulnerability for sexual exploitation. No doubt, globalisation expands the opportunities for unprecedented human advance for some but shrinks those opportunities for others and erodes human security. (Sengupta, 2001: 31-39).

Process of Human Trafficking

The process of human trafficking is a long chain with demand and supply at the beginning and end of the chain.

In between this long chain are a number of people who earn their commissions out of the woman being trafficked. These include, the spotter, recruiter, buyer, seller, harbourer, financier, brothel keeper, pimp and clientele. Trafficking is driven by a constant demand for women's and children's bodies (for commercial sex work), and which is constantly met with the supply of marginalised women who are denied equality and opportunity of education and gainful economic employment. Trafficking process is further perpetuated by traffickers who are able to "exploit human (women) misfortune with near impunity." (Phiney, 2001 as quoted in Sen and Nair, 2005, 9). Shelly, also supports this notion and argues that the process of human trafficking can be explained with a simple demand and supply model (Shelly, 2010, 37). According to Shelly, globalisation has accelerated rates and incidences of trafficking cases all over the world. She attributes this growth in trafficking to liberal economy, lesser government control and less state intervention and modern means of communications which have collectively diluted the security across borders and facilitated the illegal and criminal activities, including drugs, arms and human trafficking (Shelly, 2010, 42-43).

In Indian context, Sen and Nair (2005) also note similar patterns where globalisation has led to an openness of borders (interstates and with neighbouring countries such as Nepal) and means of communications and transport are made available at a cheaper cost, and increasing use of modern telecommunications such as internet and mobile phone are some of the factors attributing to the rise in cases of trafficking since 1980s (Sen and Nair, 2005).

To begin with, the process of human trafficking has both demand and supply sides- demand for criminal and illegal purposes and supply of poor, underprivileged persons. According to available data, over 80 per cent of the victims trafficked included women and young girls (Sen and Nair, 2005, 124). Of these, more than half of the victims were trafficked to brothels, for the purpose of commercial sex work (Sen and Nair, 2005, 124). A continuous demand for and a constant supply of victims keeps running the vivacious cycle of trafficking at any given time. The factors like poverty, underemployment, lack of awareness and vulnerability of women and girls ensure their constant capture and exploitation. The demand and supply parts of trafficking are linked through a certain route. A route of trafficking therefore is a step-by-step process as to how the victims are captured, held back, transported to a different location and finally put to various forms of uses and abuses. India is a major source, transit and destination point across the globe. Among Indian states, Andhra Pradesh is the largest source for trafficking, followed by Karnataka, Tamil Nadu, West Bengal, Odisha and Maharashtra. Sen and Nair cite poverty, unemployment and the low social status of women and their vulnerability as the main determinants of a source place. Moreover, a majority of source places are remote rural areas (48.1 per cent) as compared with exclusively urban areas (3.8 per cent) (Sen and Nair, 2005, 122).

In contrast with source areas, the demand areas included both rural and urban places, including metros as well as small townships. This indicates towards a universal demand for victims and further accelerates the process and magnitude of trafficking. Delhi and Maharashtra are main destinations. But the list of destination places is exhaustive, and it includes big cities as well as small towns all over the country, Alwar (Rajasthan), Mangalore (Karnataka), Gorakhpur and Benaras (Uttar Pradesh) to name a few. The route of trafficking may be internal (within national and state borders) as well as external/ international (across national borders). However, nearly 90 per cent of trafficking in India occurs within different states. On the other hand, nearly 10 per cent of trafficking occurs cross-borders. Bangkok, South Africa, and Dubai are some of the place were cross-border trafficking takes places from India. (Sen and Nair, 2005,122). The route of trafficking can be broadly divided in three distinct parts, namely source (or origin), transit (or transport) and destination. The source (origin) refers to the place where victims are identified and captured. The transit part refers to one or more places where the victims are held and/or transferred during the act of trafficking, prior to reaching their destination. The destination refers to the final place where victims are put to various forms of exploitation, mostly to sexual and economic exploitation. This is one-time source-transit-destination process at any given time. A victim may be subjected to the same route multiple times, depending upon the selling and re-selling of the victims through various hands.

The victims are trafficked by various methods, offers of money and employment being the most common amongst them. According to various studies, the traffickers use following common methods: (i) job offers in different sectors such as domestic servant, agricultural and/or industrial labour, (ii) promising jobs in media/ fashion/ film industry, (iii) making false promises of marriage (in case of adolescent girls and young women), (iv) making other false promises. The most common tools employed in trafficking are through deception and coercion (Sen, 2005). However, it is found through various studies that in most cases, the traffickers befriend the victims and lure them into false promises of money, marriage and job etc, thus using illusion and deception as their main tools. According to a study, nearly 80 per cent of the victims were trapped through deception. On the other hand, lesser than five per cent of victims were trafficked by using physical coercion (Sen and Nair, 2005, 121).

Commodification of human beings in the third world

Globalisation, the new form of capitalism has encouraged the alarming spread of free mobility of capital, technology, goods, sex tourism and trafficking of women. As the sovereignty of the nation-states has been compromised under globalisation, national policies are greatly influenced by international politics, affecting in turn, the citizens within each national territory. Neo liberalism's three pillars, Privatisation, liberalisation and restructuring have impact on the daily lives of women. Women have been pushed into free trade zones to work under exploitative conditions. Thousands of families have been displaced and forced to migrate in search of better livelihood. In this rapidly shifting paradigm, the state, instead of helping the poor, marginalised and socially disadvantaged people, has gradually withdrawn from essential sectors like healthcare, education, power and water.

Capitalist globalisation today involves an unprecedented "commodification" of human beings. In the last three decades, the rapidly growing sex trade has been massively "industrialised" worldwide (Barry, 1995). This process of industrialisation, in both its legal and its illegal forms, generates profits amounting to billions of dollars. It has created a market of sexual exchanges in which millions of women and children have been converted into sexual commodities. This sex market has been generated through the massive deployment of prostitution in the emerging economies, the unprecedented expansion of the tourist industry (Truong, 1990).

The industrialisation of the sex trade and its globalisation are fundamental factors that make contemporary prostitution qualitatively different from the prostitution of yester years. "Consumers" in the economic North now have access to exotic and young, very young bodies worldwide, notably in Brazil, Cuba, Russia, Kenya, Sri Lanka, Philippines, Vietnam, Nicaragua, and given the trafficking of children, in their own countries. The sex industry is diversified, sophisticated, and specialised: it can meet all types of demands. The liberalisation of the economy in the wake of globalisation in the third world has vastly diminished traditional livelihood means for the poor. Most of the women trafficked come from drought prone areas or from agricultural background and their farm lands have not been able to sustain the livelihood of their families for more than six months of a year. The conversion of large tracts of agricultural land for commercial aqua production, the diminishing viability of traditional livelihood skills, lack of education and skills for alternative means of income all reduce such victims to a situation of no other option but to enter into the sex trade (Pande, Rekha, 2006, 35).

Another factor, which confers a qualitatively different character on the current sex trade, is the fact that prostitution has become a development strategy for many third world countries. Under obligations of debt repayment, numerous Asian, Latin American, and African States were encouraged by international organisations such as the International Monetary Fund (IMF) and the World Bank (WB) to develop their tourism and entertainment industries. In each case, the development of these sectors inspired the development of the sex trade. In certain cases, as in Nepal, women and children were put directly on regional or international markets (notably in India and in Hong-Kong) without the country experiencing a significant expansion of local prostitution. In other cases, as in Thailand, local, regional, and international markets developed simultaneously (Barry, 1995). We can see that, in every case, the "goods" in this market move transcontinentally and transnationally from regions with weak concentrations of capital toward regions with stronger concentrations.

Human Trafficking: Statistical Data

One of the issues in tapping and presenting actual data on trafficking at global as well as local levels is the unavailability of data, or under-representation of cases of trafficking due to lack of proper identification, reporting and visibility. According to a fact sheet published by the United States National Human Trafficking Resource Centre: Actual statistics [on trafficked persons] are often unavailable and some may be contradictory due to the covert nature of the crime, the invisibility of victims, and high levels of under-reporting. Further obstacles include inconsistent definitions, reluctance to share data, and a lack of funding for research and standardisation of data collection (Polaris Project).

Thus, we see that there is a scarcity of actual data on human trafficking. This is particularly true for countries like India where trafficking is seen as a sensitive issue and talking and reporting about the same in an open manner, specifically in case of women and young children, is still a taboo. Same holds true for remote locations, such as villages and townships, which serve as the main origin for trafficking on a daily basis and yet there are various obstacles in collection of data in these places. These obstacles include lack of adequate resource persons, reluctance on the part of local people to talk about such issues, difficulties in identification and rapport building with the victims of trafficking (particularly in the case of women and children), unwillingness on the part of the victims to recall and share their experience and risk factors involved in carrying out a study on trafficking.

It is very difficult to give exact figures about the actual numbers of women and girls involved in trafficking. Besides this, trafficking of women and children is just the end result of a long chain, which involves a large number of persons. Whenever we talk of trafficking, three aspects that need to be focused are transit, destination and the whole supply chain and only then can the issue be understood in its various dimensions. The girl being trafficked is only one of the constituents of this and just focusing on her will not help in understanding the issue. Trafficking is a very dynamic business and newer forms of exploitation are discovered every day. Since commercial sex work is carried out right across the country in hotels, brothels, lodges, cinema halls, parks, along major roads and highways, it is impossible to provide actual facts and figures. Added to this is the fact that apart from regular operators, there are also such forms as contract workers, call girls, part time operators seeking supplementary income, escort service, masseurs and the like. Electronic media particularly internet and print media facilitates the very nature of this business which has to be conducted with a certain ambiguity and secretiveness. Earlier, prostitution was centralised and confined to red light areas but now it is becoming more decentralised. There is a close relation between trafficking and the spread of AIDS epidemic and we are sitting on a time bomb.

Hence, this issue deserves all the attention and it is high time we take it with all seriousness.

However, the data available on human trafficking worldwide is based upon the available resources such as International Labour Organisation (ILO), UNICEF, US Department of States including the Polaris Project, various country reports as well as reported cases of human trafficking all over the world.

Human Trafficking Worldwide

According to the International Labour Organisation (ILO), nearly 2.5 million people are estimated to be engaged in forced labour activities all over the world at any given time as a result of trafficking. This includes forced sexual exploitation as well. Moreover, 161 countries are reported to be actively affected by human trafficking, by their virtue of being an origin/ source, transition or destination point (Report, ILO, 2007). The majority of trafficked persons are young, between 18 and 24 years of age and they are mainly trafficked for the sexual and economic exploitation. According to ILO report nearly 43 per cent of total trafficked persons are subjected to commercial sexual exploitation and of these nearly 98 per cent are women and young girls. Secondly, nearly 32 per cent of all victims are put to forced labour activities and of these, nearly 56 per cent are women and girls. (International Organisation of Migration, 2007).

Human Trafficking in India

Although it is difficult to estimate and obtain exhaustive data on human trafficking in India, owing to the same factors as mentioned in reference with data on human trafficking worldwide yet India is generally perceived and accepted as a source, transition as well as destination country for trafficking. According to a study, nearly 150,000 women and children are trafficked from South-Asia regions on a yearly basis and majority of them are from, through, or to India. This confirms India's position as a source, transition as well as destination point of trafficking. It is also estimated that nearly 90 per cent of trafficking is internal, between different states and regions. According to a media report, 378 of 593 districts of India are affected by trafficking. A majority of these cases are from within states, that is inter-state trafficking (A.D.B., 2003).

A close examination of the source-transit-destination patterns in different Indian states reveals that poverty and illiteracy are the biggest markers of the source points. On the other hand, the destinations pointed are marked with high migrant population, industrial and commercial infrastructure and transport hubs. For example, states of Andhra Pradesh and Odisha serve as source places whereas states of Delhi and Goa are the major destination points within India.

Women's Movement and the issue of trafficking

It was primarily due to the efforts of the women's movement that this issue was highlighted. It was from the 1990's that trafficking of women was recognised as an organised enterprise by local and international criminal groups that use frauds and violence to entice and employ women (Kempadoo and Doezenma, 1998, Skrobanek *et.al.*, 1997). Women's groups and academicians first drew public attention to the phenomenon and to its cruel and exploitative nature, pointing out the ongoing practice of buying and selling women and children as property and their sexual and violent abuse in addition to their horrific living conditions. These were investigations on the scene carried out by NGO groups and academics. The media was also instrumental in exposing the exploitative and criminal characteristic of the business and its roots in international organised crime (Outshoorn, 2004). Unlike the issue of prostitution, trafficking received a lot of media attention and the attention of the NGO's and the women's movement. It was during the end of the nineteenth century and the early decades of the twentieth century that feminists all over the world raised their voices against trafficking of women across international boundaries for the purpose of prostitution. Consequently, under feminist impetus, a series of international agreements were adopted between 1903 and 1949 (Jeffreys, 1997, 7-34). The United Nations Convention for the suppression of the traffics in person and the exploitation of the prostitution and others popularly referred to as 1949 Trafficking convention declared that trafficking was incompatible with the dignity and the worth of the human person and endangers the welfare of the individual, the family and the community. By 1996, only 71 countries had signed it and this achieved little in terms of combating trafficking. There was no unit with in the United Nations that had responsibility for monitoring compliance with the convention (Chiang, 1999, 348). It was only recently that a comprehensive international approach to trafficking came about as a result of the United Nations Trafficking protocol of 2000. It identifies the main cause of trafficking to be poverty, underdevelopment and lack of equal opportunities.

Causes for Trafficking

Available literature points to poverty as the single biggest cause for trafficking. In the Indian contexts, states with lowest rates of economic growth and highest levels of poverty are also the biggest source points for trafficking. It is also argued that feminisation of poverty leads to an increase in demand for illegal supply of cheap female labour, and thus increases the magnitude of women trafficking. Studies also cite globalisation and unequal rate of development as one of the main reasons for trafficking across the borders, owing to a greater mobility of people and good and a rapid growth of means of communication and transport (Shelly, 2010, 37).

Other prominent cause for trafficking in India is the caste factor. According to a study by the National Commission for Women (NCW), nearly 60 per cent of women in sex-work belong to scheduled castes and 30 per cent were from scheduled tribes (India Country Report, 2008). Another evidence may be drawn from the practice of Devdasis in central-south regions of India, namely Maharashtra, Karnataka and Andhra Pradesh where minor girls are subject to serve in a temple and eventually subject to sexual and emotional exploitation (Charpenel, Yves, 2012).

Women and young girls are the most vulnerable victims of trafficking. Their low socio-economic status, lack of education and employment opportunities and their commoditisation as sex-objects are some of the secondary factors, other than poverty, which play a significant role in trafficking of women and girls. On the other hand, patriarchal socio-cultural practices may directly or indirectly induce the trafficking of women and girls. Demand for dowry can be attributed to both as a cause and a method of trafficking on the pre-text of a promise of a lump-sum dowry in return for their daughters' services.

Similarly, the practice of ritual-slavery such as devdasis may reinforce trafficking in certain places where the socio-cultural and religious exploitation of women and young girls is largely accepted. For instance, 14 out of 22 districts in Andhra Pradesh are reported with cases of devdasis and a majority of these districts also have poor socio-economic demographers, such as poverty and illiteracy, which are big factors in initialising human trafficking.

Impact of Trafficking

Trafficking is "one of the worst abuses of human rights." Consequently, the impacts of trafficking are the most derogatory to the humankind. The most prominent impact of trafficking is exploitation of the victims. Trafficked men, women and children are exploited in various ways, such as domestic work, bonded labour, agricultural labour, commercial and industrial labour, begging rackets, organ trade, forced prostitution, sex tourism and forced marriages (Khan, 2004). In majority of cases, the victims are lured and deceived into these activities for the return of a handsome amount of money. But in reality, the victims are enslaved and forced to provide their services, economic as well as sexual, for almost free. They are subject to constant trauma and poor living conditions and often end up compromising with poor physical and emotional well-being and low standards of living. According to available data, trafficked persons, owing to their sexual exploitation tend to get HIV-AIDs and STDs more often. (Ghosh, 2009, 716-738) This trend is particularly observed in the case of commercial sex workers. Other prominent diseases affecting the health of commercial sex workers (and/or trafficked persons) are tuberculosis and malaria (Ghosh, 2009, 716-738).

On the other hand, the socio-economic impacts of trafficking are miscalculation of the income generated from the employment of the victims of trafficking in various activities. Most of the income generated through the act of trafficking as well as through the employment of trafficked victims is put back to the criminal circuits and largely to illegal activities, such as arms and drugs dealings and trafficking. (Shelly, 2010). This implies not a under-representation of income and revenue, but also poses a serious threat to the peace and security across the globe.

Objectives of the Study

The broad objective of our study was to examine and look into the problems and issues related with women victims of trafficking, with a special focus on two Indian states, namely, Andhra Pradesh and Telangana.

The study has following main objectives:

- To study the trafficking of women and girls for sex work with focus on Telangana and Andhra Pradesh.
- To trace the journey of the trafficked victim and their rehabilitation and re-integration processes.
- To analyse the anti-trafficking measures and intervention of the government in addressing the problem of trafficking of women, with specific focus on legal frameworks and policies.
- To analyse the role and anti-trafficking measures of the Police.

- To examine the role and intervention of the Non-government Organisations (NGO's) and Community Based Organisations (CBO's) in addressing the problems of trafficking of women.

Methodology

Our research methodology employed a triangular method that is a combination of quantitative and qualitative data along with case studies. Data for this study comprises of both primary and secondary data. Data was obtained through an extensive survey of the sample population and quantitative as well as qualitative information extracted from the data.

An interview schedule was designed and implemented for the purpose of collection of data. Where ever we could we taped the interviews but by and large this was not allowed. Based upon different sources of data, three different interview schedules were prepared, that is, the victims of trafficking (schedule (I), the police (schedule (II) and NGO and CBO personnel (schedule (III). Each of these schedules aims at understanding the issue and problem of trafficking and its impact from the perspective of each resource persons, i.e. the victims of trafficking, the police and NGO's and CBO's.

Data Collection

We identify the following stages in our data collection and report writing:

- In stage one; information pertaining to trafficking in general is collected from different sources, which include literary surveys, survey of NGOs, Government agencies and Departments.
- In stage two, a detailed questionnaire was administered to seek information on the victims of trafficking.
- Recognising the limitations of the formal questionnaire, interviews and field observations were employed. Informal discussions and limited observations whenever possible were done.

- Data was collected from the social activists, NGOs and consultants.
- The research data was analysed and with general and specific findings, strategies and suggestions for policy input and follow up actions were made.

Sample size

We were able to get a data of 300 respondents from Telangana and Andhra Pradesh. These included 225 victims whom we found in various shelter homes or working elsewhere after being rehabilitated, 30 police officials and 45 NGO persons who were very actively involved in the whole task of rehabilitating these girls and women.

No.	*District*	*Victims*	*Police*	*NGO's*	*Total Number*
1.	Warangal	**21**	**3**	**5**	29
2.	Khammam	**20**	**2**	**3**	25
3.	Karimnagar	**12**	**2**	**2**	16
4.	Nellore	**11**	**2**	**2**	15
5.	Tirupati	**24**	**4**	**4**	32
6.	Anantapur	**23**	**1**	**3**	27
7.	Ongole	**27**	-	**1**	28
8.	Vijayawada	**8**	**4**	**2**	14
9.	Adilabad	**6**	-	**2**	8
10.	Rajmundry	**8**	-	**2**	10
11.	Visakhapatnam	**10**	-	-	10
12.	Ranga Reddy (Vikarabad)	**11**	-	**2**	13
13.	YSR Kadapa	**7**	-	**2**	9
14.	Kurnool	**7**	-	**1**	8
15.	Guntur	**8**	-	**1**	9
16.	Hyderabad	**22**	**12**	**13**	47
	Total A.P.	**225**	**30**	**45**	**300**

Hypothesis

Today more and more women, especially from weaker backgrounds are being pushed into trafficking.

Due to the existing difference between women and men's access in knowledge, skills, responsibilities, concerns and control over resources, women are affected widely by the global process and experience increasing marginalisation and pauperisation. Majority of these women live in abject poverty, without adequate food, clean water, sanitation, healthcare or education. The lives of a large number of women who were earlier poor are blighted by poverty and robbed of dignity in a world of growing wealth and material plenty. Due to an increasing poverty, women are migrating from one region to another in search of jobs. Unable to find these, they are being pushed into prostitution and trafficking. Hence, with increasing impact of globalisation, more and more women are turning to trafficking as a source of income for survival or are pushed into it.

Significance of the Problem and Justification in Investigation

We find major changes occurring in South Asia and India. Today, one can see that women are being squeezed out of marketing and vending spaces become parking spaces. Agricultural land is diminishing as a result of population growth and commercialisation in many States, whereas in coastal areas of AP, agricultural land is being utilised more and more for prawn cultivation. Fishes dwindle and global tenders are making local labours and skills obsolete. The dominance of rich nations, multinational corporations and international capital over market resources and labours in developing countries through trade, aid and technology transfer has greatly weakened the capacity of nation states and governments to promote human development and offer protection to poor people. The worst hit in this transformation is the informal sector, marked with income disparities and dominated by the poor and the underprivileged. Even among the unorganised sectors, it is the women who are affected the most. Unable to find any avenues of survival, they are pushed into trafficking and HIV/AIDS has emerged as a major problem in both Telangana and AP. Though everyone is now talking of globalisation and its impact, there is hardly any study on trafficking which looks at the empirical data and see the trends in order to help policy-makers take decisions. It cannot be denied that there is an irreversibility of the reform process that has already been initiated. So, there is an urgent need to look at alternatives and suggest remedial measures, policy inputs and other administrative inputs.

Stake holders and partners who assisted this study are:

1. Shaheen- Society for women's development. This NGO works on women's empowerment issues among the Muslim community.
2. Cova, *Confederation of Voluntary Associations,* Old City, Hyderabad-29.
3. The Andhra Pradesh Mahila Samta Society is a Govt/ autonomous body under the Ministry of Education and works throughout Andhra Pradesh but has its head office in Hyderabad. It specialises in imparting gender training focuses on capacity building, and developing self-help groups.
4. AP States AIDS Control Society, Government of Andhra Pradesh, Sultan Bazar, Koti, Hyderabad-95. This is a Government of India organisation that looks into the issue of AIDS in Andhra Pradesh.
5. Chaitanya Mahila Mandali, Secunderabad :12-10-399/ 2A, 1st Floor Opp to Suresh Theatre, Sitafalmandi, Secunderabad - 500061 AP India.

Chapterisation

This book is divided into eight chapters.

Chapter 1: ***Introduction,*** introduces the concept and issue of trafficking of persons in general and that of women (including children and young girls) in particular. It examines the magnitude of the problem of human trafficking on global as well as national and regional scale. This chapter also gives a general picture of human trafficking.

Chapter 2: ***Key Legislations related to trafficking,*** looks into the legislation and laws related to trafficking at the International level and in India.

Chapter 3: ***The material context of trafficking,*** provides a detailed study of the field. It begins with a look at South Asia and moves on to examine the socio-demographic profile of Indian states, specific mention of Telangana and Andhra Pradesh. It also examines the issues and vulnerability of regions to trafficking.

Chapter 4: ***Profile of Trafficked victim,*** *discusses* in detail the life, issues and perspectives of the victims of trafficking, when we found them.

Chapter 5: ***Life Experiences, Re-habilitation and the aftermath,*** looks at the life of the victims and their history of being trafficked and the rehabilitation and other issues connected with this.

Chapter 6: ***Institutional Response on Trafficking,*** examines the role of the Police, Non-Government Organisations (NGO's) and Community based organisations (CBO's)

Chapter 7: ***Case Studies.***

Chapter 8: ***Summing Up*** summarises the study and presents major findings and observations.

Human trafficking is a serious threat to humankind and it is one of the biggest and constantly growing criminal activities all over the world. The mere purpose of trafficking that is exploitation of underprivileged persons for economic and/or sexual purposes points to the loopholes in the existing constitutional and legal framework puts a big question mark to the ethical promises of individual life with dignity and independence. In case of women and young girls, the impact and consequences of trafficking grow manifold, given their vulnerable situation, their commodification as sex-objects and their forced marginalisation in the socio-cultural and economic parlance. India is no exception to this trend and is emerging as a major source, transition and destination point for trafficking.

References

A.D.B. Asian Development Bank, 2003, *Combating of Trafficking in Women and Children in South Asia: Regional Synthesis Paper for Bangladesh, India and Nepal. Bangkok,* http://adb.org/sites/default/files/pub/2003/combating-trafficking-south-asia-paper.pdf, accessed, 3rd February, 2016.

Basler, Patrick, 2005, *Forced Labour and Human Trafficking: Estimating the Profits,* Working Paper. Geneva: International Labour Office. http://www.civilandhumanrights.org/documents/Forced_Labor_and_Human_Trafficking_-_Estimating_the_Profits.pdf, accessed 20th March, 2015.

Barry, Kathleen, 1995, *The Prostitution of Sexuality,* New York: New York University Press.

Chakravarti, Uma, 1985, "Of Dasas and Karmakaras: Servile Labour in Ancient *India,*" In Utsa Patnaik and Manjari Dingwaney (eds.), *Chains of Servitude: Bondage and Slavery in India*, Madras: Sangam Books, pp. 35-75.

Charpenel, Yves, 2012, *Sexual Exploitation Prostitution and Organised Crime,* Paris. http://www.fondationscelles.org/pdf/rapport_mondial/sexual_exploitation_prostitution_Fondation_Scelles.pdf accessed, 2nd February, 2016.

Chiang, Lois. 1999, 'Trafficking in Women', in K. D. Askin and D. M. Koening (eds) *Women and International Human Rights Law* (Vol. 1), pp. 321–64. Ardsley, NY: Transnational Publishers.

Farr, Kathryn, 2005, *Sex Trafficking: The Global Market in Women and Children.* New York: Worth Publisher.

Gail, Kligman and Stephanie, Limoncelli, 2005, "Trafficking of women after socialism : To Through and from Eastern Europe", Social Politics: *International Studies in Gender, State and* Society, 12 (1), pp. 118-140.

George, Annie, U Vindhya, Sawmya Ray, 2010, *Sex Trafficking and Sex Work: Definitions, Debates, and Dynamics- A Review of Literature.* Economic & Political Weekly, Vol. XLV (17), pp. 64-74.

Ghosh Biswajit, 2009, Trafficking in Women and Children in India: Nature, Dimensions and Strategies for Prevention. T*he International Journal of Human Rights* 13:5, pp.716-738.

Hawthrone, Susan, 2004, *Wild Politics: Beyond Globalisation.* Women Studies International Forum, Vol. 27, pp. pp. 243-259.

Huda, S. 2006, *Sex trafficking in South Asia.* International Journal of Gynecology and Obstetrics, Vol. 94, pp. 374-381.

International Organisation for Migration, 2007, *Counter- Trafficking Database,* http://www.iom.ch/jahia/webdav/shared/shared/mainsite/activities/ct/iom_ctm_database.pdf, accessed, 21st March, 2015.

Jana,Samarjit, Nandinee Bandopadhyay, M.K. Dutta, 2002, *A Tale of Two Cities: shifting the paradigm of anti-trafficking programmes.* Gender and Development, Vol. 10 (1), pp. 69-79.

Jeffreys, Sheila, 1997, *The idea of prostitution,* Spenifex, North Melbourne.

Kara, Siddharth. 2010, *Sex Trafficking: Inside the Business of Modern Slavery.* New York: Columbia University Press.

Kempadoo, Kamala and Jo Doezema, (eds), 1998, *Global sex worker: Rights, resistance and redefinition,* Routledge, London.

Kofi Annan, 2007, Address to the House of Parliament. London. 8 May.

Maggie Black, 2007, *Women in Ritual Slavery, Devadasi, Jogini and Mathamma in Karnataka and Andhra Pradesh, Southern India,* Anti-slavery International. http://www.antislavery.org/includes/documents/cm_docs/2009/w/women_in_ritual_slavery2007.pdf, accessed on 21st March, 2015.

Mohanty, Chandra Talpade, 2003, *Feminism without Borders: Decolonizing Theory, Practicing Solidarity,* Duke University Press Books.

Okonofua, F.E. Ogbomwan, S.M. Alutu, A.N. 2004, *Knowledge, attitudes and experiences of sex trafficking by young women in Benin City, South-South Nigeria.* Social Science & Medicine, Vol. 59, pp. 1315–1327.

Outshoorn, Joyce (ed) 2004, *The politics of prostitution: Women's movements, Democratic states and the Globalisation of sex commerce,* Cambridge University Press, U.K.

Pande, Rekha, 2014, "Human Security, Globalisation, and Trafficking of Women and Children in South Asia", in, *Globalisation, Development and Security in Asia,* (ed) Zhquin Zhu, Foreign Policy and Security in an Asian Century: Threats, strategiés and Policy choices, Vol. 1, (ed), Benny The Cheng Guan, World Scientific. Hackensack, N.J. U.S.A. pp. 277-296.

Pande, Rekha, 2008, "Ritualised Prostitution: Devdasis to Jogins- A few case studies", in *Prostitution and Beyond, An analysis of sex work in India* (eds), Rohini Sahni, V. Kalya Shnkar and Hemant Apte, Sage Publications, New Delhi, pp.101-117.

Pande, Rekha, 2006, Globalisation and trafficking of women and Children, *Samyukta,* A Journal of Women's studies, Vol. VI, No. 2, pp. 31-47.

Pande, Rekha, 1, 2006, Devdasis, in J.S. Grewal (ed), Religious Movements and Institutions in Medieval India, Vol. VII, Part, 2. in D.P. Chattopadhyay (general editor), *History of Science, Philosophy and Culture in Indian Civilisation,* Oxford University Press, New Delhi, pp.493-504.

Pande, Rekha, 2004, At the service of the Lord- Temple girls in Medieval Deccan (11th to 17th centuries), in *Deccan Studies,* Vol.II, No. 2, July-December-pp. 25-43.

Pande, Rekha, 2001, The Social costs of Globalisation : Restructuring Developing World Economies, *Journal of Asian Women's Studies,* Vol. 10, December, Kitakyushu Forum, Japan. pp.1-14.

Penttinen, Elina, 2008, *Globalisation, Prostitution and Sex trafficking,* New York, Routledge.

Polaris Project, Human Trafficking Trends in the United States: National Human Trafficking Resource Center 2007–2012, https://polarisproject.org/sites/default/files/Human%20Trafficking%20Trends%20in%20the%20US%2011-21-13.pdf accessed 2md February, 2016,

Report, Trafficking in Persons, 2005, U. S. Department of States. Office to monitor and combat trafficking in persons.
http://www.state.gov/j/tip/rls/tiprpt/2005/46606.htm, accessed 2md February, 2016,

Report, Trafficking in Persons, 2008, U. S. Department of States. 8th edition. Washington DC: U. S. Department of State.

Report, International Labour Organisation. 2007. Forced Labour Statistic Factsheet.

Report, International Organisation for Migration. 2007. Counter-Trafficking Database.

Report, India Country Report to Prevent and Combat Trafficking and Commercial Sexual Exploitation of Children and Women, 2008, Ministry of Women and Child Development Government of India, p. 24.

Ritzer, George, 2010, *Globalisation : A basic Text,* London, Wiley Blackwell.

Samarasinghe, Vidyamali and Burton, Barbara, 2007, "Strategizing Prevention: a Critical Review of Local Initiatives to Prevent Female Sex Trafficking". *Development in Practice,* 17:1, pp. 51-64.

Sengupta, Chandan. 2001, *Conceptualising Globalisation : Issues and Implications,* Economic and Political Weekly, Vol. 36 (33), pp. 3137-3143.

Sen, Sankar, 2005, *Trafficking in Women and Children in India,* New Delhi: Orient Longman Pvt. Ltd.

Sen, Sankar and P. M. Nair. 2005, *Trafficking of Women and Children in India.* New Delhi: Institute of Social Sciences.

Skeldon, Ronald, 2000, 'Trafficking: A Perspective from Asia', in Reginald Appleyard (ed.) *Perspectives on Trafficking of Migrants,* New York: International Organisation for Migration, United Nations, p. 22.

Skrobanek, S. Nataya, Boonpakdee and Chutima Jantareero, 1997, *The traffic in women: Human realities and the International sex trade,* Zed Books, London.

Shelly, Louis, 2010, *Human Trafficking: A Global Perspective.* Cambridge, UK: Cambridge University Press.

Truong, Thanh-Dam, 1990, *Sex, Money and Morality: Prostitution and Tourism in Southeast Asia*, London: Zed Books.

UN Palermo Protocol, 2000, Also known as UN Protocol to Prevent, Suppress and Punish Trafficking in Persons, Especially Women and Children Article 3. http://www.ohchr.org/EN/ProfessionalInterest/Pages/ProtocolTraffickingInPersons.aspx, accessed, 28th March, 2015.

U. Vindhya and V. Swathi Dev, 2011, "Survivors of Sex Trafficking in Andhra Pradesh : Evidence and Testimony" *Indian Journal of Gender Studies* 18(2), pp.129–165.

Wang, Yi. 2005, *Anti-Human Trafficking Program in Vietnam.* Oxfam Quebec, Hanoi, pp. 1-29.

Chapter 2

Key Legislations Related to Trafficking

India is a signatory to most international human rights instruments relevant to trafficking in persons and trafficking in women and children. These include the Convention for the suppression of traffic in persons, Trafficking Convention, the International Covenant on Civil and Political Rights (ICCPR) and anti-slavery conventions. It has also ratified the Convention on the elimination of 'All forms of Discrimination against Women' (CEDAW) and the Convention of the Rights of the Child (CRC). Articles 34 and 35 of the CRC directs State parties to take all appropriate national, bilateral and multinational measures to prevent the abduction, sale or traffic of children for any purpose or in any form and specially charges signatories with the protection of children from sexual exploitation and abuse. The Indian constitution also prohibits trafficking in persons. Article 23, of the Fundamental Rights states, traffic in human beings and other similar forms of forced labour are prohibited. Article 39, guarantees equal treatment of men and women and obligates the state to ensure that the health and strength of workers, men and women and children are not abused and that all children are protected against exploitation. Article 42, provides protection against inhuman working conditions.

International Conventions with regards to trafficking

International law is a powerful conduit for combating human trafficking. The most reputable and recent instruments of international law that have set the course for how to define, prevent, and prosecute human trafficking. Instruments that have dealt with human trafficking date back to the abolition of slavery.

In 1885, the National Vigilance Association (NVA) was established to set up an international organisation that would be able to oppose the international network of traffickers. The NVA, which had lobbied for British legislation to contain provisions for trafficking committed in foreign countries, formed the International Association for the Suppression of the White Slave Trade in 1899 in response to the discovery (Gorman, Daniel, 2007, 12).

In 1902, Delegates from 16 European nations met in Paris to draft an agreement for an international law on prostitution – the International Treaty for the Suppression of the White Slave Trade. Various white slavery offices were established throughout Europe after the convention. There was a lot of discussion that took place in this convention on white slavery but no decision was taken on majority and minority age with regards to trafficking. In 1904 in the convention on white slavery the lacuna was that it did not address other women and confined itself to only white women. Again the Convention of 1910, discuss the issue of consent but the lacuna was that it only focused on the issue of physical movement and migration and not on exploitation.

By 1919, the Association suspended its actions and reformed into the International Bureau for the Suppression of Trafficking in Women and Children (IBSTWC). In 1921, however, the League of Nations officially took over the issue of white slavery. It is important to note the League changed the crime's name from 'white slave trade' to the 'traffic in women and children' to stress that no victim would be discriminated or neglected on the basis of their race or ethnicity.

Trafficking in women first emerged on the international political agenda when the League of Nations began to address white slavery in 1921. While the 1921 Convention contained provisions for forced prostitution, it did not protect adults of either sex from being procured as prostitutes if they consented and stayed in the country, nor did it make keeping a brothel an offense. The IBSTWC continued to lobby Convention signatories to pass legislation making trafficking a crime and to protect children. The result was the 1927 Report, which gathered information from both traffickers and prostitutes to produce a detailed account of how the trade operated (Gorman, Daniel, 2007, 12). The term was assigned various definitions over time, but by the late nineteenth century, white slavery's meant the procurement by use of force, deceit or drugs – of white women or girls against her will for prostitution (Walkowitz, 1992, 247).

The abolitionist struggle over slavery in the United States significantly influenced early campaigns against prostitution, and later, the rhetoric of white slavery in the late nineteenth century. For some reformers, white slavery meant that all forms of prostitution, voluntary or coerced, was a form of sexual slavery, while others saw white slavery and prostitution as distinct but related issues (Willis, 1912). However, these conventions became a precursor of various conventions that followed. They include provisions within the Slavery Convention (1926) and the Supplementary Convention on the Abolition of Slavery, the Slave Trade, and Institutions and Practices Similar to Slavery (1956).

The 1933, International Convention for the Suppression of the Traffic in Women of the Full Age was employed under the League of Nations and recapped the wish to more completely secure the suppression of trafficking in women and children. (1933 Convention). This convention followed up on the recommendations contained in the Report to the Council of the League of Nations by the Traffic in Women and Children Committee on the Work of its Twelfth session. Article 1 of the 1933 Convention extends the punishable requirements of trafficking to include 'attempted offences, and within the legal limits, acts preparatory to the offences in question'. Additionally, the term 'country' is widened to include the colonies and protectorates of the parties concerned, as well as the territories under them. For the first time this convention reiterated trafficking as an International act and a covered act carried out in another state.

In 1937, another Convention was set up but due to the outbreak of the World War II, this could not be completed.

In 1948, the Universal Declaration of Human Rights, also included segments against the trafficking of persons.

The 1949, Convention for the Suppression of the Traffic in Persons and of the Exploitation of the Prostitution of Others was an important instrument for it saw prostitution as an accompanying evil of trafficking. This is a resolution of the UN General Assembly. The preamble states: "Whereas prostitution and the accompanying evil of the traffic in persons for the purpose of prostitution are incompatible with the dignity and worth of the human person and endanger the welfare of the individual, the family and the community." The Convention supersedes a number of earlier conventions that covered some aspects of forced prostitution. Signatories are charged with three obligations under the 1949 Convention: prohibition of trafficking, specific administrative and enforcement measures, and social measures aimed at trafficked persons. The 1949 Convention presents two shifts in perspective of the trafficking problem in that it views prostitutes as victims of the procurers, and in that it eschews the terms "white slave traffic" and "women," using for the first time race- and gender-neutral language. However, this convention was not very successful for many states did not ratify this. There was a lot of divergence of opinion among the different states as what trafficking meant. This is not surprising, as one of the fundamental problems in combating trafficking until then had been the lack of international consensus on a definition and thus on precisely which practices should be combated. Underlying this lack of consensus are two diametrically opposed views on sex work. The depth of this controversy was reflected in the presence of two opposed NGO-lobbying blocs, representing two types of feminist response to sex work and, consequently, the issue of how to define trafficking in persons. One sees all sex work as trafficking per se. The other view holds that conditions of (forced) labour in all industries, including the sex industry, should be addressed.

Additional tools of international law that include, the International Covenants on Civil and Political Rights, 1966 and the Convention on the Elimination of all Forms of Discrimination Against Women 1979. These instruments laid the foundation for the contemporary conventions and efforts to eliminating trafficking.

The 2000, Protocol to Prevent, Suppress and Punish Trafficking in Persons, especially Women and Children (also referred to as the Trafficking Protocol or UN TIP Protocol) is a protocol to the Convention against Transnational Organised Crime. It is one of the three Palermo protocols, the others being the Protocol against the Smuggling of Migrants by Land, Sea and Air and the Protocol against the Illicit Manufacturing and Trafficking in Firearms. The protocol was adopted by the United Nations General Assembly in 2000 and entered into force on 25th December 2003. As of December 2014, it has been ratified by 166 parties. It was this protocol that gives a definition for the first time of trafficking. India signed this protocol on 12th December, 2002 and it was ratified and accepted by it on 5th May, 2011. This is a very important convention because for the first time there was a definition of trafficking.The definition was discussed at all eleven sessions and was hotly contested every step of the way. Informal meetings and specially scheduled lunch time meetings were held almost daily by a (closed) working group of governmental delegates devoted to discussing proposed definitions and trying to find middle ground after no headway was made during the plenary meetings. Central point of debate was the question whether trafficking should be defined by the nature of the work involved or by the use of deceit and coercion. The inclusion of force or deception as an essential element of trafficking signifies an important departure from the abolitionist perspective. The definition finally agreed upon allows a certain interpretative leeway for its enforcement by signatory nations. This was necessary in order to achieve consensus in such a large meeting. However, it does mean that, although the Protocol leaves governments free to treat sex work as legitimate work, it (also) does not prevent them from further criminalising sex work and sex workers in the name of combating trafficking. In addition, the Protocol does little to protect the rights of trafficked persons, leaving it to the discretion of the signatory countries whether to arrest, prosecute and deport them or provide them with protection and assistance. (Melissa Ditmore and Marjan Wijer, 2003, 87).

It is this definition that has been generally accepted as far as trafficking is concerned. The act of trafficking refers to the mobilisation and displacement of persons from one place to another through deception or coercion, leading into their physical as well as economic exploitation. The United Nations Palermo Protocol (2000) defines Human Trafficking as:

- "Trafficking in persons" shall mean the recruitment, transportation, transfer, harbouring or receipt of persons by means of the threat or use of force or other forms of coercion, of abduction, of fraud, of deception, of the abuse of power or of a position of vulnerability or of the giving and receiving of payments or benefits to achieve the consent of a person having control over another person, for the purpose of exploitation. Exploitation shall include, at a minimum, the exploitation of the prostitution of others or other forms of sexual exploitation, forced labour or service, slavery or practices similar to slavery, servitude or the removal of organs;

- The consent of a victim of trafficking in persons to the intended exploitation set forth in subparagraph (a)...shall be irrelevant where any of the means set forth in the subparagraph (a) have been used;
- The recruitment, transportation, transfer, harbouring or receipt of a child for the purpose of the exploitation shall be considered "trafficking in persons," even if this does not involve any of the means set forth in the subparagraph (a) of this article;
- "Child" shall mean any person under 18 years of age. (UN Palermo Protocol, 2003, Article 3).

A large number of International conventions after this like the CEDAW, Rights of Child look upon trafficking as exploitation. The UN Trafficking Protocol is very important for it defines for the first time, recruitment, transportation, transfer, harbouring and receipt.

Tier Placements

The United Nations has placed all the countries in the World in different Tiers with regards to trafficking.

In **Tier 1** are those countries whose governments fully comply with the Trafficking Victims Protection Act's (TVPA) minimum standards. The most important among these include, Australia, Austria, Belgium, Canada, Denmark, Finland, France, Germany, Iceland, Ireland, Israel, Italy, Korea South, Netherlands, New Zealand, Norway, Sweden, Switzerland, United Kingdom, and United States of America.

In **Tier 2,** are countries whose governments do not fully comply with the TVPA's minimum standards, but are making significant efforts to bring themselves into compliance with those standards. The absolute number of victims of severe forms of trafficking is very significant or is significantly increasing. There is a failure to provide evidence of increasing efforts to combat severe forms of trafficking in persons from the previous year or the determination that a country is making significant efforts to bring itself into compliance with minimum standards was based on commitments by the country to take additional future steps over the next year. India is listed in the Tier II list of the United Nations which includes countries which have failed to combat human trafficking. Other countries include, Afghanistan, Albania, Bangladesh, Bhutan, Brazil, Egypt.

In **Tier 3** are countries whose governments do not fully comply with the minimum standards and are not making significant efforts to do so. These include, Central African Republic, Cuba, Iran, Korea North, Kuwait, Libya, Malaysia, Russia, Saudi Arabia, Syria, Thailand, Uzbekistan, Venezuela, Yemen, Zimbabwe.

Laws in India

The Indian constitution specifically bans the trafficking in persons. Article 23 in the Fundamental Rights section of the constitution prohibits traffic in human beings and other similar kinds of forced labour. Though there is no concrete definition of trafficking like in International law trafficking is understood to involve, movement, transportation of a person by means of coercion or deceit and consequent exploitation leading to commercialisation.

The two principal laws that address trafficking and prostitution are the Suppression of Immoral Traffic in Women and Girls Acts of 1956 (SITA) and the Immoral Traffic in Persons Prevention Act of 1986 (ITPPA) but colloquially called as PITA as an amendment to SITA. Neither law prohibits prostitution per se, but both target of the female practitioner of prostitution. The language of the law defined prostitution as female, thereby exempting males in prostitution from criminalisation. While a woman arrested for soliciting could be imprisoned for a year, a pimp for three months the men were let off Scott free. This law addressed only street prostitution and the prostitution behind closed doors was left alone. ITPPA recognises nine punishable conditions, including brothel keeping, living off brothel earnings, procuring, detaining, activity in the vicinity of public places, seducing or soliciting. It hence recognises that men and children can also be sexually exploited. While it expands police power to prevent trafficking, it also recognises the potential abuse of power, such as verbal, physical and sexual harassment by police during raids.

The role of different government and international agencies, such as Ministry of Women and Child Development, Ministry of External Affairs, National Human Rights Commission, National Commission of Women, UNICEF, UNIFEM, United Nations Office on Drugs and Crimes (UNODC) is also significant in identifying, providing guidelines and institutional support and combating cases of Human Trafficking.

Prior to comprehending the Act and its provisions one would elucidate India's tolerationist nature to 'prostitution' which was not centred on 'prostitutes' rather had a very sexist understanding of it. Cunha (1987) argue that the "It was based on the premise of man's aggressive and uncontainable sexuality and polygamous nature, considered 'natural and biological' giving rise to prostitution. Prostitution thus preserved the family structure and prevented rampant rape." Socially 'prostitution' is an ostracised phenomenon and women involved in it are socially castigated. (Cunha, 1987).

Two widely mentioned Supreme Court judgements, Vishal *Jeet v. Union of India in 1990* and *Gaurav Jain v. Union of India in 1997* are considered instrumental in initiating government action on the issue of commercial sexual exploitation (DWCD, 1998). The judiciary is accused of playing a role in secondary victimisation through its mode of questioning during court procedures and the long and tedious processes involved. The legal system is perceived to be formidable by the victims rather than being a deterrent to those who commit offences (DWCD, 1996). Depending on the sensitivity of the judges, judgements, range from supporting the victims to aggravating their harassment (United Nations 2001). The approach is that of a stereotypical one wherein the ascription of harmful and dehumanising aspect to sex work and other related activities has a problematic approach to the discourse of trafficking. It is stated so because if the conceptualisation of sex work is problematic by the law-makers then the whole approach of anti-trafficking discourse becomes flawed. Presumption of the actors in the institution of sex work as a criminal activity validates the states conflation of sex work with transnational organised crime. Therefore, the anti-trafficking discourse of the state both national and international is based on the analysis of sex work as institution regimented or rooted in coercion, discrimination and inequalities. (Koteswaran XV). Thereby one could argue that the anti-trafficking laws has an unidirectional impact on eliminating or preventing human trafficking and has a strong assertion of uprooting sex markets. (Koteswaran XV).

The Indian Parliament recently enacted the Criminal Law (Amendment) Act, 2013 (CLA). Although primarily concerned with targeting rape and sexual assault, the Bill incorporates a range of other offences dealing with violence against women many of which the Indian Penal Code, 1860 (IPC) did not envisage. Two such offences relate to trafficking, an area of considerable policy and legal reform internationally. Specifically, the new Section 370 defines the offence of trafficking thus replacing the prior Section 370, which dealt with the buying or disposing of any person as a slave. The new Section 370 criminalises anyone who recruits, transports, harbours, transfers or receives a person using certain means (including threats, force, coercion, fraud, deception, abduction, abuse of power, or inducement) for purposes of exploitation. Exploitation in turn is not defined but is said to include any act of physical exploitation or any form of sexual exploitation, slavery or practices similar to slavery, servitude, or the forced removal of organs. Punishment ranges from 7 to 10 years' rigorous imprisonment with fine. This is further enhanced and graded depending on whether the victim is an adult or minor, if more than one person or minor is trafficked, if the trafficker is a repeat offender and whether the trafficker is a police officer or public servant. Recognising that targeting the demand for trafficked labour is often crucial in the fight against trafficking, Section 370A criminalises anyone who engages a trafficked minor or adult for sexual exploitation.

Flaws in the implementation of trafficking laws

Implementation of laws relating to trafficking of women and children and child protection reveals various flaws in the implementation process as well as non-implementations of various important aspects of law. In the existing trafficking law in Section 13 there is a provision of appointment of Special Police Unit to enforce the law but this provision remains only in the statute book and is ignored by most of the states in India. There is no definition of trafficking in the existing laws, giving opportunity to the offenders, to escape from criminal liability. The existing Trafficking law is accused oriented ignoring the rights of the victims. There is a provision of the Special Court for trial of Trafficking cases, but no such courts are being constituted.

The priority placed by our law enforcement agency on illegal immigration has resulted in treatment of cross-border trafficking as criminals. When police raid brothels women are often detained and punished and subjected to human rights abuses in jail. A few victims dare testify against the traffickers or those who hold them fearing retribution for themselves and their families since most occasions the prosecutors do not offer stays of deportation or adequate protection for witnesses. In some cases, police and other governmental authorities accept bribes and collude with traffickers by selling fake documentation.

Trafficking is now a problem that affects virtually every country in the world. Generally, the flow of trafficking is from less developed countries to more developed countries or towards neighbouring countries with marginally higher standards of living. Trafficking is as organised criminal activities and also a trans-national organised crime, but our criminal justice system and the law enforcement agency is not equipped to combat such organised crime of trafficking.

Even in India, generally a girl is booked and the traffickers are let of Scott free, to recruit another woman or child and there is no attempt at breaking the entire network. The prostitute or the trafficked victim should be treated as a victim than an accused. The term used for the prostitute should be VOCSE Victim of commercial sexual exploitation. Similarly when a person is rescued from a brothel, such a operation should be called rescue and not raid.

Trafficking and HIV/AIDS

Human rights are universal and apply to all individuals in every sector of society. Denying human rights to any one person perpetrates an injustice that has ramifications far beyond the local level. Indeed, it cripples globally-supported attempts to stem the spread of a plague that has no regard for gender, age, race, marital status, sexual orientation, immigration status, or religion. HIV/AIDS policies and programmes at the global, national, and local levels must support universal access to prevention, treatment, and care in order to effectively address the pandemic. This requires a staunch adherence to basic human rights, without judgment or hesitation. Policies cannot, for any reason, bar any individual or group from accessing necessary health services—it is both immoral and automatically handicaps the HIV/AIDS prevention effort (Change, 2010).

In 2007, the Government of India estimates that, around 2.3 million people in India are living with HIV. Of these, an estimated 39 per cent are female and 3.5 per cent are children. The HIV prevalence at antenatal clinics was one per cent in 2007. This figure is smaller than the reported 1.26 per cent in 2006, but is still highest out of all states. HIV prevalence at STD clinics was very high at 17 per cent in 2007. Among high-risk groups, HIV prevalence was highest among men who have sex with men (MSM) (17 per cent), followed by female sex workers (9.7 per cent) and IDUs (3.7 per cent). In Manipur, prevalence of HIV is perceived as high as 32 per cent. HIV is no longer confined to IDUs, but has spread further to the general population. HIV prevalence at antenatal clinics in Manipur exceeded one per cent in recent years, but then declined to 0.75 per cent in 2007. Estimated adult HIV prevalence is the highest out of all states, at 1.57 per cent (Chetty, Priya, 2012).

Today, AIDS is the third biggest killer in the world. Everyday, 14,000 new infections occur. Of these, 2,000 infections below 14 years age (primarily through vertical transmission). Out of the 12,000 infections occurring in the age of 15 years and above, 50 per cent of infections (i.e., 6,000) occur in the age group of 15-24 years - young people in the centre of the epidemic. First reported case of HIV/AIDS in India was detected in Chennai in 1986. Estimated number of HIV Positive people in India - 5.13 million. (1/9th of the Global HIV infections). India's epidemic is strikingly diverse among and within states. HIV is a generalised epidemic in Maharashtra, Andhra Pradesh, Karnataka, Tamil Nadu, Manipur and Nagaland. There is a close relationship between trafficking and the spread of AIDS. This is a predictable and inevitable epidemic. (Chauhan, Sanjay Singh, 2015, 133). It starts with sex workers or drug users and is a *Low Level Epidemic.*

The spread of AIDS and awareness about it has effected trafficking in more than one way. There is a demand for more young girls, who can be sold as virgins and therefore AIDS free. There is also more customer demand for clean girls particularly virgins. Girls who test positive for AIDS are immediately dismissed and visibly sick and without money are either ostracised by their families or unwilling to go home. A newspaper Reports an infected girl saying, "I am not living even now. So how does it matter if I die" (Times of India, 1994, 5). These women are powerless to negotiate any terms of sex in order to protect themselves from HIV infection. They have virtually no say over whether or not to service a particular customer, the number of customers to accept in a particular day, condom use, etc. In Bombay, according to the calculations of an organisation of Nepali brothel staff there are about 20,000 Nepalis in the city's flesh trade; other agencies estimate that the actual number is closer to 50,000. Most of these women and girls work for Nepali *gharwalis* (madams), and almost all are illiterate. Seventy per cent are thought to belong to ethnic minority groups such as the Tamang, Gurung, Magar, and Sherpa. Women and girls from Nepal's Hindu majority communities constitute about 10 to 15 per cent. Twenty per cent of Bombay's brothel population is thought to be girls under the age of eighteen, and at least half of them may be infected with HIV. (Human Rights Watch, 1995, 66).

Women and girls are the primary victims of the nexus of the global epidemics of sex trafficking and HIV/AIDS. As sex trafficking victims, women and girls are more vulnerable to HIV infection because of their lack of choice with regard to high-risk sexual activities. Similarly, HIV infection is spread through international and local sex trafficking. Findings from south will not necessarily generalise to regions with different HIV transmission dynamics and commercial sex trades. But at least one lesson comes out clearly that, sex trafficking is not only a human rights crisis, but also exacts a devastating toll on the health and well-being of women, girls and communities.

References

Chauhan, Sanjay Singh, 2015, The HIV/Aids Epidemic in India, Research Journal of Science and Technology, Volume : 7, Issue : 2, pp. 133-138.

Change, 2010, *Human Trafficking, HIV/AIDS, and the Sex Sector Human Rights for All,* Center for Health and Gender Equity (CHANGE) and Center for Human Rights and Humanitarian Law at American University Washington College of Law. http://www.genderhealth.org/files/uploads/change/publications/Human_Trafficking_HIVAIDS_and_the_Sex_Sector.pdf, accessed, 11th February, 2016.

Chetty, Priya, 2012, Project Guru, http://www.projectguru.in/publications/state-wise-details-of-aids-in-india/ accessed, 3rd February, 2016.

Gorman, Daniel. 2007, "Empire, Internationalism, and the Campaign against the Traffic in Women and Children in the 1920s". *Twentieth Century British History,* Oxford University Press, p.12.

Cunha, Jean D. 1987, Prostitution in a patriarchal society: A critical review of the SIT Act", *Economic and Political Weekly,* 22 (45) pp. 1919-1925.

DWCD, 1998, Situation Report on trafficking of children for prostitution. New Delhi: New Concept Information Systems Pvt. Ltd. Department of Women and Child Development, Ministry of Human Resource Development and Government of India.

Koteswaran, Prabha. (ed), 2010, *Sex Work.* New Delhi: Women Unlimited.

Human Rights Watch, 1995, https://www.hrw.org/legacy/about/projects/womrep/General-138.htm Accessed, 3rd February, 2016.

International Convention 1933, http://ec.europa.eu/anti-trafficking/sites/antitrafficking/files/1933_international_convention_en_1.pdf, accessed 29th March, 2015.

Melissa Ditmore and Marjan Wijer, 2003, The negotiations on the UN Protocol on Trafficking in Persons, *Nemesis,* pp.79-88, http://www.bayswan.org/traffick/NEMESIS_Ditmore.PDF accessed, 29th March, 2015.

Times of India, 1994, p. 5.

Walkowitz, Judith R., 1992, *City of Dreadful Delight: Narratives of Sexual Danger in Late Victorian London.* Chicago: University of Chicago Press.

Willis, W. N.,1912, *The white slaves of London.* London: S. Paul.

Chapter 3

South Asia: The Material of Context of Trafficking

South Asia is home to around a fifth of world population. It consists of India, Pakistan, Bangladesh, Sri Lanka, Nepal, Bhutan, Maldives and the British Indian Ocean territories. From the civilisations of 5,000 years ago to the present day, South Asia has hosted countless numbers of cultures, creating a land with diverse beliefs where modern concerns mesh with traditional values. The region has often seen conflicts and political instability, including wars between the region's two nuclear states India and Pakistan. Most of the South Asian Countries were under direct or indirect European Colonial subjugation at some time or the other and hence due to their experiences of Colonialism and exploitation they have not been able to keep up with the development of Capitalism in the world. Most of the region gained independence from Europe by the late 1940s. Though today this region is characterised by high economic growth for the past 10-15 years yet poverty is also a reality along with illiteracy, backwardness and a large population.

At the dawn of the new millennium, South Asia is a land of juxtapositions. While some South Asians reside in villages, farming and raising families in the same manner as their ancestors, others have moved to the cities. Wherever they live, most maintain their cultural identities and families are very strong. However, today the gap between the haves and the have not's has only increased with globalisation creating two distinct worlds and family structures. All South Asian cultures are patriarchal and the major concerns today are a decline in the sex ratio, early marriage, increasing gender violence and trafficking of girls and women. In the absence of a State support structure, the family plays a major role in this culture (Pande, 2010).

Even a cursory glance at South Asia's demographic and cultural profile forces us to confront its diversity of caste, religions, political structures, philosophical systems and cultural practices. Historically, while the region has only rarely been welded together in one political unit, even the innumerable kingdoms herein often found themselves at the helm of diverse populations, and constantly evolved systems to check potential contradictions. Through outthis long history there were endowments to places of worship frequented by different religious groups, such as *dargahs* (Islamic shrines), groves and *mandirs* (Hindu temples), were made not only by emperors, but also by provincial rulers such as Shivaji (in Marathwada), Tipu Sultan (in Mysore) and Ranjit Singh (in Punjab) (Bose *et. al.,* 1999). Thus, while pluralism and civil society partnerships pluralism was a fact of the South Asian socio-political and even economic system, (merchant guilds coexisted with tribal sustenance mechanisms), it was not informed by any democratic vision of society by the state and there is a lot of diversity (Pradhan *et.al.,* 2006, 55).

South Asia is among the world's most vulnerable regions to both natural and human made disasters. The region recorded 15 out of the 40 major disasters in the world from 1970 to 2000. Over the last 25 years, disasters have killed nearly half a million people in South Asia besides inflicting colossal financial damages worth US$ 59,000 million. Over 60,000 people were killed by Tsunami in India, Sri Lanka and Maldives. The October 2005 earthquake killed at least 73,000 people and severely injured or disabled another 70,000 and rendered 2.8 million homeless in northern parts of Pakistan. The rehabilitation cost of 2004 Tsunami disaster for India, Sri Lanka and Maldives is estimated to be US$ 3 billion. The overall cost associated with the October 2005 earthquake is estimated at approximately at US$ 5.2 billion. Although some of the South Asian countries have begun to implement strategies for disaster mitigation or risk reduction, there still is need for an all-round paradigm shift to proactive measures in the approach to disaster mitigation (Sahni and Ariyabandu, 2003, IX). To this natural disaster is now added a human made disaster in the form of trafficking. South Asia is emerging as the main centre of human trafficking for domestic work, child labour and sex trafficking of women and girls for prostitution.

South Asia has emerged as the poorest, illiterate and least gender sensitive regions in the world. The problems of women living in these poor and illiterate regions are compounded by the existence of patriarchal societal order (Haq, 2000). The pervasive gender disparity exists in this region which effects access to education, health and employment. In situations of armed conflict, communal violence, women and girls are increasingly targeted for attack, mistreatment and rape because in these cultures there is a very strong notion that the honour of men reside in its women and one can get at the men by targeting the women. Masculinity is defined at the women's expense. So they are worst hit in caste wars and communal clashes. The violence against women is a manifestation of the unequal power relationship between men and women. The normality of violence and the wide acceptance of it by society trivialises any talk around it and refuses to take it seriously (Pande *et. al.*, 2008, 123).

Asia is identified as the increasing ground for trafficking in women and children. To quote "UNICEF maintains that the numbers being trafficked in Asia represented nearly half the world total — and that South Asia is bearing the brunt." (Huda, 2006: 375). According to Crawford and Kaufman (2008), Asia is estimated to contribute to 250,000 cases of trafficking for Commercial Sexual Exploitation (CSE), which is lesser in magnitude as equated with Central Europe and that is 175,000. Similarly, Crawford, Kaufman, and Gurung (2007) accede that sex trafficking in East and Southeast Asia is upsurging to an extent that it contributes nearly a quarter of the worldwide cases of trafficking for CSE [Crawford, Kaufman, and Gurung, 2007: 99). However, lack of concrete data on trafficking generates many myths that need serious interrogations. (Brown, 2000), Farr (2005), Crawford, Kaufman, and Gurung (2007) and others.] To quote "...that trafficking is usually for the purposes of prostitution, when there is evidence of the use of trafficked persons as domestic workers, or in factories. An assumption that most trafficking incidents start with kidnapping is also false, as coercion or deception by traffickers frequently occurs as part of a migration experience." (ADB, 2003: 12)

Historical Background to Trafficking

A close examination of the historical trajectory of trafficking is also instructive of the degree to which today's global problems were global problems a century ago. South Asia was under Colonial domination for a long period of time and mass migrations, and rising economic inequality, were also significant features of this society. Many of these victims were caught in the nets of traffickers because their rural communities were increasingly marginalised in the global economy or because, as women, their economic prospects were particularly bleak. Understanding that the trade in humans is not substantially different today than it was 100 years ago or that enforcement regimes are strikingly similar to those tried before World War II informs us that that the issues faced by policy-makers, law enforcement, non-governmental actors, and others leading the fight against human trafficking have deep historical roots and therefore great staying power that must be appreciated if there is to be any hope of achieving significant results. We also need to focus on trade. Kerala in India has a long history of trading with the Arab regions and many of these men come and have temporary marriages with the local girls and leave them once they have to return. Again, in this region migration is not a new phenomenon. For centuries, people have left their homes in search of better lives elsewhere. In the last decade, the process of globalisation has enhanced the "push-pull" factors which drive migrants' desires to seek more gainful employment abroad. This has caused an unprecedented amount of migration. Criminal networks which smuggle human beings for financial gain increasingly control the flow of migrants.

All countries in Asia experience both emigration and immigration—and often transit migration. But it is possible to differentiate between mainly destination countries (Brunei, Hong Kong, Japan, Singapore, South Korea, Taiwan), countries with both significant immigration and emigration (Malaysia and Thailand), and mainly source countries (Bangladesh, Burma, Cambodia, China, India, Indonesia, Laos, Nepal, Pakistan, Philippines, Sri Lanka, and Vietnam). Today, South Asia is the locus of extensive migrations that link cities and villages in the region to diverse places that cut across the concerns of governments, policy-makers, migrants themselves and their families. Large migration streams already occurred at the outset of South Asia's post-colonial history, when millions fled communal violence on both sides of the Indian-Pakistani border.

Historically, if we look at human trafficking it is nothing but a modern form of slavery. The defining element of trafficking is the force, fraud, or coercion exercised on the person by another to perform or remain in service to the master. Human trafficking has its roots in the phenomenon of slavery. History reveals about innumerable people transported to live under some kind of bondage, either by force or through abduction.

Genealogy of human trafficking could be traced back to the practice of 'slavery', which in itself has a long and extensive history, having started with human civilisation. A practice that most part of the world accepted, viz. Mesopotamia, China, Egypt, India, sub-Saharan Africa, and America (Masci, 2004: 282). It went global during the fifteenth century, with the

European explorers discovering new territories, and the Dutch, Spanish, Portuguese, French, and English establishing colonies all over the world. From the mid-1500s to the mid-1800s almost nine million Africans were shipped mostly to Latin America (Masci, 2004: 282). The term trafficking therefore, denotes the process by which individuals become enslaved (Zimmerman, 2010, 82). With their initiation, practice of 'slavery' became massive. One can state that the essential articulation of human trafficking since its inception has been a 'modern day slavery', therefore the genealogy of the discourse of human trafficking has been ascribed to the practice of slavery that has a long and extensive history, having started with human civilisation. A major proportion of the world geography was under the massive practice of slavery, which had a tremendous extent with European, exploring new territories in the world and establishing colonies. Therefore, the practice of slavery took a tantamount size with the spread of colonisation.

Attempts by various abolitionist groups were made to eradicate the practice of slavery during the eighteenth and nineteenth century. However, it was only after the Civil War that worldwide attempt to abolish slavery was made, making it an illegal practice. (Masci, 2004: 282). It was outlawed through various international agreements such as the Slavery Convention of the League of Nations of 1926; the Convention required the signatory countries to work for the abolition of Slavery. However, though a number of international legal mechanisms banned 'slavery', yet it seems to persist in the present century. It is present in the forms of labourers, domestic servant, indentured labour, sex slaves, and others. An estimated 27 million people around the world today are living under some form of slavery, and the great majority, including most women trafficked for prostitution, are victims of debt bondage slavery. (Farr, 2005: 25).

In India, especially in Telangana and Andhra Pradesh traditional forms of prostitution are prevalent such as among the Joginis, Marthammas, Dommarras, and Basarvis etc. The system of Devadasis where girls are dedicated to temples historically from tenth century onwards and never marry prevailed. With the coming of colonialism and the absence of patronage to the temples from eighteenth century onwards we have Devadasi who enter into prostitution. The transition of these groups into new molds of trafficking has been easy (Pande, Rekha, 2006, 453).

Migration and trafficking

It is important to understand that trafficking and other forms of exploitation occur within well-worn migratory pathways. Trafficking occurs as part of the migration continuum; many trafficked people consent to the initial movement through a facilitator or move of their own accord and it only becomes evident at their destination that they have been deceived and are being exploited. In the case of trafficking, the primary objective of the offender is the exploitation of a person for labour or services at the destination. Although both trafficking and smuggling are processes that involve the movement of people, put simply, smuggling involves a transaction which ends once the person is delivered to their destination. Around the large scale of undocumented or unregulated labour migration, which results in a blurred distinction between trafficking and smuggling. The widespread movement of women as wives and domestic workers, in addition to sex and entertainment work; the trafficking of children for labour, sexual exploitation, and adoption; and the strong link between prostitution and sex tourism can be seen (Piper, 2005: 208).

Migration discourse, in all its forms, focuses on issues such as poverty, violence and push-pull factors; the exploitation and victimisation of the migrants is often central to the analysis. The ideology of anti-trafficking does not recognise that migrants have been displaced by practices that have resulted in the loss of their land and/or livelihoods through international trade liberalisation policies, mega-development projects, the loss of employment in capitalist labour markets, or war (Sharma, 2005, 89). Inevitably exploitation exists but when the issues of trafficking and migration are brought together, conditions that make up the many reasons for which women migrate are given very little attention and the concept that women do make decisions based on choice (albeit constrained) is typically ignored. It needs to be further investigated as to whether all women, trafficked or prostituted, are incapable of choice and, therefore, are never able to exercise agency –which is not to deny the structural changes that are part of the push/pull factor.

Labour migration takes two forms, legitimate and irregular, and may be intra-national or international. In the case of women on the subcontinent, both are intended to be temporary, unless it is connected with marriage. What began as a process previously dominated by men in search of work is now part of the phenomenon of "feminisation of migration" (Skeldon, 2000: 8), which has been going on at an increasing rate globally in the twenty-first century. Forced labour also takes two forms, sexual and non-sexual, and women can be subjected to both. In the case of South Asia, they are often related to a greater or lesser degree, depending on the work for which the woman was trafficked. Given that for women in Asia generally it seems to be more economical and quicker to proceed through informal and often illegal channels to obtain regular labour than to pass through legitimate official channels and because women have fewer resources financially than men on the subcontinent and often do not have the means to carry out the lengthy paper work required. Trafficking takes place within and between the countries of the subcontinent, with India and Pakistan acting as transit countries for wider international trafficking. Trafficked persons may set out as legitimate migrant labour from Bangladesh or Nepal to India, but may end up far from where they intended, either in India or elsewhere in the world. In South Asia, Bangladesh and Nepal are the main originating countries for trafficking, although India and Pakistan are countries of destination or transit to other regions, and trafficking is rife in both (Wright, 2008: 36).

Human smuggling and trafficking complicates and adds a criminal dimension to the issue of cross-border migration. The latter is a complex social phenomenon that is influenced by economic, political, socio-cultural, historical and geographical factors and accelerated by the rapid pace of globalisation. Economic determinants, especially poverty and economic disparities are the prime motivation for migrants to leave their countries of origin. Over the last ten years, the issue of illegal migration has been increasingly linked to organised criminal groups that now largely control the smuggling and trafficking of people. An example of the transnationalisation of criminal groups is the spread of the organised gangs throughout the world or more so into the non-traditional regions where new networks are forged and one of the examples of this is the coining of the term 'narco-terrorism', that explores the interface between terrorism and drug trafficking, a term in vogue since the mid-eighties. Although we live in a globalising world, migrants increasingly face restrictive immigration policies and reduced legal immigration opportunities. This leads to a growing reliance on illegal methods to either enter or remain in a specific country.

Information Communication and Technology (ICT) and its impact on sex trafficking

The development and advancement of information communication technologies (ICT's) have revolutionised the way people communicate and share information. Technologies have made communicating and accessing information more efficient and effortless. Unfortunately, the benefits of technologies enable traffickers to more easily recruit, harm, and exploit victims/ survivors without fear of being arrested and prosecuted. Today sex trafficking is greatly simplified by the growing technological advance. In this sense, technological revolution has been providing means and tools to the crime of trafficking in women and children. Prior to the internet, traffickers were forced to reach consumers and conduct business through underground networks. Due to the anonymity of the internet, both traffickers and consumers can conduct business online with minimal risk of being identified. The result is an increased market and consumption in the trafficking in persons industry (Linda Baker, *et. al.,* 2013, 3). Traffickers can use pre-paid, disposable, or pay-as-you-go mobile phones to text information, send photos, or communicate directly with consumers in real-time without the restriction of physical location. Traffickers can also use mobile phones and the GPS tracking systems to maintain constant contact and monitor the whereabouts of victims (Vitale, K., 2012). The consumer market has expanded through exposure to the internet, where photographs and profiles of literally thousands of women and a vast array of sex tourism sites can be viewed (Farr, 2005, 22). One of the attractive features of ICT is that it helps traffickers remain anonymous and therefore provide a fine platform to conduct the business of trafficking. The affordability and access of global communications technologies allows users to carry out these activities in the privacy of their home. The increase in types of media, media formats, and applications diversifies the means by which sexual predators can reach their victims. Traffickers have taken advantages of varied technologies to "stalk victims, transmit illegal materials, and avoid detection by law enforcement." (Maltzahn, 2006, 4).

The print media, even advertisements in newspapers act as a medium of heightening the business of trafficking by luring opportunities for better job in "exciting cities", travel and matchmaking agencies also help recruit potential victims in the destination countries. Pimp and traffickers use various technologies not only to attract victims but also they use these technologies to advertise victims and attract customers. Therefore, various technological advances, have posited the world with varied developments- such as improved and convenient mobility, hassle free transactions, improved industry and so forth. Information, Communication Technologies have a revolutionary and fundamental impact in our society. However, the exploitation of information and communication technology has been sought for various crimes, one of which is sex trafficking that have transcend across the globe. Therefore, possible efforts are required to help controlling the fast spread of sex trafficking.

Women and children may be subjected to sexual exploitation by using internet as a tool for promoting and selling images or services. Various web sites are used for sharing sexual materials online. Recently, the internet has become the most effective tool in the prostitution of women. The women are tricked or forced into performing sex acts for digital photos that appear on globally accessible web sites. The internet offers several ways to sell sex and allows global sex syndicates to recruit women from all over the globe, all of which contribute to the 'globalisation' of the sex trade. (Cabrera, 2007, 3).

One can state that satellites channels that are broadcasted across the world also become a site or a medium of source for exploitation of trafficked women. Images made, using trafficked women may be transmitted to viewers through these venues. New cable Networks use satellite transmission to deliver hundreds of channels and pay-per-view delivers content on demand. Cable companies consider that the more sexually explicit the content the greater the demand. (Chawki, and Wahab, 2005).

Pornographic video is another medium of sexual exploitation. Videos of sexually exploited and trafficked victims are shot and shared across the globe for sexual pleasure of customers viewing it. Digital videos are common forms of exploitation of trafficked victims. Therefore, ICT as a medium of sexual violence simplifies the marketing of women. Hence, one can state that- sex trafficking industry has taken huge advantage of ICT developments to enhance and flourish their business of children and women trafficking.

Technology is constantly evolving and providing traffickers with new opportunities for exploitation. However, these same technologies used by traffickers can become a powerful tool to combat trafficking in persons. In order to keep pace with the rapid evolution, it is important for counter-trafficking responses to maintain constant vigilance and assert the use of technology in the strategy to prevent human trafficking. A major concern in South Asia is that many countries will not be able to meet the costs of maintaining and supporting new technology strategies in order to interrupt and prevent trafficking across borders or that local law enforcement will not receive appropriate training or the basic equipment needed to properly investigate and prosecute trafficking cases.

India emerging as Source, Transit and Destination Country

India is fast becoming a source, transit point as well as a destination area for traffickers. A substantial body of newspaper reporting as well as reports of voluntary agencies suggested that apart from Nepal, Bangladesh and the poverty-stricken districts within India, trafficking from the Commonwealth of Independent States (CIS) countries was also on the increase. This was a significant pointer towards the complex, organised nature of the crime (Sen, Nair, 2004,1). A major kind of flow has also become a serious bilateral issue in India that is the stream of illegal immigrants from various neighbouring countries like Bangladesh, China, and Pakistan to India. India shares a border with these nations running through the Indian states of West Bengal, Assam, Meghalaya, Tripura, and Mizoram. This border is longer than the one India shares with China. Indian officials have alleged that continued illegal immigration from Bangladesh has altered the demography of India's border areas resulting in ethnic imbalance, electoral irregularity, and loss of employment opportunities for Indian nationals (Ganguly, 2003: 544-56).

There are four very well established routes through which trafficking takes place in Andhra Pradesh and Telangana. These include,

The Mumbai Network

- The first is from Guntur, Visakhapatnam, East Godavari to Vijayawada, Hyderabad and Mumbai.

- The second direct from Hyderabad to Mumbai.
- The third from Cuddapah, Guntakal to Mumbai.
- The fourth from Vijaywada, Warangal, Karimnagar, Nizamabad, Khammam, Hyderabad and Mumbai.

The Delhi Net Work

- The first one is from Anantpur to Daund, Bangalore, Hyderabad to Delhi.
- The second from Guntakal, Warangal and Tirupati to Delhi.
- The third from Chittor to Vijaywada, Warangal, Tirupati, Delhi.
- Fourth, Kurnool to Warangal to Delhi.
- East Godavari to West to Vizag to Delhi.
- Hyderabad to Delhi.

The Kolkata Network

- First from Bapatla, Vizag to Rajahmundry to Ongole to Vijayawada to Kolkata.
- Second from Anantpur to Bangalore to Hyderabad to Kolkata.

The Goa Network

- First, Kurnool, Hyderabad to Guntakal, to Hubli, Londa to Vasco.
- Second from Eluru, Tadpatalligudam, Ongole, Chilakaluripet, Medmetta, Mangalgiri, Machalipatnam, Vizianagaram to Vijayawada to Vasco.
- Third Kakinada, Rajahmundry to Samalkot to Vijayawada to Vasco.
- Fourth, Vijayawada to Vasco.

Over the years one can see an increase in traffiking in many states.

Assam situated at the foothills of eastern Himalayas, is the largest state in northeast India. Assam being on the periphery of the country stands vulnerable to trafficking of women and children. Its peculiar geography is one of the prime reasons for human trafficking. The rationale for this is that, being in the northeastern region of the country, it is one of the overlooked states of the country, which henceforth has amounted to its slow economic development. Connected to mainland India by the thin 'chicken neck' area – the peculiar geographical location of Assam makes it more vulnerable to infiltration and insurgency resulting in slow economic growth. Over the decades, Assam has witnessed large scale migration of the local population to the comparatively richer parts of the country. The growing need for better livelihood options and employment has turned Assam into a fertile place for human traffickers and in the past few years, thousands of young men and women of the state have fallen prey to the designs of traffickers and have been exploited as cheap labour. Over 1,500 children have disappeared from Assam between 2011 and 2012, and most are now living in subhuman conditions somewhere in north India, as forced sex workers, domestic helps or underage wives in women-starved states. According to the latest data of the State Crime Records Bureau, altogether 1,071 female and 494 male children have gone missing in Assam in 2011-2012, the highest in the Northeast.

Poverty is on the rise, which has resulted in the increased cases of human trafficking. On 3rd March 2007, the Daily Agradoot published a report which stated that during the period from 2001 – 2006, as many as 4000 people of the state have gone missing. What happened to those people? Did they fall prey to traffickers? In the early months of 2004, the National Human Rights Commission (NHRC) carried out a detailed investigation to comprehend the growing menace of human trafficking in India and put forward certain recommen-dations to counter the problem. (Dibasri Mazumdar, 2016).

Further, Assam's economic development is lagging behind than the rest of India and the gap is widening. In 1998, the average per capita income for the country was over 1.8 times that of Assam. Assam is a less industrialised state. A major portion of its economy is dependent on agriculture. Nearly 70 per cent of the population depends on its earnings. The 2011 census reports that 88 per cent of the total geographical area of Assam is available for agricultural cultivation. During 2010-11 the State domestic product contributed from agriculture was nearly 25 per cent. Therefore, one can argue that though agriculture is the principal sector of the economy yet it has not developed largely. The growth rate of agriculture is neither enough to generate a surplus capital for investment nor enough to create purchasing power.

Besides considering the secondary sector, the state relies on petroleum industry and natural gas. Tea industry is also one of the major industries of the State. The state produces about 15.6 per cent of the world's total tea. In India, the total contribution of the state is 55 per cent. Apart from these major industries, the state continues with its traditional industries such as weaving, pottery looms, bell metal and brass-metal works, spinning of endi, muga and mulberry silk, and manufacture of ivory products. Therefore, the overall industrial economy of the state does not reveal an upward trend. The fact accounting to this is that- number of factories existing in the state contributes to only 1.23 per cent of the total number of factories existing in the country. Absence of industries and factories in the state can be accounted to inadequate infrastructure, lack of well-developed markets, and geographical isolation of the region.

Besides this Assam has seen a lot of conflict which has added to the underdevelopment of the region. With the forceful implement of Armed Forced Special Power Act, 1958 (AFSPA) in the states of North-East, the situation of conflict has grown manifold. Armed Force Special Power Act, 1958, gives the armed forces special power to raid any civilians home without any warrant. They can even carry out encounter of a person on the basis of mere suspicion. It has been in North-East for 48 years, first in Assam to combat Naga rebellion in undivided state of Assam. The act literally gave the central security forces the power of life and death over ordinary people (Hazarika, 2010). Assam for that matter, have been undergoing the situation of conflict since late 1970s to present date. The Anti-Foreigner Movement of late 1970, considered as epic moment in history of Assam, was mainly spearhead by the organisations such as The Assam Sahitya Sabha, a literary organisation of Assam, which promotes the culture and literature of Assam and this movement tried to stop the increasing illegal immigration of people from neighbouring country, Bangladesh. The movement resulted in signing of Memorandum of Settlement (MoS) between the representatives of Government of India and the agitating leaders which came to be known as Assam Accord in 1985. But with the signing of the treaty, conflict situation in Assam have not come to an end. The separatist movement of ULFA also holds importance in the history of Assam along with different forms of ethnic conflicts among different communities. The Bodo-Adivasi conflict, Bodo-Muslim conflict is of significance as large numbers of families have been displaced from the 1990s till 2012, when conflict between these com-munities occurred based on ethnicity and identity. All this has lead to underdevelopment of the region and poverty.

The problem of conflict as a result of political instability, social unrest, identity movements, class struggle, and ethnic fragmentation in the Indian state of Assam (districts of Kokrajhar, Bongaigaon, Dhubri, Goalpara and Udalguri) have resulted in high magnitude of internal displacement and migration of communities from their settled lands. This conflict induced displacement had given rise to a new social problem in the form of trafficking of women and children in this conflict stricken areas, thereby reinforcing the main argument that internal conflict encourages the internal displacement of individuals from networks of families and communities and their access to "economic safety nets" visible in the form of networks that are transnational and partially invisible (Akee *et.al.,* Khamis; 2010). It is during this time of conflict which makes trafficking in person much easier for traffickers because of the breakdown in law and order situations, lapse in border control initiatives and actions with understaffed police persons in the area.

Marked by nascent levels of industries, poor-infrastructure, weak-communication, low-agricultural productions, the economic growth of Assam has not percolated since the mid-nineties. This, therefore had resulted in increased poverty in the state. The State's economy is affected by a long stranded chronic poverty. The decadal growth of population, the high incidence of inequality in the distribution of income, and the ever-increasing price level has set Assam towards the increasing problem of poverty. The poverty rates in the state show that at least 116.4 lakh persons in the state live below the poverty line. This figure has been increasing at a high rate from 7.8 million in 1983 to 9.5 million in 1999-2000. Further, Percentage of poverty in Assam is highest as compared to all other states of northeast.

The present status of women in Assam holds an asymmetry and inequity vis-à-vis that of men. The position of women in Assam is not different from that of women in other regions of the country. The gender gap in the state is prominent and brought out at all levels. The overall status of women vis-à-vis men reveals of the glaring inequality between them. Gender inequity is visible in the wide gender gaps in literacy rates, reflected in sex ratios, gender-based violence such as domestic violence and rape is on the increase in the state. For instance, the number of dowry deaths and violence is increasing in the State. In the last couple of years, Assam has seen an increase in the number of dowry deaths. Similarly, government sources in February 2011 at the State Legislative Assembly revealed the rise in rape, domestic violence, and dowry cases.

Moreover, Assam is a state inflicted with the problem of ethnic conflict, and insurgency, which had resulted in great violence in the state. For instance, in Nellie massacre, 2,191 people lost their lives. Mobs slaughtered people, mostly women and children. Though the agitation halted with the Assam

Accord, it resulted in the creation of many new insurgent groups, one of the most prominent being the United Liberation Front of Assam (ULFA). Thereby the effects of violent situations created by insurgent groups marginalise women and subject them to various forms of vulnerable situation. For instance, the aftermath of violent actions result in destitution of many families and in turn taking shelter in relief camps. Research shows that relief camps have been the main source of supply for traffickers seeking for 'fresh merchandise' (women). They strive in taking advantage of the vulnerable position of these women and utilise them for their own selfish motives. The best examples from Assam are from the districts of Kokrajhar and Karbi Anglong. In conflict situations, girls are asked to sacrifice their education on grounds that it is unsafe for them to venture out in the public space. Nagaland is a good example of this form of educational exclusion.

Therefore Assam has emerged as one of the major sources of sex trafficking. One observes that the state circumscribes the possible factors grounding human trafficking for commercial sexual exploitation (CSE) - such as geographical isolation, economically backward identity, political unrest, illiterate population, and gender discrimination. These reasons essentially make Assam a source country for trafficking of girls and women to other metropolitan and bigger cities.

India is also facing problem of a large number of Bangladeshis emigrating from Bangladesh into all states of India, but their proportion is much higher in North East states, particularly Assam and Tripura and in August 2012, India saw one of the worst communal violence in Assam due to this.

Bangladeshi infiltration remains unchecked and illegal immigration continues to be a sensitive issue, exploited by vested political interests. It is widely believed that Islamic militancy has been consolidating because of unabated Bangladeshi immigration. Ineffective border management has emerged as a major irritant in India-Bangladesh relations because of concerns about smuggling, illegal immigration, trafficking in women and children, and insurgency. India's plan has led to strong resentment in villages that straddle the dividing line and trade in both directions. Smugglers on both sides also stand to lose with the erection of this fence. Organised criminal gangs and syndicates often with powerful political and communal influence and patronage have cropped up at different places along the border. The quickening pace of urbanisation and the heightened mobility resulting from the development of road links are contributing factors.

A culture of consumerism and materialism distorts family needs and individual desires. Bangladeshi migration has assumed alarming proportions leading to ethnic clashes and the observations of the Supreme Court of India that this is a security threat is a notable observation. While the 'brothels' were the earlier destination for many of the trafficked Bangladeshi women, the skewed sex ratio has opened up newer destinations. In many of the villages of Haryana it is a common sight to see a large number of able bodied unmarried young men who are unable to find a bride and these youth are seen as potential trouble makers and as a result there is a demand for Bangladeshi women here and this is the subject of many articles in magazines that have labelled this phenomenon as a sort of a 'cottage industry'. This is akin to trafficking for the women are just left at the mercy of a patriarchal culture which undervalues girls and find themselves in an alien new culture and environment where they do not even speak the language but a kind of respectability is given to this by the women wearing insignias of marriage and considering herself married to the man in the house.

Trafficking in Nepal is a byproduct of the country's appalling poverty and it is mostly low caste women who are the worst victims of human trafficking (Brown, 2011). By 2001, the amount spent annually on anti-trafficking initiatives in Nepal was 52.5 million dollars and this initiative shows the increasing international recognition of the problem in Nepal (Crawford, 2010, 115). This estimates show that the 5000-7000 Nepali girls and women are trafficked across borders to India each year and currently there are 150,000- 200,000 women and girls in various Indian cities (Deane, 2010, Datta, 2005, Samarsinghe, 2008). The open border agreement between Nepal and India was designed to facilitate trade and transit between the two countries but it now enables traffickers to easily transport victim from Nepal to India because of the 1,740 miles open border between both these countries.

When caught receiver countries such as India usually adopt a legalistic immigration approach, and this gives little consideration to the fact that the woman trafficked is a victim. For a country like India, with many thousands of recent illegal immigrants from Bangladesh, men as well as women, governments have taken a tough stance on this matter because they do not want to be perceived as being soft on immigration that might lead to an uncontrolled rush into India from neighbouring states. The rights of the trafficked woman or child simply gets lost in this process, and it does not matter whether the person has been trafficked for prostitution or forced labour; there is not much sympathy for the victim and it is generally left to NGOs to try to sort out the mess.

Odisha is situated in the east coast of India and shares its borders with the states of Madhya Pradesh, Chhattisgarh, Bihar, Jharkhand, West Bengal, and Andhra Pradesh. Bay of Bengal forms its eastern coastal boundary. The state comprises the highest ST population after Northeastern states and 45 per cent of the geographical area in the state is scheduled area with Districts of Gajapati, Kandhamal, Keonjhar, Koraput, Malkangiri, Mayurbhanj, Nabarangpur, Rayagarh and Sundergarh having a Schedule tribe population of more than 40 per cent of their total population. Odisha is home to about 62 tribes and 93 Schedule Castes making their proportion in total state population 22.21 per cent and 16.20 per cent respectively. The north-western districts (Sundergarh, Keonjhar, and Mayurbhanj) account for 35.3 per cent of Odisha's tribal population and the south-western districts (Koraput, Kalahandi, Phulbani, and Balangir) account for another 39.4 per cent (Odisha,UNDP, 2004). The state is among the poorest in India with the state of Infrastructural development lagging far behind. Poverty level and illiteracy are important factors in Odisha's human trafficking.

Sex trafficking of women is highly rampant not only for the sex trade but also for other forms of non-sex-based exploitation which include servitude of various kinds as domestic labour, industrial labour, begging, organ trade and false marriage. Many contributing factors are there to women's sex trafficking which include economic deprivation, lack of employment opportunities, frequent natural calamities, illiteracy, social status and political uprisings and the like. In the case of women the factors expand to many a variations like male preference, dowry demands, Misogyny, domestic violence, destitution, alcoholism, and so on. It is also a fact that girls are found more vulnerable as they are looked upon as more expandable than the rest of the population. Often young girls become sex slaves and are forced into prostitution.

In spite of high concentration of scheduled tribes in the state who, due to their marginalised status, are prone to exploitation, a relatively low number of trafficked women are from tribal populations. The majority come from poor and landless families. Eighty per cent of those trafficked are illiterate (Pandey, B.*et.al.*, 2002). Odisha is a major source state for Trafficking of Women for commercial sexual exploitation. Due to poverty, women, taking to commercial sex is not new in Odisha. According to Lalitha, a social activist, child trafficking in Odisha is an open secret. Families, irrespective of their caste, sell their children for mere Rs 100 so they can get their next meal. The children are either married off to old men or they work as bonded labour (Shakti Vahini., 2003). The incidents of child trafficking increased after multinational companies took over large areas of fertile land for mining and to set up other industries. Increasing level of trafficking was reported in Odisha after the super cyclone in 1999. A Task Force on Women and Violence (TFWV) study found that the people living within the community are the first links in the trafficking chain that takes the recruits to the sex trade because of their familiarity with the local families. In particular, they can recognise those in economic distress. They know exactly which families to target. They know which family is poor; which has too many daughters for whom dowry arrangements are not possible; the family that has suffered the death of the breadwinner, is in debt and simply cannot cope. They also know which woman is deserted by a husband or lover; who is pregnant; a widow; or whose image is tarnished. They know the family that cannot or is indifferent to protecting its daughters. Many girls are also fooled by false promises of marriage, followed by desertion after being sexually exploited. And they may have other reasons too. The TFWV study also found a clear involvement of police and politicians in trafficking (Bahuguna, 2004).

The Odisha State Commission for Women, found that five coastal districts had become vulnerable to trafficking and labour exploitation in general, especially with road and rail connections providing easy access into and out of the state. Following the cyclone, 21 of the 30 districts in Odisha have been sucked into this network, extending the geographic scope of trafficking within Odisha. The main sourcing districts though remain the coastal districts of Bhadrak, Jagatsinghpur, Cuttack and Jajpur as well as tribal dominated border districts of Koraput, Rayagada, Nuapada and Mayurbhanj. (Jeni, Manipadma, 2003). The trafficking for Odisha, is mostly to the states of Uttar Pradesh (Brothels, coerced marriages, brick kilns), Madhya Pradesh (coerced marriages, brick kilns), Punjab (coerced marriages, bonded labour in agriculture and domestic maids), Haryana (coerced marriages, bonded labour in agriculture, stone quarries, brick kilns), Chhattisgarh (coerced marriages, brick kilns), Andhra (Brick Kilns, Chilly farms), metropolises of Mumbai, Delhi or Kolkata (Brothels and domestic services).

A study by an NGO in Odisha, says 80 per cent of the victim families are landless; and 70 per cent of those trafficked are illiterate. Dowry-related problems lead more and more poor girls into getting duped by false promises to marry; 49 per cent of the women victims were deserted by men after being sexually used. Families refuse to take them back for fear of social approbation and spoiling the marriage prospects of younger sisters. The study also showed that times of hardship are the 'best season' for recruitment; and for Odisha, hard times seem endless. Nearly half the population is under the poverty line (ISED, 2000). The girls being trafficked from Odisha rarely land directly in the final destination place, in case of direct prostitution. For the purpose of coerced marriage majority are apprehended directly, by their buyers at first time through pimps. The modus operandi is of both kind, the buyer going along with the pimp to the girls locality and the girl brought to buyers locality by pimps. The majority of girls trafficked from Odisha are for prostitution mainly in smaller cities. For coerced marriage girls from Odisha are taken to Bihar, Uttar Pradesh, Haryana and Punjab. Girls from Odisha are also trafficked for labour purposes in brick kilns, and construction work who are subjected to all sort of physical, economical, moral exploitation including sexual and prostitution. The trafficking in Odisha is directly related to the overall backwardness of the state both economically and socially. The most effected districts are Balasore, Malkangir, Nayagarh, Kendrapara, Nabaranpur, Nuadpada, Koraput, Rayagada, Ganjam and Puri (Shakti Vahini, 2003,).

Most of the districts in Odisha have typical features of trafficking. In districts like Nayagarh and Kendrapada, trafficking is seen in the form of marriages. Sundergarh district is the source for young girls migrating as domestic help and are often found in exploitative situation. The remote tribal belts and coastal districts are known for migration of its population. Ganjam, almost 40 per cent people migrate every year. Ganjam is the southernmost coastal district of Odisha with typical costal and tribal belt together. Coincidentally this district also has the highest HIV infected population and is the highest populated district. In most of the villages in Balasore district parents sell their daughters for money.

In Bengal in 2011, more than 13,000 women and children were untraceable. Where did they go? Were they abducted? Were they sold for money? Are they still alive? There are no answers. The year before, around 28,000 women and children went missing and 19,000 of them remained untraceable. The recent report of United Nations Office on Drug and Crime (UNODC) titled 'Anti Human Trafficking, 2013' revealed that out of over 19,000 women and children reported missing in West Bengal in 2011, only 6,000 could be traced. Bengal, with a huge porous international border (2,217 kms with Bangladesh, 92 kms with Nepal and 175 kms with Bhutan). On the northern side districts like Darjeeling, North and South Dinajpur, Cooch Behar and Malda having international borders with Bangladesh, Nepal and Bhutan are identified as trafficking prone. The districts of North and South 24 Parganas are other vulnerable areas prone to trafficking on the southern side. Children and women from Bengal are mostly trafficked to Delhi, Mumbai and Pune, revealed the study. After this the destinations are Haryana, Uttar Pradesh, Rajasthan and Punjab. Some new destinations that have been identified are Ahmedabad, Bangalore and Haridwar, the report found after ten months of intensive consultations with various government and non-government stakeholders (Shakti Vahini, 2014).

India's Northeastern States of Manipur, Nagaland, Arunachal Pradesh and Mizoram are bordering with Burma's western states such as Chin State and Sagaing Division. North-East India connected with mainland India with a chicken neck secludes the region and makes the region further isolated. Further biased treatment of the central government, there has been growing riots and insurgencies in the region. Here, trafficking of women and children takes place within the states in the region and other states in India, and also across the borders of Myanmar, Bangladesh and Nepal due to poverty and unemployment, declining traditional economy, militarisation and armed conflict, urbanisation, migration, displacement, proximity to the international border and influx of security personnel, businessmen. The region, rich in natural resources is regarded as a hotspot of biodiversity. North-East is a miniature of India as it is the abode of many ethnic groups. Ethnic conflicts and internal armed conflict in North-East region have cause wide scale trafficking of different kinds. Large numbers of children in conflict areas are recruited as comrade by the rebel forces. It is also revealed by the returnees (surrendered) girls' rebels forces that most of the times they were made to perform sex to their superior/commanders and other leaders of rebel groups visiting the camps and perform sex for blue films. Such films were made in order to raise fund to run the rival camp in the deep jungles. Most of the films are sold to the foreign countries. It is one of the biggest blue films making network operating in the North-East region (Nedan Foundation, Report). Poverty and lack of employment opportunities in the North-East region is also one of the root cause of the problem. Searching for employment, driven by poverty and insecurity of life has forced many women and girls to move in uncertain destinations with unknown persons. In such situation the girls mobility has been trapped by the traffickers as such agents put them into exploitative condition without having any means to return to their respective home towns (Ninghorla Zimik T, 2015, 35).

The other reasons contributing to trafficking in North-East India are seen to be closure of several tea gardens and loss of livelihood, acute poverty, natural disaster and displacement. existence of fake placement agencies both in the source and destinations, lack of awareness and illiteracy, demand of girls for marriage in Haryana, Punjab and Rajasthan, demand of domestic helps in metros are other reasons. Poor implementation of policies/right to education bill and integrated child protected skills, Poor policing by the law enforcement at the source states, Inaction of police against the traffickers also add to the woes. Trafficking is also due to social evils like dowry, down grading of daughters and child marriages, lack of sustainable job opportunities and large family size (Deboleena Sengupta, Pallabi, Deka).

Trafficking discourse in India

Though India symbolically is held accountable to the conventions it ratifies, the UN protocols lack legal power in India's dualist system. In order for these conventions to be legally binding, the government must make an explicit enactment of a statute to internalise them within the central and state legal structures (SHRDC, 2012: 45). India has integrated trafficking into its legal framework, but maintains a bias towards criminalising trafficking for sex work rather than for any other means. The National Network of Sex Workers in India has frequently called for the need to distinguish between consenting and trafficked sex workers, arguing that "punitive laws and policies have fueled the stigma and discrimination resulting in extreme forms of violence against sex workers by State and non-State actors; further exacerbated by the denial of access to justice." The National Network of Sex workers points out that, the suggestion that criminalising clients of sex workers is an anti-trafficking solution is not supported by evidence. In fact, as is being seen in the case of Sweden where the purchasers of sexual transactions are criminalised, it exposes sex workers to increased violence. The Supreme Court of India in *Budhadev Karmaskar v. State of West Bengal,* stated that along the recognition of prevention of trafficking and rehabilitation of sex workers who wish to leave sex work, it is essential that conditions conducive for sex workers to live with dignity in accordance with the provisions of Article 21 of the Constitution, must also be recognised. The distinction between sexual exploitation and consensual adult sex work is very significant as it enables sex workers and their advocates to legally contest oppressive and forced sex work towards creation of safe and dignified work. (National Network of Sex workers, 2013).

The dividing line between the two, prostitution and trafficking is very thin. All trafficking ends in prostitution, where as a prostitute may not necessarily end in being trafficked. What separates the two is the element of force and deceit, which may not necessarily be the case in prostitution and it include an element of consent and willingness. India's Constitution and penal code contain 20 provisions on trafficking (NIHR, 2000: 4). The main piece of legislation in India's trafficking policy is the Immoral Traffic Prevention Act (ITPA), which limits trafficking to acts perpetrated towards women and children for prostitution (ITPA, 1956). It specifies that the consent of the victim being trafficked is irrelevant, thereby making it difficult to distinguish between a consenting sex worker, a person being exploited in sex work having willingly migrated, and a non-consenting sex worker. Trafficking is thus framed within the purview of right and wrong, whereby the act of prostitution is inherently deemed illegal. This view is also reflective of societal perceptions; as an opinion article in the newspaper DNA states, "Contrary to what a section of society believes, no woman chooses prostitution, but is forced into it due to the lack of choices available to her." (Gautam, 2014)

The frameworks in human trafficking reveals a gendered and exclusionary approach to India's trafficking policy discourse, which doesn't allow for an integration of non-sex trafficking as a normative phenomenon. Despite the lack of empirical evidence to support the extensive focus on trafficking for commercial sex work, Indian and South Asian policies continue to emphasise it's occurrence in the region, specifically of women being trafficked from Nepal to India for sex work. Anti-sex trafficking initiatives are largely guided by the moral assault of sex work on human dignity. (Purohit, Bhumi, 2015, 12).

It was in the 1980's that the Indian women's movement took up the issue of violence against women especially in the context of the dowry-related violence and during this debate, many other issues like battering, rape, sex determination, and sexuality came to the forefront. Debates around 1980's based on the experience of non-middle class women integrated and seen as bringing out and enlarging opposing between the sexes nakedly, unlike other forms of gender-based oppression such as lower wages for working class women (Gangoli, 1998). By and large, there was reluctance to debate on issues of non-marital sex relations and prostitution was alien to many middle class women's experiences and was not addressed. Many feminists accepted monogamy as the accepted norm and socially accepted parameters of women's public behaviour and morality. In fact, there was an unwritten understanding that anything sexual is obscene and that respect for women is equivalent to treating them as asexual (Agnes, 1995, 137-38). The attaching of marital sexual ideology into the trafficking discourse, essentially displaces the tripartite standard of force, fraud and coercion as the central criteria by which human trafficking is defined. Rather than defining trafficking with reference to force, fraud, or coercion, the reference point shifts to the ideal heterosexual marriage. (Zimmerman, 2010, 94)

Socio-economic issues in exploitation

Trafficking of women and children is just the end result of a long chain, which involves a large number of persons. A dysfunctional home environment, break-up of the family, marital discord, physical abuse, sexual abuse, drug use, family pressures, large families, families facing uncertain times, children in substitute care, gender discrimination within the family, desertion by husbands, husbands 'acquiring a second or a third wife makes people vulnerable to trafficking (Sen and Nair, 2004, 9). Discriminatory practices and social exclusion exacerbate the vulnerabilities of groups like Scheduled Tribes, Scheduled Castes, Other Backward Castes, ethnic minorities, tribal communities, undocumented migrant workers, stateless people or people in refugee camps.

Whenever we talk of trafficking, three aspects that need to be focused are transit, destination and the whole supply chain and only then can the issue be understood in its various dimensions. The girl being trafficked is only one of the constituents of this and just focusing on her will not help in understanding the issue (Pande, 2006, 34). Trafficking is a very dynamic business and newer forms of exploitation are discovered every day. Since commercial sex work is carried out right across the country in hotels, brothels, lodges, cinema halls, parks, along major roads and highways, it is impossible to provide actual facts and figures. Added to this is the fact that apart from regular operators, there are also such forms as contract workers, call girls, part time operators seeking supplementary income, escort service, masseurs and the like. Electronic media particularly internet and print media facilitates the very nature of this business which has to be conducted with a certain ambiguity and secretiveness. Earlier, prostitution was centralised but now it is becoming more decentralised. There is a close relation between trafficking and the spread of AIDS epidemic and we are sitting on a time bomb. Hence, this issue deserves all the attention and it is high time we take it with all seriousness.

Trafficking is a multi-dimensional problem encompassing a whole range of economic, social and cultural issues which are varied and highly complex. Most of the victims are trafficked with the promise of better jobs, better career prospects and marriage. Some are inducted forcibly through abduction. Poverty and deprivation, secondary status accorded to women in society, prejudice against the girl child, weakening of the family structure, changing public attitude towards sex and morality, the caste structure, urbanisation, migration and the growing consumerism are some of the factors that have contributed to trafficking. Economic impoverishment provides the ideal ground for exploitation. It is no surprise therefore that nearly 70 per cent of victims come from drought-prone areas in AP (The Velvet Blouse, NCW, 1997).

References

A.D.B. Asian Development Bank, 2003, *Combating of Trafficking in Women and Children in South Asia: Regional Synthesis Paper for Bangladesh, India and Nepal. Bangkok,* http://adb.org/sites/default/files/pub/2003/combating-trafficking-south-asia-paper.pdf, accessed, 3rd February, 2016.

Agnes, Flavia, 1995, *Report, State, Gender and the rhetoric of law reform,* Centre for Women's Studies, Bombay, S.N.D.T. University.

Akee, R, Basu, A.K, Chau H.N, Khamis M. 2010, "Ethnic Fragmentation, Conflict, Displaced Persons and Human Trafficking: An Empirical Analysis", *Discussion Paper No. 5142.*

Bahuguna, N., 2004, November 4, HumanTrafficking Escalates, from http://www.boloji.com/wfs6/wfs1053.htm. Retrieved November 4, 2009.

Bose, S. and A. Jalal, 1999, *Modern South Asia,* Delhi: Oxford University Press.

Brown, Louis, 2011, *Sex slaves : The trafficking of women in Asia,* London, Palgrave, Macmillan.

Brown, Louise, 2000, *Sex Slaves: The Trafficking of Women in Asia.* London: Virago Press.

Cabrera, Marion Bernadette G. 2007, The Role of Cyberspace in Marriage Migration in Asia: Claiming Spaces for Intervention. *Women in Action,* Vol. 3, pp. 51-56.

Chawki, Mohammad Judge and Wahab, Mohammad, "Technology is a double edged sword: Illegal human trafficking in the information age. www.droit-tic.com/pdf/chawki_wahab 3 pdf accessed on 16th april 2016.

Crawford, Mary, 2010, *Sex Trafficking in South Asia: Telling Maya's story,* New York, Routledge.

Crawford, Mary and Michelle R. Kaufman, 2008, 'Sex trafficking in Nepal: Survivor characteristics and long-term outcomes', *Violence against women* 2008; 14 (8): 905-917.

Crawford, Mary, Michelle R. Kaufman, and Alka Gurung, 2007, Women and Children Last: The Effects of the Maoist Insurgency on Gender-based Violence, in Mahendra, Lawoti (ed.), *Contentious Politics and Democratisation in Nepal*, pp. 95-119. New Delhi: Sage Publications.

Chiang, Lois, 1999, "Trafficking in women", in K.D. Askin and D.M. Koening (eds) *Women and International Human Rights law* (Vol. 1), pp. 321-64, New York, Transnational Publishers.

Datta, Parnati, 2005, "Nepal female migration and Trafficking", *Journal of Social Science,* 11(1), pp. 49-56.

Deane, Tameshine, 2010, "Cross Border Trafficking in Nepal and India_ Violating women's Rights", *Human Rights Review,* 11, pp. 491-513.

Deboleena Sengupta, Pallabi, Deka, Her body, her rights: In reference to women trafficking in North East India, https://www.academia.edu/9154140/HER_BODY_HER_RIGHTS_In_ Reference_to_Women_Trafficking_in_North_East_India accessed, 13th February, 2016.

Farr, Kathryn, 2005, *Sex Trafficking: The Global Market in Women and Children,* New York: Worth Publisher.

Gangoli, G. 1998, "Prostitution, Legalisation and Decriminalisation. Recent debates," *Economic and Political Weekly*: 504-05.

Gautum, Nishat, 2014, DNA, *How India Inc can help combat human trafficking* http://www.dnaindia.com/analysis/standpoint-how-india-inc-can-help-combat-human-trafficking-1959083, accessed, 12th February, 2016.

Haq, Khadija, 2000, *Human Development in South Asia:* The *Gender Question,* Oxford University Press, http://mhhdc.org/wp-content/themes/mhdc/reports/HDRSA%202000.pdf Accessed, 25th April, 2014.

Hazarika, S. 2010, "In the times of Conflict the real victims are Women". *The Peripheral Centre: Voices from India's Northeast.*Ed. Preeti Gill. Zubaan: New Delhi. 66-79.

Huda S. 2006, Sex trafficking in South Asia, Jaranal of Gyncology and Obstretricst, Vol. 94, pp. 374-381.

ISED, 2000, Institute of Small Expertise and Development, *Report on Trafficking of Women and Children. Institute for Socio-Economic Development.* Bhubaneswar.

Jena, Manipadma, 2003, *Trafficking in Overdrive* http://www.boloji.com/index.cfm?md=Mobile&sd=Articles&ArticleID=6351 accessed, 17th February, 2016.

Linda Baker, Marcie Campbell, 2013, *Information Communication Technologies and Trafficking in Persons,* The Learning Network Brief, Centre for Research and Education on Violence against Women and Children, London, Ontario. http://www.learning-toendabuse.ca/sites/default/files/Baker_Campbell_Trafficking_ and_Technology.pdf accessed, 12th February, 2016.

Masci, David, 2004, *Human Trafficking and Slavery*, CQ Researcher, Vol.14 (12), pp. 273-296.

Maltzahn, Kathleen, 2006, Digital Dangers: Information and Communication Technologies and Trafficking in Women. *APC WNSP and AWID "Issue Papers",* pp. 1-12.

Mazumdar, Dibasri, "Human Trafficking in Assam." *Eastern Panorama,* http://www.easternpanorama.in/index.php?option=com_content&

amp;view=article&id=173:human-trafficking-in accessed, 23rd February, 2016

National Network of Sex Workers — India, 2013, Statement. http://www.nswp.org/sites/nswp.org/files/Statement-national-network-of-sex-workers-India.pdf accessed, 12th February, 2016.

Nedan Foundation, Trafficking & HIV/AIDS, North East report, http://nedan.in/reports-1/trafficking-and-hiv-north-east-report accessed, 13th February, 2016.

Ninghorla Zimik T. 2015, Human trafficking in north east India, *International Journal in Management and Social Science*, Vol. 03, Issue-06.

NCW, 1997, *The Velvet Blouse, Sexual exploitation of children,* National Commission for Women, New Delhi.

Odisha, UNDP, 2004, *Human Development Report*, Government of Odisha.

Pande, Rekha, 2014, "Human Security, Globalisation, and Trafficking of Women and Children in South Asia", in, *Globalisation, Development and Security in Asia,* (ed) Zhquin Zhu, Foreign Policy and Security in an Asian Century: Threats, strategies and Policy choices, Vol. 1, (ed), Benny The Cheng Guan, World Scientific. pp. 277-296.

Pande, Rekha, 2010, Gender issues in South Asia, with special reference to India, Challenges in the new Millennium, in *Family in Development, Hopes and Challenges,* (Eds), Simon Polinder, Evert Jan Brouwer and Hank Jochesen, Just development Series, Prisma, Shaker Publishing, Netherlands, pp. 47-58.

Pande, Rekha (with Bindu, K.C. Mumtaz Fatima, Nuzhath Khatoon), 2008, "Narratives of domestic violence, Reconstructing masculinities and Feminities", in Singh, Manjit and D.P. Singh (ed), *Violence –impact and intervention,* Atlantic Publishers and Distributors, New Delhi, pp. 121-140.

Pande, Rekha, 2006, Globalisation and trafficking of women and Children, *Samyukta, A Journal of Women's studies*, Vol. VI, No. 2, pp. 31-47.

Pande, Rekha 1, 2006, Devdasis, in J.S. Grewal (ed), *Religious Movements and Institutions in Medieval India*, Vol. VII, Part, 2. in D.P. Chattopadhyay (general editor), *History of Science, Philosophy and Culture in Indian Civilisation,* Oxford University Press, New Delhi, pp. 493-504.

Pandey, B., Jena, D., and Mohanty, S 2002, *Trafficking in Women in Orissa, Institute for Socio-Economic Development (ISED).*

Piper, Nicola, 2005, "A Problem by a Different Name? A Review of Research on Trafficking in Southeast Asia and Oceania," *Special Issue of International Migration*, 43(1/2) pp. 203-233.

Pradhan, Uma, and Indrajit Roy, Pluralism and civil society partnership perspectives from Uttar Pradesh and Nepal, *Contemporary South Asia,* 15(1), March, 2006, pp. 55-74.

Purohit, Bhumi, 2015, Morality vs. reality: examining intentionality in India's human trafficking policy, Malangs South Asia Essay. http://www.area-studies.ox.ac.uk/sites/sias/files/documents/Morality%20vs%20Reality-Examining%20Intentionality%20in%20India's%20Human%20Trafficking%20Policy.pdf accessed, 12th February 2016.

Sahni, Pardeep and Ariyabandu, Madhavi Malalgoda, 2003, Eds. *Disaster Risk Reduction in South Asia,* New Delhi: Prentice-Hall of India Private Limited.

Samarsinghe, Vidyamali, 2008, *Female Sex Trafficking in Asia: The Resilience of patriarchy in changing world,* New York, Routledge.

Sen, Sankar and Nair, P.M. 2004, A Report on Trafficking of women and Children in India, 2002-2003, Vol. I, Institute of Social Sciences, Human Rights Commission and UNIFEM, New Delhi.

Sharma, Nandita, 2005, Anti-Trafficking Rhetorica and the Making of a Global Apartheid, *NWSA Journal,* Vol. 17, No. 3, States of Insecurity and the Gendered Politics of Fear (Autumn) Published by: The Johns Hopkins University Press, pp. 88-111.

Shakti Vahini, 2003, *Female Foeticide, Coerced Marriage and Bonded Labour in Haryana and Punjab.*

Shakti Vahini, 2014, Anti trafficking in India and south Asia – national legal research desk – a Shakti Vahini research initiative, https://traffickingnews.wordpress.com/tag/west-bengal/ accessed on 13th February, 2016.

SHRDC, 2012, SAARC Human Resource Development Centre, Human Trafficking Situation in SAARC Region: Bridging the Gaps. Karachi.

Skeldon, Ronald, 2000, 'Trafficking: A Perspective from Asia', in Reginald Appleyard (ed.) *Perspectives on Trafficking of Migrants,* New York: International Organisation for Migration, United Nations, p. 22.

Vitale, K., 2012, Barricading the information superhighway to stop the flow of traffic: Why international regulation of the internet is necessary to prevent sex trafficking. American University *International Law Review,* 27(1), 91-131.

Wright, Denis, 2008, "Forced Labour, Trafficking and Migration of Women in South Asia," UNEAC Asia Papers No. 24, pp. 33-43. http://www.une.edu.au/asiacentre/PDF/No24.pdf. Accessed on 9 June 2012.

Zimmerman, Yvonne C. 2010, "From Bush to Obama: Rethinking Sex and Religion in the United States' Initiative to Combat Human Trafficking" *Journal of Feminist Studies in Religion,* 26 (1) : 79-99.

Chapter 4

Profile of Trafficked Victims

Trafficking is a very dynamic business and newer forms of exploitation are being discovered every day. The very nature of this business requires it to be conducted with certain secretiveness and ambiguity. It is very difficult contacting these women and hence we approached the Police and the shelter homes and we had to start backwards and first meet the Staff in the shelter homes. After several visits and having made some rapport with the staff and the girls we could slowly approach them and ask them to share their lives with us.

The scope of this study is limited to those victims whom we found in the Shelter homes and those who consented to have interactions and give interviews. In few cases, victims who were identified for interaction did not respond or on the day of interview walked out. Some brothels and spa centres where trafficked victims were suspected to be currently working refused to participate in the study. In this study, victims were identified and approached with the intervention of police or NGOs or both. In such cases, interactions and interviews with trafficked victims were indirectly controlled and monitored by NGO/ police personnel up to some extent. They were also present at the time of interview and they reserved the rights to stop any interaction/ interview in the middle in case they suspected the victims were getting stressed or if they showed any signs of discomfort, re-trauma, and uneasiness.

Hence, we had to resort to various measures to get the details of our respondents. Some victims came forward and gave us the interviews. Few allowed us to tape their conversations. When we were refused permission to record the interview we came home and noted the details. We also participated in a number of group discussions in the shelter homes. We often coincided our visits on the day that had been fixed up for weekly checkups by the doctor and the councillors. In all we could get the data from 225 victims. The data on socio-demographic profile of victims includes information on their age at the time of interview, their education and current employment details, their religion and caste, and their current relationship as well as residential patterns.

Table 1: Age of Victims (at the time of Interview)

Sr. No.	*Age of Victims (in years)*	*Number*
1.	Less than 10	nil
2.	11-20	16
3.	21-30	63
4.	31-40	81
5.	41-50	48
6.	51-60	12
6.	61-70	04
7.	70 and above	01
	Total	**225**

Majority of victims when we interviewed them were in the age group of 21-40 years of age at the time of interview. Hence they were still in the prime of their lives. Although there were young victims in transit/ shelter homes, those who were less than 10 years of age but permission to interview them was not granted. The youngest victim in our study was 13 years and the oldest victim was above 70 years at the time of interview.

Table 2: Current relationship status of victims

S. No.	*Current Relationship Status*	*Number*
1.	Unmarried (never-married)	26
2.	Married	148
3.	Widowed	22
4.	Divorced	06
5.	Separated	09
6.	Any other (Specify)	02
7.	No response	12
	Total	**225**

Majority of women were married at the time of interview. Few women did not want to reveal their current relationship status. In majority of cases, women victims got married after they were rescued from trafficking. In majority of cases, women victims were unmarried at the time of trafficking, and they got married after their rescue and re-integration programmes. Hence, it is wrong to state that the trafficked woman never get married. As our case studies will show some of these respondents had kept their earlier lives a secret while in some cases the husbands knew about the women being trafficked.

Table 3: Religion of victims

S. No.	*Religion*	*Number*
1.	Hindu	149
2.	Muslim	46
3.	Christian	14
4.	Sikh	02
5.	Atheist	04
6.	No response	10
	Total	**225**

Majority of victims were Hindu. The second largest group of victims is Muslim. Few victims did not disclose their religious status. On the other hand, few victims claimed to be atheists.

It may be noted that a majority of women were religious (86 per cent) as compared with those who claimed to be atheists (5 per cent).

Table 4: Caste of victims

S. No.	*Caste*	*Number*
1.	General	75
2.	Scheduled Castes	70
3.	Scheduled Tribes	40
4.	Other Backward Classes	16
5.	No response	24
	Total	**225**

Few victims did not wish to disclose their caste affiliations. Of the 225 victims, majority of victims, 126, belonged to scheduled castes, scheduled tribes and other backward communities. Twenty four victims refused to give us their caste break up and some were not aware of their caste and hence we were not sure how many of these again belonged to general, SC, ST or OBC castes.

Table 5: Current residence of victims

S. No.	*Current Residence*	*Number*
1.	Rural Areas	82
2.	Urban Areas	143
3.	No response	00
	Total	**225**

Majority of victims were residents of city or urban areas. This was due to the fact that all the rescue homes established by the NGO's were located in urban areas. It may be noted that the victims currently residing in urban areas have their roots / parental homes in villages and townships. However, they are currently settled in urban areas.

Table 6: Education level of victims

S. No.	*Education Level*	*Number*
1.	Illiterate	85
2.	Below 10th Standard	74
3.	Intermediate	40
4.	Graduate	09
5.	Post-graduate	01
6.	No response	16
	Total	**225**

Majority of the victims in our study were illiterate, followed by those who are marginally literate (below 10th). At the time of trafficking, majority of these women were either school drop-outs or never went to schools. Only some women were studying in junior / high school level classes at the time of their trafficking (less than 10 per cent). It was interesting to note that few trafficked women had taken up studies after being rescued and had passed their exams and others were studying towards an exam.

Table 7: Current occupation/ employment of victims

S. No.	*Current Occupation*	*Number*
1.	Unemployed	24
2.	Student	08
3.	In training	59
4.	Salaried job	65
5.	Daily wage earner	58
6.	Self-employed	11
	Total	**225**

Majority of women reported to being in salaried works, including that of a housemaid and office jobs as janitors, peons etc. About equal number of women reported to be engaged in daily wage earning. These included industrial labourers, piece rate workers in garment and manufacturing industries and construction site labours. Another considerable number of women were currently undergoing training for vocational courses. This training includes tailoring, embroidery work, bakery, jute and cotton handicrafts, pottery and making of sanitary napkins. It may be noted that women currently undergoing training were residing in shelter/ transit homes and their training was a part of their daily life. Only few women were self-employed as small scale vendors and shopkeepers. Reasons for unemployment among women were health issues and family constraints or they had recently shifted to the shelter home and were still trying to recover from their ordeal and get beck to normalcy.

We also wanted to know about the present economic status of the victims and how much they were earning.

Table 8: Monthly income of victims

S. No.	*Monthly Income*	*Number*
1.	Less than 1000	07
2.	1001-2000	26
3.	2001-3000	65
4.	3001-4000	81
5.	4001-5000	14
6.	More than 5000	01
7.	No income/ currently unemployed	31
	Total	**225**

Majority of women are earning between Rs 3001-4000 per month. Currently unemployed also includes students who are not earning at the time of interview. Income of women in shelter homes was also accounted for. This income is generated by their in-training work and products. It may be noted that in most of the cases, the money earned by these women is handed over to them at the time of their release from the homes.

Hence, in our sample size, most of the trafficked girls, whom when we met and interviewed were between the age of 21 to 41. Majority had married, once they were rescued and hence it is wrong to state that none of these girls or women will ever get married. Most of these girls were Hindus and came from Schedule castes, Schedule Tribes and backward communities. Majority of these were illiterate or educated up till 10th class or had dropped out at different stages. Currently at the time of interviews they were residing in urban areas but they had their roots in rural areas. The rehabilitation home was providing them some training and giving some money but this was certainly not enough. They earned about Rs 3000 to 4000 per month. They were earning salaries through works such as that of a housemaid and office jobs as janitors, peons etc. About equal number of women were reported to be engaged in daily wage earning. It included industrial labourers, piece rate workers in garment and manufacturing industries and construction site labours. Another considerable number of women were currently undergoing training for vocational courses. This training includes tailoring, embroidery work, bakery, jute and cotton handicrafts, pottery and making of sanitary napkins. It may be noted that women currently undergoing training were residing in shelter/ transit homes and their training was a part of their daily life and an attempt towards rehabilitation.

Chapter 5

Life Experiences, Rehabilitation and the Aftermath

This chapter highlights life and experiences of women as victims of trafficking and looks back into their lives when they were trafficked. It includes their duration as trafficked victims, main reasons for trafficking and methods of trafficking. It may be noted that "no response" category includes incomplete data or the women and girls were too young to remember anything and hence could not give an answer.

Table 9: Age when trafficked

S. No.	*Age when Trafficked*	*Number*
1.	Less than 10 years	42
2.	11- 15 years	93
3.	16- 20 years	36
4.	More than 20 years	12
5.	No response/ cannot recall	42
	Total	**225**

Majority of victims were trafficking at the young age of 11-15 years. Few victims could not recall their exact age at trafficking, the reason being that they were probably too young (below 6 or 7 years) at the time of trafficking, hence they could not recall their age. Hence, majority of the victims in our study were children when they were trafficked. As noted by an NGO activist, Ramani, "*Most of cases of trafficking of girls happened at the vulnerable age of 10 to 15 years. These girls were either school dropouts or assisting their parents at home and were trafficked on the pretext of earning money for family. Another common reason for trafficking for this age group is to dupe young girls in love affairs and then trap them in trafficking.*"

Table 10: Duration in trafficking

S. No.	*Duration in Trafficking*	*Number*
1.	Less than 1 year	40
2.	1-5 years	29
3.	6-10 years	76
4.	More than 10 years	36
5.	No response/ cannot recall	44
	Total	**225**

Majority of women lived as victims of trafficking for 6-10 years. These women were at the prime of their youth (18-28 years) during this period of time. Majority of these women were trafficked for sexual work/ prostitution. The victims who did not respond or could not recall or did not want to remember their days in hell as pointed out by a respondent.

Table 11: Reason for trafficking

S. No.	*Reason for Trafficking*	*Number*
1.	Personal reason (including false promises of love/ marriage)	37
2.	Economic reasons	42
3.	Wish to support family (including work for own dowry)	40
4.	Forced in trafficking by parents/ family	68
5.	No response/ cannot recall	38
	Total	**225**

This table shows the reasons cited by victims for their trafficking. It is very difficult to quantify in numbers the reasons for their being trafficked for each one had some times more than one reason but we wanted to quantify this in order to get rough idea. It is evident that majority of women were trafficked on the pretext of earning money for their families. One of the main reasons to send young girls was to earn as much money as possible for their dowry. Of course, the parents were also kept in dark and the girls were eventually pushed into sex work. Some victims cited personal reasons such as love affairs and promises of marriage to encourage them to leave home and accompany the leading person. The so-called lover/ suitor turned out to be a trafficker in majority of cases. What was surprising, that many of these girls were also forced by their parents and family into trafficking. The girls told us that the trafficker was very well known to their family and he or she would visit their homes on a regular basis. Often the parents and families agreed for this girl to go with the trafficked person. Bhagya told us, "*Anna was a regular visitor to our house whenever he came from the city. He used to tell me that I am your uncle. In fact, after few visits I started looking forward to his visit for he would bring a lot of gifts, new clothes, chocolates for me and some food stuff for my parents. He even brough cigarettes for my father who was smoking beedis and very proudly he would smoke these cigarettes. He would tell us stories about his life in Chennai and how everyone was rich there and he used to meet the film stars on a regular basis and he knew many of them. I was very keen to see some of these film stars. He then fooled my parents to send me to Chennai for he will get me a good job as a maid servant and I can lead a very happy life and send money to my parents on a regular basis. My parents were very convinced and I was so excited when I left with him. We never reached Chennai but I was imprisoned in a room for days and raped on the first day and after that I travelled to many places of which I do not even know the names and every night I had many men coming to me. I cried a lot but I never saw Anna after this.*" Hence, one reason that emerges is the economic necessity of the families and in this situation the girl becomes dispensable and a source to add to the income of the family.

Table 12: Method for trafficking

S. No.	*Method for Trafficking*	*Number*
1.	Through false promises of job/ money	91
2.	By deception (love/marriage)	38
3.	By force	58
4.	No response/ cannot recall	38
	Total	**225**

We also wanted to find out how these girls were trafficked and how they were coerced. The main methods employed by traffickers were false promises of employment and false promised of love and marriage. Where the victims have indicated "by force" as a method of trafficking, they meant to say that the parents forced them to accompany the leading persons because they promised money. In this way, traffickers rarely used force as a method of trafficking; they mainly relied on deception and false promises to lure away victims. In majority of cases, parents of young girls were lured by traffickers/ leading persons to send their girls away. In turn, parents used force, emotional blackmailing and even physical abuse to send the daughter away, against their wishes.

Table 13: Purpose for trafficking

S. No.	*Purpose for trafficking*	*Number*
1.	Economic- domestic work	06
2.	Economic- industrial work as labour	18
3.	Prostitution	141
4.	Both economic and prostitution	20
6.	No response	40
	Total	**225**

This table brings out the difference between cited reasons for trafficking and the actual reason and purpose of trafficking. In the previous table, economic reasons were cited the most common reasons for initiating the trafficking process. As it turns out, the actual or real reason for trafficking is sexual work/ trafficking for prostitution. The victims and their families were told false reasons (economic) to drive them away from home and later on the victims were pushed into sex trade.

Table 14: Methods of control over trafficked victims

S. No.	*Methods of control over trafficked victims*	*Number*	*Percentage*
1.	Control on life (including mobility/ earnings)	176	78.57
2.	Further recruitment to work for themselves/ others	130	58.04
3.	Through physical force (including sexual exploitation)	196	87.11
4.	No response	194	86.20

Again it is very difficult to quantify for many respondents stated more than one reason. The victims were suppressed and controlled by traffickers. The most common methods of suppression included verbal and physical abuse, beating, and sexual exploitation. In majority of cases, the traffickers or the agents of victims controlled their earnings. The mobility of victims was also suppressed and they were always under the close supervision of their masters/ owners. The master/ owners here are the brothel owners where the trafficked victims were residing and exploited for sex trade.

Table 15: Social-psychological status of victims in trafficking

S. No.	*Social- Psychological status of victims in trafficking*	*Number*	*Percentage*
1.	Life controlled by others	174	77.68
2.	Abuse- physical as well as verbal	178	79.91
3.	No control on own money and earnings	183	81.70
4.	Poor health conditions	186	83.04

(*Contd...*)

5.	Constant feelings of fear/ depression and hopelessness etc.	189	84.38
6.	Felt in constant custody of others	172	76.79
7.	Unable to move freely (control on mobility)	188	83.93
8.	Forced to work in pitiable conditions	190	84.82
9.	Forced to work against own wish and ability	192	85.71
10.	Felt deceived	190	84.82
11.	Felt exploited	194	86.61
12.	Denied food when refused to work	170	75.89
13.	Denied basic amenities such as personal hygiene	177	79.02
14.	Felt homesick	193	86.16
15.	No response/ unregistered response	30	13.39

This table registers victims' experience and their condition in brothels and such other places of exploitation and sex-trade. Often the responses of victims to these questions were monosyllabic, that is they responded in Yes or No and did not provide details on nature of their conditions and treatment as victims of trafficking. Since these were sensitive issues and victims were prone to get re-traumatized by mention of difficult situations, any further probing into these areas was not done. In addition, accompanying police or NGO staff member also discouraged further probing into sensitive areas, least the victims may be stressed or face trauma again by talking about such issues. We only had few girls who could tell us the details of their lives and were not traumatized by talking about their past.

Table 16: Age at rescue

S. No.	*Age at Rescue*	*Number*
1.	Less than 10 years	13
2.	11- 15 years	35
3.	16- 20 years	77
4.	More than 20 years	62
5.	No response/ cannot recall	38
	Total	**225**

Majority of women were rescued when they were 16-20 years of age. Second largest group of women were more than 20 years at the time of rescue. Women who were trafficked at a relatively younger age (less than 10 years or so), had difficulty in recalling the specific details, such as age at trafficking, age at rescue.

Table 17: Key agents in rescuing and rehabilitation

S. No.	*Key Agents in Rescuing and Rehabilitation*	*Number*	*Percentage*
1.	Self (refers to self-motivation)	139	61.07
2.	Family members	107	47.55
3.	Police	194	86.22
4.	NGO	196	87.50
5.	Individual/ community members	46	20.44

Police and NGOs played a key role in identifying and rescuing victims of trafficking. Family members meant father, mother, brothers, sisters, husbands, uncle and aunts. The role of family member in rehabilitation of rescued victims does not present a good picture. In about half the cases, the family members (parents/ siblings/ husbands) were ashamed of victims' presence in the house. They did not wish to take them back because they were seen as a black spot in family. Only in about half of cases reported, the family of victims played a positive role in their re-integration process. They provided emotional support to victims and also safeguarded their well-being. Shilpy, told us, "*I did not want to face them after all this. I carried a bad name. But still they took me. My parents were crying when they saw me. My mother was praying to God every day for my return. My family stood for me. I thank God for giving me such a nice and caring husband. He accepted me even after knowing the bad things that had happened to me.*" On the other hand we also had families that did not give support: Sneha, told us, '*The NGO madam called my family to meet me. But they did not come to meet me and said I was dead for them. However, the NGO madam went to my house and brough my parents to see me. I was crying when I saw my mother but they did not love me because I was a bad spot for them. I was a big black spot on their name and izzat (honour).They refused to take me back and said I was dead for them. I can understand their point of view for once I go home every one in the village will look down upon them and there would be no way my two younger sisters could be married. I accepted my fate and thought it better that my parents think I am dead."* Few others like Bhanu reached home and again had to leave. *"My husband did not keep me in the house. He always shouted at me and said that I was useless for him. My husband took me under force of Police and NGO people and did not say any thing in front of them. But very soon he started abusing me and calling me by all bad names. He also wanted me to start sex work again, so that I could bring some money to him. When I refused, he beat me badly saying I had done this work earlier and why was I now not doing it. He did not give me any food or money and used to beat me a lot. So one day when he was not there I ran away from home"*.There were many other stories of how the victims wanted to escape but there was no escape for them. Rani told us, *"I wanted to run away. But everywhere they (brothel owners and pimps) kept an eye on us. We were not allowed to go out. If we went out for some shopping or even to temple, Maalkin's bodyguards were always with us. There was no way we could escape their eyes. Every night I prayed to God that someone will come and rescue me."*

Table 18: Skill building-training and employment opportunities

S. No.	*Skill-building Training and Employment Opportunities (with reference to shelter home)*	*Number*	*Percentage*
1.	Skill building	190	84.82
2.	Vocational training	187	83.48
3.	Preparing for Jobs	180	80.36
4.	Studies/ formal education	14	6.25

This section refers to the opportunities provided to victims in shelter homes. Majority of victims received some vocational training to enable them to earn money in future. Training included tailoring, embroidery, piece rate work, bakery items, making sanitary napkins, baby diapers, jute and cotton bag making etc. Others were being prepared for a job such as worker in a factory, as a peon or of a security guard. Majority of women were able to find a regular employment after their trainings. Some women also continued to work as housemaids, daily wage earners/ labourers along with their trained work. The main reason for doing double work is that they did not have regular source of income from their training, or they felt it did not fetch enough money. Some young victims were continuing their school education with assistance from NGO/ shelter homes.

Table 19: List of aid received by victims

S. No.	*Types of Aids received by Victims*	*Number*	*Percentage*
1.	Psychological counselling	189	84.38
2.	Financial aid	136	60.71
3.	Medical aid	192	85.71
4.	Vocational training	186	83.04
5.	Job opportunities	180	80.36

Victims received financial assistance as well as emotional counselling during their stay in shelter homes. Financial aid included those who have received a grant/ aid in their name. Besides this there were a number of victims who had applied for but did not receive the grant till date (till the date of their respective interviews) are not included in this particular data table.

Table 20: Main sources of aid and assistance

S. No.	*Main Source of Aid and Assistance*	*Number*	*Percentage*
1.	Government	141	62.95
2.	NGOs	196	87.50
3.	Community members	60	26.79
4.	Any other/ foreign aid	32	14.29

The main sources of financial aid are government and NGOs. The NGOs also arranged for additional funds from charity drives, different fund raising activities. NGO and its members are cited as the main source of counselling and emotional support. Community members also participate in well-being of the victims. Although their contributions are mostly indirect, such as donation of money, old clothes, food supplies and books etc. Community members make their contribution with NGO interventions.

Table 22: Health profile of victims (HIV-AIDS and STDs)

S. No.	*Indicators of Health Profile*	*Number*	*Percentage*
1.	General awareness of health	166	74.11
2.	Awareness of HIV/ AIDS	173	77.23
	Tested for HIV/ AIDS	58	25.89
	HIV/ AIDS positive cases	01	0.45
3.	Awareness of STD	143	63.84
	Tested for STD	96	42.86
	STD positive cases	26	11.60
4.	Health check-ups	143	63.84
5.	Medical aid in check-up and treatments	159	70.98
6.	Health counselling	148	66.07
7.	Self-perception on health- Healthy	54	22.11
	Self perception on health- unhealthy	138	60.61

Majority of victims are aware of HIV/ AIDS and STDs. But most of the times, victims did not reveal their actual health status on HIV/ AIDS and STDs. Only one victim affirmed to be HIV-AIDS positive and 26 victims were positive for STD. STD is an acronym for sexually transmitted diseases. The term refers to diseases like chlamydia, herpes and gonorrhea. These diseases are spread through sexual contact with patients who have this disease. HIV is the virus that spreads through a number of means such as through blood transfusion, from a pregnant mother to a child and through the sharing of unsterilised syringes and needles and sexual contact is one of the reasons. Unprotected sex is one of the main reasons that causes the transmission of STD. Most of the respondents had unprotected sex and had no control over this aspect of their lives.

The NGO staff confirmed more than one-third cases to be HIV and AIDS positive and told us that they were being treated for this.Victims on the other hand did not wish to reveal such information, may be due to shame and uneasiness to share such details. Since the victims did not confess the same, it was not taken into account. Only the cases where victims themselves confirmed to be suffering from HIV/ AIDS and STDs, we recorded only those cases. We did not go through the health records of the victims available with the NGO. Majority of victims view themselves as unhealthy. It may be noted that they often mix physical and emotional well-being together and infuse it in their perception of health. So in most of the cases, the victims are reported to be physically as well as emotionally unhealthy. Vani told us, "*I do not feel very healthy. I have regular headaches and body pain. I don't feel very good about myself. I always feel low and have this headache which is there continuously. My head is always hurting. Though I have been prescribed a lot of medicines but somehow I am not able to get over this problem. Due to this I also cannot sleep well and often get up at odd hours.*"

Table 22: Contact with family

S. No.	*Contact with family*	*Number*	*Percentage*
1.	Able to contact family	148	65.77
2.	Not able to contact the family	77	34.22

Table 23: Reintegration with the family

1.	Total Respondents able to contact	148	
2.	Total numbers reintegrated	43	29.05
3.	Total Numbers not reintegrated	105	70.94

In majority of cases, women victims were able to contact with their family (parents and/or husband). Police and NGO played a key role in making contacts with family. However, the rate of successful re-integration is much lower. The main reason for this is that family members did not wish to accept the victims, and viewed their past life (as victims of trafficking and sexual workers) as a shame on family. In few cases, where the victims were trafficked at a very young age (below 10 years), it was difficult to trace their roots and family details. At the time of interviews, such victims are either under surveillance of shelter homes, or reintegrated as individuals. In the cases where victims' families refused to accept them, these victims were independently established in main stream society with help of NGO.

Table 24: Knowledge about victims' trafficked status

S. No.	*Knowledge about victims' trafficking status*	*Aware*		*Not aware*	
		Number	*Percentage*	*Number*	*Percentage*
1.	Parents	113	76.35	35	15.63
2.	Husband	24	10.71	149	66.52
3.	Children	nil	nil	152	67.86
4.	Friends- current	12	5.36	147	65.63
5.	Neighbours- current	08	3.57	138	60.61
6.	Fellow workers	19	8.40	181	80.80
7.	NGO activist/ counselors/ Police	194	86.61	nil	nil

Parents and husbands were contacted and informed of the victims' trafficked status. It was noted that majority of victims after their reintegration did not reveal their past life to their children, friends, neighbors and coworkers. NGO and police members were fully aware of victims' past life and trafficked status. In fact, police and NGO members played a key role in identifying and approaching victims for this study.

Table 25: Attitude towards re-integration

S. No.	*General Attitude*	*Attitude with Self*		*Attitude with Others*	
		Number	*Percentage*	*Number*	*Percentage*
1.	Comfortable	166	74.11	124	55.36
2.	Un-comfortable	34	15.18	41	18.30
3.	Isolated	84	37.50	39	17.41
4.	Indifferent	76	33.93	87	38.84
5.	Friendly	151	67.41	137	60.16
6.	Unfriendly	40	17.86	19	08.48
7.	Helping	157	70.09	154	68.75
8.	Non-helping	33	14.13	28	12.50
9.	Any other (specify)-reserved	161	71.88	128	57.14
10.	No response in any single category/ Incomplete responses	54	24.11	54	24.11

Majority of victims cited to be comfortable with their current surroundings. They see themselves as friendly being helpful towards others. This shows their positive attitude. Some victims also reported to have reverted into isolation, indifference and even uncomforting state of mind. But these are occasional state of affairs. In their assessment of other's attitude, majority of victims perceived themselves to be comfortable with other members of society. Majority of victims cited that they tend to be reserved and do not open up in case they feel any conversation will lead to their past life. This could be one of the main reasons of non-disclosure of information and personal details from victims.

Table 26: List of main issues and problems in re-integration process

S. No.	*Main issues and problems*	*Number*	*Percentage*
1.	Poverty	195	87.05
2.	Lack of education	168	75.00
3.	Trauma	191	85.27
4.	Guilty	179	79.91

(*Contd...*)

5.	Shame	192	85.71
6.	Blame oneself for trafficking (victims)	182	81.25
7.	Rejection by family/ society	181	80.80
8.	Gender bias	179	79.91
9.	Lack of self-confidence in victims	186	83.04
10.	Lack of good employment opportunities	190	84.82
11.	Discontinuation of facilities due to fear of exposure	187	83.48
12.	Lack of financial aid	176	78.57
13.	Under reporting of facts (on parts of victims)*	68	91.89
14.	Lack of proper counselling*	69	93.24
15.	Re-trafficking	178	79.46

Poverty, lack of education and lack of adequate employment opportunity and regular sources of income are cited as main issues in their reintegration. Many victims felt that a major issue was that they would get back into the same rut and be trafficked again. Re-trafficking of victims was one of their major concerns.

Table 27: Role of main agencies in re-integration process

S. No.	*Role of Agencies*	*Agencies*	
		Number	*Percentage*
1.	Self	139	61.07
2.	Family	107	47.55
3.	Government	132	58.93
4.	NGOs	196	87.50
5.	Police	194	86.22
6.	Laws	173	77.23
7.	Community members	46	20.44
8.	Media	108	48.21

Majority of victims acknowledged their own role in the re-integration processes. To quote Venkataamma, "*God has helped me to come out of that situation. Now I must try to be happy and not think of past life. In counselling Sirs and Madams always told us that God will help us if we help ourselves. I feel it is true."* The victims viewed NGO and government agencies including shelter homes as main agencies for their re-integration. The role of family in reintegration process is equally important. It was noted that regardless of the fact whether family assisted in their reintegration or denied them/ refused them, the victims acknowledged role of family in successful re-integration. To quote Mani, *"Of course, you cannot do without family. If they help you, you are good. If they do not help, you are lost. My family did not help me. I feel my life would be better if they helped me a little. After all, I was their blood and I always have this feeling of being let down by my family for no fault of mine."*

As data shows, victims did not perceive community members as main sources of assistance and re-integration. This fact is partially true and is countered by Police and NGO personnel. They say that community members often contribute indirectly towards orphanages, old age homes and even for victims of trafficking. They contribute by means of money, clothes and food etc, but their contributions are kept anonymous most of the times and they do not get an opportunity to interact directly and freely with the inmates. But as the perception of in-mates/ victims is concerned, they do not see them as main source / agencies in their lives.

Table 28: List of main issues and constrains experienced by victims

S. No.	*Main Issues and Constrains Experienced by Victims*	*Number*	*Percentage*
1.	Poverty	195	87.05
2.	Lack of education	168	75.00
3.	Lack of financial assistance	182	81.25
4.	Lack of proper economic opportunities	187	83.48
5.	Rejection by family (mainly parents)	108	48.21
6.	Guilt about not disclosing past to husband and in-laws	179	79.91
7.	Negative feelings such as fear, depression,	190	84.82

(Contd...)

8.	Problems in adjusting with family	176	78.57
9.	Problems in marriage	153	68.30
10.	Gender discrimination	189	84.38
11.	Poor health	183	81.76

Poverty, lack of education and lack of suitable employment are main reasons. Gender-discrimination is also cited as one of the main issues. On the part of victims, negative feelings such as fear, guilt, shame and depression are also noted. One significant observation is that victims do not disclose about their past life to their family members. They make conscious effort to bury their past experiences. But at the same time, it gives way to guilt and being untruthful to family which they find difficult to suppress. To quote Mala, *"My family is nice to me. I am now married. But I know I lied to them about my past. I do not know how they will react if they find out about where I have been in the past. Every day I live in fear that someone from my past will come and point a finger at me. I know my husband will not keep me anymore if he knows that I was a sex-worker".*

Table 29: Victims' responses to main issues and constrains

S. No.	*Victims' response to main issues and constrains*	*Number*	*Percentage*
1.	Try to solve the issue	179	79.91
2.	Accept as it is/ accept as destiny	176	78.57
3.	Have faith in God	190	84.82
4.	Blame oneself for the present day situation	136	60.71
5.	Try not to think of the past	185	82.59

A majority of the victims try not to think about their past life and their traumatic experiences. Victims also indicated their faith in God, in whichever religion they are practicing. According to many, they feel that God is always helping them. To quote Lalitha, "*God has led me so far. I thank him all day and night. May be I was put in trouble due to my own bad karma. But God helped me out of it and I think the worst is over. God has given me hope to live. When I was in brothel, then also I was praying to God to get me out of that hell and I feel he has listened to my prayers."*

Table 30: Family/ personal life of victims post re-integration

S. No.	***Personal Life of Victims***	***Number***	***Percentage***
1.	Happy	138	60.61
2.	Unhappy	80	35.71
3.	Live under constant fear (fear of being recognised/ re-trafficked)	176	78.57
4.	Guilt of keeping family in dark (guilt of not telling the truth)	165	73.66

Most of the respondents reported to be happy with their present life. It was noted that a majority of victims reported to live under constant fear of being recognised as ex-sex-workers. Fear of re-trafficking was also noted among these victims. Victims were happy with their respective families, but at the same time they also expressed the guilt feelings for keeping their families in dark about their past lives. To quote Sarla, "*I know what I am doing is for the safety of my family. I do not want my children to be blamed for what I did. But sometimes I feel sorry and feel shameful for not telling them the truth. I am living far away from City, and I will not go back there. But still I fear that someone from City will find out about me and tell my family. I see bad dreams and I cry in my sleep. When my child asks about it, I cannot tell him the truth. I only tell him that I was missing his father." (She is a widow)*

Table 31: Life Satisfaction reported among Victims

S. No.	***Life Satisfaction among Victims***	***Number of Victims***	***Percentage***
1.	Satisfied with life	113	50.45
2.	Not satisfied with life	47	20.98
3.	Cannot say	22	9.82
4.	No response	43	18.75
	Total	**225**	**100.00**

Most of the respondents reported to be satisfied with their present life. The victims also confessed to have "occasional burst of anger, sadness and negative feelings." But these feelings did not last long. According to one victims, they believed in "something is better than nothing." This tendency was observed during the interviews. To quote Ashalata, "*What I have is not enough. But at least it is not bad and full of torture like my past. Do I have any choice? With my past, my low status and no education, I do not think I can complaint about my life. I am happy with what I have. It is so much better than the past where I was living in hell. It is good. I do not have to sell my body anymore. No one plays with me and my emotions now.*"

No questionnaire or interview with the girls could unfold the trauma that the trafficked girls went through. Throughout our interviews we could often feel emotionally one with the victim and could imagine the hell that they went through. In fact, their eyes would fill with tears and it was very difficult for us to control our emotions. Many of our respondents told us many times, the hell that they were living through. Geeta told us, "*I felt like hell or I used to curse myself day and night for being in this situation. I died every day there (in brothel). Every time a customer touched me, I felt like I was dead. I was living in a hell. I had lost all hope. I missed my family. They burnt me with cigarettes and kept me locked in a room until I was obeying their wishes. They did not give me food for many days. Every morning I was beaten by my pimp, and in the night again, after the business was over, he used to have sex with me. I was just like a toy in their hands. Maalkin (lady-owner of brothel) used to give me high doses of alcohol. Other girls were also forced to drink it. Sometimes she also gave us some drugs. After getting drink and drugs, we lost all sense and they used our bodies. We worked even when we were sick. We worked when we had fever or headache. We worked even when we had our menses periods. Some customers liked it that way only. I wanted to run away but I did not know where I will go. It is same everywhere. It is same in all places.*"

Rani, told us, "*The only thing I could thank God was for giving me a roof on my head and some food in my tummy. I did not want to live anymore. I was very young to know what was happening to me. I cried all time when a man touched me. We were treated like machines. Sometimes four or five times in a day we were sent to clients. Twice I conceived from customers. And both times Madam aborted my child. She said I was too young to be a mother and if I had the baby, the customers will lose interest in me. I was ready to do what Madam wanted me to do, but only thing I asked her to meet my family once. She did not allow that. In fact, she told me much later, she did not know who my family was. Because a middleman had sold me to her. I wanted to die. Whenever a man took me to room, I used to think it will be over soon. But it was never ending. We were sad, but we were forced to do all the makeup and wear those shiny dresses. Madam and his men will twist our arms and pull our hair if we did not smile at customers.*" Venu narrated her story, "*...There was a boy whom we used to meet often in the market.. He was earning good money and told us that he can offer us a good job in Delhi. My friends and I thought of accepting the job offer, however our parents did not agree. We were so fed up with our poor economic status and this boy kept telling us how we can become very rich and have the best of clothes, food and see all the films. So one day without telling our parents, we decided to elope from our house. Our friend brought us to a house in Annkapalli. After this we did not see our friend at all. Then we were taken to one of the rooms and asked to wait. After some time a man came and again took us at night in a bus to a new place. Then we were again locked in a different room and for two days we did not get enough food. On the third day two men came and raped us one after the other. When we shouted and cried we were beaten.*"

Hence all these girls had gone through hell. These girls whose services can be repeatedly sold and resold, are the contraband of sex trafficking. Trafficking is the modern equivalent of slavery. Against their will, millions of girls like these are forced to work for the profit of others. There were instances when they were forced to drink alcohol and were given drugs so that they could deal with their body and its abuse. As a result many of these girls were now addicted to drinks and drugs and needed this on a regular basis. Recruitment agents used drugs to target those who are already in the profession or to entice non-users into recruitment. They could also keep a control over the victim in a trafficking situation. They often used alcohol and drugs as a way to punish, reward, decrease victims will to escape. Often we found that drugs and alcohol were used as a coping strategy so that, victims use drugs to dull the pain. It was very difficult to quantify this but talking to the girls made us realise how alcohol and drugs were used by the recruiter for their own benefits and finally the girls were accustomed to this. Many girls told us that their customers showed them many pornographic pictures and wanted to try new positions with them. Often after sex some of the customers forced them to sit and watch some pornographic film with them.

As we looked back at the girls who were trafficked, we found that majority of them had been trafficked at the age of 11 to 15 and again when they were less than 10 years. Hence the girls in our sample were in fact children when they were trafficked. Majority of these children had been living in trafficking for 6 to 10 years and this was in the prime of their youth. Most of them had come from poor homes and hence economic reasons were the main reasons as to why they were trafficked. The person who was responsible for trafficking them was very well known to their family and it was on the pretext of getting them a job that the parents had sent them and most of these girls landed into prostitution and sex work.

As we spent hours talking to these women who were trafficked at an age where they did not know anything about sex or exploitation, it became evident that sex trafficking starts in the head, by viewing women as objects. The portrayal and treatment of women as either property or sex objects is an affront to human dignity and creates both the supply and demand of women and girls who are traded like commodities. Trafficking, like poverty, discrimination and abuse of human rights, wears a woman's face. We need to improve access to education to increase (women's) opportunities and limit their vulnerability to the false promises of the traffickers. It is a series of acts that bring vulnerable people into the hands of criminals for the purpose of exploitation. There is a need to stop the recruitment, the transportation and the harbouring of trafficking victims. There should be attempts to stop the coercion, abduction and deception. Sex trafficking will not be eliminated until the demand is eliminated. The demand will not be eliminated until the roots of disordered sexual desire are eliminated. One of the biggest causes of disordered sexual desire is porn viewing and porn addiction. Pornography enslaves men physically and psychologically and this enslaves women and children literally via sex trafficking. Pornography is the gateway to sex trafficking. Men create the demand; women and children are the supply. If we transform the demand side, the supply side will also cease.

As we shared the heartbreaking stories of these girls and the attitude of the family and the traffickers, it became clear to us that another overriding factor in the proliferation of trafficking was poverty and the fundamental belief that the lives of women and girls are expendable. In societies where women and girls are undervalued or not valued at all, women are at greater risk for being abused, trafficked, and coerced into sex slavery. If women experienced improved economic and social status, they would be an empowered lot and trafficking would in large part be eradicated.

Chapter 6

Institutional Response to Trafficking, Role of Police, NGOs and Civil Society

We wanted to get the perspective of the Police, CBO's and NGO's also in our study. Indian law presents a strong case for protection and welfare of victims of human trafficking. In the eyes of law, human trafficking is a heinous and cruel form of atrocity against human kind. Law views human trafficking equivalent to slavery. The Constitution of India forbids Human Trafficking (Article 23).The Indian Penal Code also contains sections on Human trafficking. The Immoral Trafficking (Prevention) Act, 1956 known as ITPA is one of main legal measures to combat human trafficking in India. Another law is SITA which also dealt with the issue of trafficking. Government of India has brought in a general scheme titled "Swadhaar" in 2002 for women in difficult circumstances. It includes widows and deserted women, women suffering from HIV and AIDS deserted by families, women victims of terrorism, women prisoners released from jail and without any family support, women survivors of natural disasters, and trafficked women and girls rescued or runaway from brothels who for any reasons are not united with their families, mentally challenged women and other women who are placed in difficult circumstances. Specifically for trafficked victims/ sex-workers, Government of India has brought in a comprehensive guideline titled "Ujjawala"

Scheme in 2007 for prevention of trafficking and rescue, rehabilitation and re-integration of victims of trafficking for commercial sexual exploitation. Particularly in Andhra Pradesh, another relevant legal provision is the Andhra Pradesh Devdasi (prohibition) Act 1989. Hence, we made an effort to contact the different agencies that were involved with the issue of trafficking and in all we could get the data from 30 police officials and 45 NGO's and CBO's. In our study we had only three Community Based Organisations (CBO's) and the others 42 were NGO's.

Police and the issue of Trafficking

We were informed by the Police that raid and rescue operations are a key aspect of government interventions to address trafficking. These operations are generally carried out by law enforcement officers, such as the assistant commissioner of police. A raid and rescue team enters an identified brothel unannounced and removes underage girls, and women, by force. The girls and women are identified through the use of decoy customers. The police develops a network of informants who would provide specific information about trafficked women to be rescued from brothels. Specific information may be in the form of letters, e-mails, photographs, identification marks, addresses etc. The police try their best to give some incentive and also protection to the informant in some form or the other and maintain their confidentiality.

After the victims are rescued and recovered, the next step is that of their proper rehabilitation. It is necessary to see that the victims do not fall into the hands of traffickers again, as it often happens in many cases. Rehabilitation of rescued trafficked women is a provision within the state enacted laws of trafficking. The rehabilitation of girls or women rescued or arrested under the SITA Act 1956 was the responsibility of the protective home or corrective institution set up under the Act. However, trafficked women, girls are children who are produced under various sections of the Indian Penal Code for inflicted crimes like rape, kidnapping, abduction for illicit sexual intercourse, confinement for the procurement of prostitution and the like were sent to rescue and rehabilitation centres.

We found the higher up officials by and large sensitive to the issue. A Police officer told us, "*We see the role of police as being very crucial as we play an active role in identification, raid and rescue operations. We have the infrastructure and the means to deal with this issue but the help from NGO's is definitely a plus point.* "The police department in both Telangana and Andhra is pro-active in rescue and rehabilitation of victims of human trafficking. A very senior police officer told us, "*Police department is dedicated to this issue. We work in a close network of informers and identify potential cases of trafficking.*" In majority of cases, police conducts rescue operations. Sometimes, it works in association with NGO/ activists or media persons. The victims of trafficking who are rescued are then sent to shelter homes. Police provides the link between victims and shelter homes. They also play active role in tracing down family members of the victims through their police network and information portals. Andhra Pradesh Police has dedicated services and personnel for identification, and rescue of victims of human trafficking. Police department also conducts awareness camps and training sessions to deal with cases of trafficking. We were also told, "*Sometimes, our policemen put their own life at stake for these operations. We have dealt with armed traffickers during rescue operations.*"

While we found a large number of police officers who were well informed about this issue, we also found that among the Non Gazetted Officers, the police personnel's had a vague idea about sex trafficking. Sometimes the person interviewed would pass on the load of answering the question to the other stating that: *"It is not my department and I do not know much about it."* Another person told us, *"I have been posted to this section only recently and I am still trying to understand this issue".* These officials knew little about the distinction between forced and voluntary sex work and their attempt towards the victim showed their attitude to criminalising them for engaging into sex work.

However, these numbers were few and by and large we found the police very informative and involved with the issue.

We also found the police besides being involved in rescue was also involved in re-integration. They were clear that, trafficking is an absolute crime. The Police department has dedicated anti-trafficking cells and units. They felt that, special training should be given to minor and young victims of trafficking and the NGOs and media persons must come forward and help police department. Some police officials told us that in some cases, NGOs will not pass the information on such cases and they start their own sting and rescue operations. They do not want to involve police and system because they do not want to share its credit. It is not about taking and giving credits for humanity. What is more important here that we must work as a unit to help them. In Hyderabad a structured red light area called, Mehboob ki Mandi was abolished in 1990s. In very few areas such as in Peddapuram and Coastal AP red light areas are reported to exist. The police also recognised the fact that, there are few organised red light areas like Sona Gachi and other cities in Telangana and Andhra Pradesh. Sex-workers and brothels in these two states are scattered all over and they may be just in the neighbourhood. In this situation, active role from NGO, media and community people is crucial. The police also informed us that, existing laws do not punish clients of such sex workers and trafficked women. If there are laws to punish them more severely, it can be stopped. However, now there was a change in the vocabulary of the police. Earlier they were carrying out raid operations but now these were termed as rescue missions. Earlier the trafficked woman was seen as a culprit and she was booked under the law but now these women were referred to as Victims of Commercial sexual abuse (VOCSA).

NGO in Andhra Pradesh and Telangana with special focus on Shelter Homes

NGOs play a key role in dealing with cases of trafficking. A Director of an NGO told us, *"It is never an easy sight to see a new victim brought in. She is obviously mentally disturbed and physically harassed. We also feel a connection with her. Seeing her in such a poor condition also affects us."* Under Swadhar and Ujjawala schemes, the Government of India extends and seeks support from local NGOs in order to identify, rescue and counsel victims of human trafficking. Swadhar homes, short-stay homes, transit homes, and shelter homes provide protection and counselling to rescued women and also make attempts for their successful re-integration in society. Many NGO members and activists highlighted their key role in victims' reintegration process. Many other NGO staff told us, "*We see it as our duty to help out these women. Everyone has a right to live with dignity. We are mere tools in this. We do our best to help them."*

Majority of victims from Telangana and Andhra Pradesh are trafficked to states of Maharashtra, Chhattisgarh, Karnataka, Tamil Nadu, West Bengal- Kolkata, and New Delhi. Some victims are trafficking to Nepal, Hong Kong and Gulf countries. Trafficked victims fall prey to traffickers, customers, brothel owners, pimps. They are also regarded as fallen women by common community members who fail to see their pitiful conditions. Once a person is trafficked, he or she will never be able to get back to their formal self completely. NGOs then play a key role in rescue, rehabilitation, re-integration and counselling of trafficked victims. A worker in an NGO told us, *"Lives of women in shelter homes are far away from a normal life. They may appear happy but we know the inside story. Each of the women here is suffering from loss, trauma, stress, fear, dejection and depression."*

Prachi, another worker at an NGO, told us, "*It was not their fault that they ended up like that (victims of sexual exploitation/ human trafficking). So they should not carry the burden of it either. We are there to help them."* She further informed us, "*It is not an easy job. But I have full faith in my team and myself. We will bring them out of their depression."* Most of the NGOs recognise the fact that, Trafficking of women and children is a grave issue. Most of the cases occur due to ignorance of victims or their families. It is important to have awareness drives against trafficking of humans. Sonali another person working with an NGO told us, "*While we try to rehabilitate and provide support to the trafficked victim, we feel it is also our duty to see that this woman or in fact no other woman is pushed into trafficking. Hence, awareness drives and creation of knowledge about this subject is equally important to us*".

NGOs felt that, government needs to improve laws on trafficking and make provisions for hard punishment to offenders/ traffickers. Laws such as SITA and ITPA are good in papers, but there is a gap in its implementation. They felt that awareness programmes must be regular and taken seriously by all. It is important to tell victims that they did not do anything wrong and it was the circumstances that put them in such a situation. Building up the confidence of the victim and establishing a rapport with her takes a lot of time.

We also found that there was a hierarchy within the home. The order of hierarchy is as – Director or coordinator-social worker- the counsellor- the caretaker- the guards- the inmates. Therefore, inmates being lower in the hierarchy, have no autonomy over their lives. Anything and everything they do is in accordance to the orders of the people higher in the hierarchy. The construction of the home is based on this hierarchy. Certain spaces of the home are only meant for the coordinator and the staff of the organisation. Such spaces are not allowed to be accessed by the inmates of the shelter home. Many a times the victims had no agency.

There were very few Community-based organisation's that were involved with this issue. People (community members) also need proper knowledge and awareness on this matter. Otherwise, people are not very sensitive and they start blaming trafficked victims for polluting the society, especially in case of women victims who were caught in sex-trade. There is a need to deal with such cases with proper care and understanding and make them (victims) feel safe and secure. NGOs should not put pressure on any victims to tell their stories. Instead, focus on building self-esteem and confidence by employment training. Then they will open up slowly. Making victims meet and interact with other victims of trafficking works. They meet and share their stories and a bond is formed between them. This is true in case of women victims in rape, dowry cases also. In case of victims, trust building and winning confidence of victims is a crucial point. It may take a long time before the victims start trusting NGO personnel and open up with them. Vocational training and education are good for victims and every NGO should provide that. It helps in building confidence in victims and help her in successful re-integration. With proper training and counselling, victims can lead a life of dignity.

Media and Trafficking

In our study we found that the victims do not perceive an active role of media/ social networking in their cases. On the other hand, NGO and police personnel acknowledge the role and impact of media in awareness drives, and even in identifying sensitive / potential cases of human trafficking. Occasionally, police and NGOs get clues from media persons regarding existence and operation of a sex-racket/ trafficked cases. Police and NGOs see Media and social media as an effective platform to initiate and propagate awareness about Human Trafficking. During the fieldwork for this project, project fellow succeeded in establishing contacts with sex-workers with the help of some journalists. Further, few spa centres and brothels were also identified but they did not wish to participate in the study. Media also plays an active role in sting operations. According to an activist in Hyderabad, they successfully conducted some sting operations with help of local media and busted sex-rackets. In this process, they were able to rescue sex-workers, including trafficked women.

Community Based Organisations (CBO's) and Trafficking

When compared to the responses from police/ NGO as well as the victims, it was evident that, Community Based

Organisations (CBO's) involvement is inadequate. Nearly 70 per cent victims do not perceive active/ participative role of community in these cause. Police and NGO personnel acknowledge the advantages of the involvement of community members to the cause of anti-trafficking measure, but they also point out to certain limitations. Community members are often indirectly involved in welfare measures. Their contribution is limited to money, clothes, food supplies etc. Indirect involvement of community members leads victims to perceive their low or no interest in their welfare.

In cases where community members play an active role in identification and rescue of victims, they are kept under cover for their own safety from traffickers and their networks. As a ground reality, the associations of community members with certain other categories of welfare are highly regarded in comparison with their involvement with welfare of victims of human trafficking. For instance, a community member inclined towards children education, health, child labour, and even those associated with animal welfare are highlighted. Police and NGO personnel feel the need of awareness and sensitisation programmes to involve community members.

The rehabilitation centre work on the premise that the rescued victims should get a fair chance to lead a better life. They should be provided with shelter homes with basic facilities and given vocational training to make them self-dependent. However, these government run homes or few homes run by NGO's and CBO's (Community Based Organisations) are often critiqued for its unmanned and inadequate conditions and facilities. It has been observed that inmates of the centres have mental anxiety both before and after rescue, various hardships in the rehabilitation centres borne out of the inadequacies of these centres that inmates have to cope up with. The fundamental criteria for maintaining the shelter homes were often observed to be missing or rather insufficient for facilitating the purpose of the shelter homes. The staff is woefully inadequate. It is burdensome for a single superintendent to assume overall supervision of the institution. It is also taxing for a single social worker to handle both rehabilitative and some administrative functions. The social worker has to deal both with inmates and new admissions, making her workload gigantic. Further, we observed that the survivors of trafficking most often need strong medical and psychological care, however empirical study reveals that the psychiatrist was appointed on a part time basis (approximately one hour a day) and the interaction with the inmates does not happen on a regular basis. The inmates are in acute need of medical and psychological care because of their traumatic experiences. But the psychologist is appointed on a part-time basis and spends only 72 hours a month with them. Likewise the honorary psychiatrist spends 12 hours a month with the inmates. This by any standard is grossly inadequate. In many of the other homes there are no resident or visiting full or part-time psychiatrist, psychologist or counsellor for the inmates, although many of the inmates suffered from hysteria, insomnia, depression and the like. The medical officer visited the institution every alternate day. There was no separate private room for medical examinations. The inmates queued up and were subsequently examined behind a make-shift curtain. Adequate stock of penicillin was not available in the home for treatment of VD.

We also found few homes which were in a deplorable conditions and in which girls were physically, emotionally, and sexually maltreated and received little if any support or guidance, and CBO members have tenuous relationships with protective home managers and administrators. State-run protective homes are designed to accommodate vagrant or neglected girls in need of care and protection. Most homes are not prepared to assume responsibility for girls who are HIV positive, have drug addictions, maintain boyfriends, smoke, and expect the freedoms granted to them in the brothels. Nor do they have the capacity to offer the kind of psychological support that is essential to girls who have been removed from a brothel under duress and are away from their support network.

Once the home knows that the girl is HIV positive, she is treated like a criminal. There's no love and affection and they are treated like animals. Some organisation have very sparse knowledge of the issue yet for monetary assistance and funds executed the rescue and rehabilitation and eventually lead to increased subjugation, marginalisation of the survivors keeping them within the captive of shelter homes. Though accountability of NGO have been there, and we do acknowledge the contributions of these, yet the state should take effective auditing of NGO so as to ensure the proper working of the anti-trafficking mechanisms adopted by them. We also found few instances of state corruption, including bribes, extortion, sexual coercion, and complicity on the part of the police. We only could get hints about this and had no concrete evidence. Moreover, rescues can be traumatizing, and girls face the risk of abuse in the safe house and can be re-trafficked (Ministry of Women and Child Development 2010). Most women end up doing nothing for long periods, while those who do not wish to be rescued view the home as a prison. They are confined to the vicinity of the homes. Protective custody as practiced in South Asia is a serious violation of women's rights and it is important that governments of the region re-examine this concept, as well as the conditions in the government homes where women are kept.

Generally, Indian courts send rescued girls who are foreign nationals, for example, Nepalese or Bangladeshis, back to their countries with the help of NGOs; sometimes, they are sent to government homes. Beyond that, there is hardly any activism or inquiry. Rama, working with these cases told us, 'Very little action is taken by the police or the judiciary against the traffickers and those who are initially responsible for the violation of the rights of these women...With regard to the evidentiary procedures trafficking cases, the women and girls who are victims of the trafficking are the primary witnesses against the perpetrators. In cases involving organised crime, they are extremely vulnerable and in fear for their lives'.

The main government body dealing with protection and assistance policies and programmes is the department of women and child development (DWCD) under the Ministry of human resource development. It is the national focal point for combating trafficking in women and children in India. DWCD has corresponding departments in each state government (ADB 2002: 48). The 1990 Supreme Court judgement in the *Vishal Jeet v. Union of India* case directed the government to ensure care, protection, development, treatment and rehabilitation of the victims of commercial sexual exploitation and the setting up of a central advisory committee. In 1998, a national action plan was formulated by DWCD to combat trafficking and the commercial sexual exploitation of women. The plan covered various aspects, such as prevention, awareness raising, economic empowerment, rescue and rehabilitation and has been further strengthened in 2006 (NHRC, 2006).

Despite their limited resources, funding, training, and access to information, most NGOs studied take the lead in combating trafficking in their respective regions. The relative absence of government initiatives and assistance for trafficking victims, means that it is NGOs who have taken up the challenge of organising locally, nationally, and internationally to advocate for and meet the needs of victims, despite their limited resources. (Tzvetkova, 2002, 60). Many female victims prefer to discuss their situation in a more gender sensitive environment. For this reason, women's NGOs have often been the first line of action-raising awareness, lobbying for change, and providing assistance. The institution of NGO has made the problem locally and nationally a concerning issue for the society and it had assisted the government or the state to execute the laws and acts effectively by trying to establish rescue and rehabilitation forums for reintegration of survivors of trafficking. Moreover, NGO has also taken up effective steps to spread awareness of the programme. This is because of its decentralised and small enterprise nature which unlike the state can effectively take up actions on the phenomenon of trafficking.

This localised approach are carried out by objectives and orientation of the organisations to the social and cultural backgrounds of the respective regions that reflect the local patterns of trafficking (Tzvetkova, 2002, 61).

The Community based Organisations (CBO's) and Non-Government Organisations (NGO's) deal with the issue of trafficking of women after they are rescued though some of them work in close association with the Police and act as informants and also help in rescue work. Many of the Civil society groups look at the vulnerability of these girls and focus on reducing HIV transmission, largely by addressing structural barriers to preventing transmission—such as social stigma and police violence. They usually begin negotiations with brothel owners, family, and in most cases police only after engaging in rescue work. Most are not willing to challenge issues that compromise the rights of the trafficked victim to safety, health, and well-being. Social stigma and non-acceptability are said to the greatest obstacles to reintegration; (ADB 2002: 65; Shah, 2003). Besides the difficulties in finding alternative employment because of the stigma, any livelihood option which pays less than Rs 2,000 to 3,000 a month is not viable and the rescued girls often lapse back into commercial sex work (ADB, 2002: 65).

Most of the CBO's and NGO's that are involved with anti trafficking programmes do not address structural barriers—such as poverty and vulnerability in source sites, police violence, and criminalisation of sex work and present a nuanced understanding of the issue. Most of them have a welfare approach that they are rescuing these girls and encouraging them to lead dignified lives. Therefore, their approach does not employ an expansive understanding of sex worker engagement beyond the limited realm of the red-light district. Sex workers' participation relies on spaces outside their immediate, endangered world, which NGO's have little or no access to. In the majority of rescue cases, girls are repatriated to their natal or marital villages. Unlike police-led rescues, when

NGOs leads the process, girls are treated respectfully. These members take several steps to ensure a girl's safe return to her home. Unlike the police, for example, they ensure confidentiality and provide girls with food, one-on-one counselling, and what they often refer to as elder-sisterly love and affection. Upon a girl's repatriation, the NGO members create a story to convince village elders that the rescued girl is still chaste.

Strategies to deal with the issue of trafficking

Securing state accountability for violation of fundamental human rights is an essential element of human rights protection. An environment of increased awareness of violence against women and children had to be created to focus attention on the issue of trafficking. Concrete steps need to be taken for controlling the trade, curbing the involvement of citizens in trafficking and sexual exploitation and address the issue of official complicity and protect the women and girls against victimisation. There have to be multifaceted approach with various legislative, administrative and preventive measures to deal with the complex issue of trafficking.

Legislative Measures

There should be a wide definition of trafficking in the trafficking law i.e. in Sec. 208 IPTA in the line of recommendation of the commission of the Human Rights of UN Economic and Social Council and SAARC Convention. The present provisions of IPTA recognise the ordinary magistrate court or special courts as appropriate forum for trail of trafficking cases. There should be a provision of Special Court in each District to deal with all trafficking cases. Children Homes under Juvenile Justice Act, And Protection Home of the Trafficked Children need to be combined for the child in need of care and protection. The definition and ingredients of different offences in the trafficking law needs to be widen and more specific to include varied form of trafficking of children. The punishment prescribed for offences relating to trafficking of children is enhanced to the extent of life imprisonment and confiscation of properties and money earned by committing or aiding offence of trafficking of children.

Legislation, which is also related to prevent trafficking of children such as Foreigners Act, Emigration Act, 1963, Estradition Act, 1962, are to be suitably amended as Schedule with a new legislation in trafficking in the line of Information Technology Act 2000. A comprehensive Legislation on trafficking be undertaken which will be a self-contained in both substantive and procedural aspects. The personnel and officers empowered to implement trafficking law be assigned specific powers and obligation for aberrations and negligence of duties. The legal machinery and the framework contemplated in the Juvenile Justice Act be linked up with the law relating to trafficking of the children and to prevent other from of abuse and exploitation of children in many other laws. Trafficking also involves violations of other laws, including labour laws, immigration laws, and laws relating to kidnapping, abduction, slavery, false imprisonment, assault, battery, fraud, and extortion. Hence the definitions of these offences and the relevant legal process under Indian Penal Code and Criminal Procedure Code need review and necessary amendment in this regard.

Administrative Measures

The government has to reform its prostitution and trafficking laws to ensure that they are non-discriminatory and in line with international human rights standards particularly those designed to protect the victims of trafficking. The government should investigate and prosecute all those involved in trafficking and brothel operations, with particular attention to its own police and officials who receive payoffs or protection money from brothel owners and agents, who patronise brothels, have financial holdings in, collect rent or in any other way are complicit in the operation of such brothels. The implementing agency in the government has to increase economic opportunities for potential victims and improve infrastructural facilities to provide minimum services needed to the victims of trafficking. There is a need to provide shelter and support services to victims of cross-border human trafficking that are in this country unlawfully and ineligible for assistance. Efforts should be made to establish an inter-agency Task Force or National Task Force to monitor and combat trafficking and authorise the Secretary, Home Department of each State to establish programmes and initiatives to assist in the safe integration, reintegration, or resettlement of victims of trafficking and their children, as well as victims of cross-border trafficking without regard to such victims.

Efforts have to be made to create Trafficking Victims Assistance Fund from the sale of assets seized from and forfeited by appropriate authority under Trafficking Law and under disposal of various Task Forces to be constituted under the law. It should be made obligatory on the part of the concerned government department to include in its Annual Report information on trafficking, including a list of foreign countries that are countries of origin, transit, or destination for a significant number of victims of cross-border trafficking government and the follow up. There should be efforts to take necessary steps to disseminate information to increase public awareness of trafficking dangers and include the issue of trafficking in education curriculum at school, college and University level education.

Efforts need to be made to provide proper training and orientation of personnel involved in preventing and combating trafficking of women and children. There is a need to focus on official corruption in dealing with cases of or matters incidental to trafficking of children as the crime is increasingly perpetrated by organised, sophisticated criminal gang. Such trafficking is the fastest growing source of profits for organised criminal enterprise worldwide. Nexus between officials and traffickers contribute to the expansion of organised crime of child trafficking. Trafficking exposes victims to serious health risks. Children trafficked in the sex industry are exposed to deadly diseases, including HIV and AIDS. So there should be a proper healthcare programme for trafficked victims.

References

ADB, 2002, Combating trafficking of women and children in South Asia: Nepal report. Asian Development Bank.

ADB, 2002, Combating trafficking of women and children in South Asia: India report. *New Delhi. Asian Development Bank.*

NHRC, National Human Rights Commission, 2006, Dept. of Women and Child Development. National Inpration plan of action to prevent and combat Human Trafficking with special focus on women and Children. New Delhi

Shah, Vidya, 2003, Technical Paper on Gender, Vulnerabilities and HIV/ AIDS. Commemorating Beijing, Fourth South Asia Regional Meeting, Bhutan, 19-21 May. Delhi: UNIFEM.

Tzvetkova, Marina, 2002, "GO Responses to Trafficking in Women" *Gender and Development,* 10(1), pp. 60-68.

Chapter 7

Case Studies

In order to move away from mere numbers and give a life to these victims, in this chapter we narrate the life stories of few victims who were trafficked. We have changed the names and cities of the victim in order to protect their identity. Each of these case-studies is based upon a unique variable and explores the victims' life, her sufferings and experiences and feelings in relation with the variable in question. In majority of cases, the victims had personally requested to conceal their identity. Most of the victims consented to give their interviews as well as share their life-stories in detail only on the condition that their identity will not be disclosed.

Case 1: Sonu

Sonu is a young girl of about 18 years. But she appears older than her age. Her face is pale and her body is so thin that one can count her ribs. She breathes unevenly and often stops to cough while talking to others. Her eyes are dull, full of sadness and her face wears a worried expression. She looks very different from other average girls of her age, who are usually in the prime of their health and lively. But Sonu is different from other girls of her age. She was trafficked at the tender age of about five years and her whole life was ruined at that very point of time. As she was a little girl at the time of trafficking, she is not able to recall much about her place of origin (village etc.), her parents and family. Sonu is not able to recall the names or faces of her parents but she describes her mother as "a very good woman." She asserts that her father had sold her for money. On probing further, Sonu tells us that:

> *"The only thing I remember was that my mother was fighting with my father that day and they were talking about me. My mother was telling my father that he had no heart and he gave me for money. I was a little girl to understand any of their talk but the whole scene is printed on my mind. My mother was a very good woman. She never beat us. She never had a fight with my father before that day. But that day she was fighting with him about me."*

The traffickers sold her to a brothel in Mumbai. She stayed there for 10 years or so (she is not able to recall exact details). The owner of brothel, who was called "Madam," by everyone, trained Sonu in dancing and singing. Sonu also learned to speak Hindi and Marathi, although she never went to a school (However, Sonu claims that she was going to a school in her village and also tells that she was in the first class when she was trafficked). She could also speak little English and Telugu. There were a few other women from Andhra Pradesh in the brothel, who took care of Sonu, talked to her in their common mother tongue (Telugu) and occasionally gave her food etc. It is through her interaction with other Andhra women in the brothel that Sonu can say that she has her roots in Andhra Pradesh. And it is perhaps the only clue for us to trace her place of origin. Besides this, Sonu is also not even able to tell us about her religion and caste of her birth, but she remembers going to a Church in Mumbai with other brothel women and thus thinks of herself as a Christian only.

What Sonu remembers is her suffering and misery in the brothel. As a little child, she had a miserable life in the brothel. As she says: *"I felt lonely. I missed my mother. Every time I thought of her. I wanted to go back to her."*

Her misery was not just about being away from home, missing her mother and being put to a strict routine of singing and dance training. Her real misery began when she started as a sex-worker. She served her first client when she was just eight or nine years old. Some of her clients used to lure her with toys and chocolates, while some other used force to have sex with her. Moreover, her Madam (brothel owner) also gave her sedatives for the act. As Sonu tells us:

> "*In the beginning, I was very scared. When a man touched me, I always felt fear and started crying and shouting. They (brothel owner and perhaps the clients also) gave me something to drink and then I will sleep and do not remember anything. In the morning, I will see a man in my bed and I will start crying and shouting again.*"

As Sonu can recall, her life at brothel was bad. She always felt being controlled by her "Madam," and other women in the brothel, who were perhaps older to her. She was rescued from brothel when she was 15 or 16 years old. She stayed in a shelter home for about three years and received training in tailoring and embroidery work. After her training, Sonu is now working as a piece rate worker in a garment factory and earns upto Rs 2000 per month. She lives in a small room which she shares with two other women who are employed in the same garment factory. She wants to study in a school but is not sure when and how she will start going to a school.Though Sonu was rescued from brothel and got training and also a gainful employment, but she is not able to get rid of her bad memories. As she says: *"I will not sleep well in nights. I will get up anytime and feel fear. I miss my mother and my home but now I have a very faint memory of both my home and my mother. "*

One would naturally understand Sonu's poor psychological condition and her fearfulness, given her trauma and hardships in the brothel. But there is more to her ill-fate. She suffers from HIV-AIDS. Sonu says that she was tested twice for HIV-AIDS, once in the brothel and secondly in the shelter home.

Her tests came positive for HIV-AIDS second time. Currently, she is undergoing a treatment and receives financial support from an NGO for the same. But she does not sound hopeful on her treatment. She does not want to go to hospital regularly and does not want to tell everyone about her illness at all. Although the NGO members and doctors encourage her to receive regular treatment (as told by NGO member who assisted Sonu), she herself is not very willing to do so. As she tells us: *"(The) doctor said I have a bad fever. I need to stay in the hospital. But I do not feel good there."* What more, she does not even sound hopeful about her future life. She admits to suffer from recurring suicidal thoughts. In her own words: *"I do not want to live. Many times in a day, I want to just give my life and die. But I do not know why I do not do so."*

Sonu's story puts forward an example of the misery and hardships of victims of trafficking, particularly in the case of vulnerable young girls. The fact that she is also suffering from HIV-AIDS only worsens her condition. At present, she is receiving a treatment for HIV-AIDS but she is passive about the same. She has no concrete plans for her future life. Sonu was trafficked at a very young age (five years) and therefore she is not able to recall the exact details of names, places, duration in brothel and such other details. She does not even remember names of her parents or their village. From what information we could gather from Sonu, we may conclude that Sonu's father sold her away to traffickers for money. Her mother may not be aware of this deal or may not have given her consent to the same because she was fighting with her husband over the issue. Sonu remembers that one incident clearly and perhaps that incident had left a deep mark on mind and soul. Sonu led a miserable life in a brothel and was forced to serve her clients. She is unhappy with her present life and illness (AIDS) and has recurring suicidal thoughts. Although she is currently under treatment, but she has lost all hopes to recover and settle down in life in future.

Case 2: Jaya

Jaya looks about 30 years, but she does not know her real date of birth. She currently lives in Karimnagar, but cannot recall her original place of birth apart from the fact that her village is "somewhere near Guntur." She does not even know who her parents are and how they looked. She was trafficked by a woman and was send off to Mumbai for sex-work. "*I was very little when that woman took me. I only remember getting on a train and we were travelling for 2 days and 2 nights. She told me we were in Mumbai.*" Jaya recalls that she stayed in brothel for roughly 10 years. During her stay in brothel, she also served as a private housemaid to the owner of brothel. And at the same time she was sexually exploited. In her words: "*I used to do all house stuff. I cleaned, cooked, washed clothes, and pressed feet of madam in night. Late in nights, when her lover came, he used to sleep with me.*"

For Jaya, it was a double horror. As she was put to "entertain the customers," and when the day was over, she was supposed to please the semi-owner of the brothel, who was so-called lover of brothel-madam. In Jaya's case, she was not allowed to interact much with other regular girls of brothel, she was always kept inside madam's quarters and in her words, "*Only when some VIP customer came, madam will ask her to go to him.*" The reason Jaya gives for this is her fair complexion and fine features. She said that her Madam did not keep her for all, but only for few selected customers. Since Jaya could not recall her family, and there are no documents such as childhood photo etc; she could not reunite with her parents. With the help of NGO, she is now settled in Karimnagar and married a man who was a widower with three kids. But Jaya has no complaints regarding this matter. As she says: "*At least I have a roof over my head and a place to call home. My husband knows about my past life, but his children do not know anything at all. We decided to not have children of our own, as it may divide my attention. He married me just to take care of his children and fulfill his needs. But I am happy that I have a man to look after me."*

Case 3: Chelamma (ex-Devdasi)

Chelamma is a lean woman. She has lost all her teeth but when she smiles, she looks pretty. Chelamma appears to be nearly 70 years but she is active and alert for her age. She served as a Devdasi. On her request as well as on request of the NGO member who led us to her, her personal details are kept confidential (her real name, current residence etc.). Chelamma recalls little about her initiation to Devdasi rites. She said she must be around six or seven years when it happened. But she remembers the fine details such as "*heavy clothes, jewellery, flowers and garlands,*" with which she was decorated. For a girl of her age, it was a fancy and luxury and she was naturally attracted to "*all the attention she got.*"

However, life was not so rosy after that. After serving as a Devdasi for few years, she was discontinued and replaced with another girl. Her hardships did not end there, as she was soon taken to a brothel in New Delhi. She does not supply details on how she ended up in the brothel and who took her there. She does not want to talk about her family either. She feels deserted. She feels her life would have been normal if she was not taken as a devdasi in the first place. To quote her *"I was a simple girl. I did not want much in life. I did not ask them to put me high as devdasi, and now I think that my life would be good if I was still a simple girl from the village."*

Although the derogatory, mal-practice of Devdasi has been legally abolished in the state of Andhra Pradesh, yet we come across such live examples such as Chelamma who are "pushed into ritual slavery" in the name of religious and social patriarchal rituals. Chelamma is right in asking us back, "*Why is this so that always a woman will become Devadasi, and a man would never be heard of becoming a Devadas? From the early days we all are told that God is one and He treats everyone as same and I also believe that there is no injustice in the eyes of God, and no injustice in his home (here, she referring to temples as God's home on earth), but then we (women) are put through this custom and not men. I do not understand why this (practice of Devadasi) is for women only?"*

Case 4: Teena

If women are hit worst by human trafficking, among them are those who are caught in the vivacious cycle of trafficking. Teena is such one case. She was studying in 8th standard, when her parents send her away to city. She was asked to earn money to support her family. She faced lot of issues in the beginning, as she was lost in a new world, new language and culture. But these details were not important to her, as no one heard her yelling and crying in the brothel. She pleaded with her madam and even to her customers to let her go, but they did not listen to her. *"I did not understand what they said. They did not understand what I was trying to tell them. All of them looked like foreigners' to me. But we all understood what I was supposed to do. No matter what I said and how much I cried, they exploited me."*

Teena got lucky once when she was rescued during a police raid in brothel (in Mumbai). She started working as a housemaid in a suburb area. But soon after that, she was again pushed into trafficking by her lover. Teena does not offer much details here but only says: *"I trusted him blindly. I loved him so much and he sold me again into sex work."* After spending 12 years in the brothel, Teena is now settled in a city in Telangana. She work as a housemaid. Though she is married now, but she will not talk much about her married life. But she is thankful to God to who *"finally heard all my prayers and got me out of hell."*

Case 5: Durga Amma

In the narrow lane abutting the holy Kapila Teertham in Tirupati, Chittoor, sits a small flower-shop. In the first glance, this shop looks similar to many other shops surrounding it, all of them displaying fresh flowers, coconuts, incense sticks and such other religious offerings and one is likely to pass it without a second glance. But in that tiny shop, sits a woman with a warm smile on her face and her eyes full of expectations that some devotees passing by her shop might just stop and buy flowers from her shop so that she makes enough money for her daily bread. This woman is Durga Amma, aged about 38 years and of a fragile frame. She looks much older than her age and attributes it to her own hardships. As she says: *"Where is time to look good? And for whom? I feel safer this way only. The way I look is partially because of my tough life and partially because of my own wish."*

This arouses a question as why Durga would want to look unattractive and older than her age? On inquiry, it is revealed that she was victimized because of her good looks and perhaps this is one of the reasons why she does not want to groom herself now, as it reminds her of her terrible past. Durga was trafficked at the age of 10 years from her village in coastal Andhra Pradesh. She was trafficked on the pre-text of getting a "decent, house-maid's job in Mumbai, with a nice family," and instead sold to a Mumbai- brothel for Rs 5000. As she recalls: *"Anna and Akka (referring to her traffickers) told my parents that I will get a good job in Mumbai because I was good-looking and smart. They said that a girl like me is wanted in big cities like Mumbai where I can work in a big house with ease and keep the masters happy."*

Durga spend nearly 10 years in the brothel. As a sex-worker, she served 5 to 10 clients on a daily basis who had a preference for her over other girls in the brothel because of her good looks and docile nature. In the words of Durga *"I kept crying every day and requesting men not to use me and my body, but they always said that they gave money to spend time with her and use her."* Durga was disgusted with her good-looks and yet she had to *"put on her make-up everyday and attract men."* If she refused to entertain men, she was beaten and denied food by the owners of the brothel. She recalls an incident when she was just 12 or 13 years old and suffering from high fever and yet put to serve a client. The more her clients and the brothel owners praised her good looks, the more she loathed herself. As she says: *"They thought I will be happy to hear that I am beautiful. But they did not know that I was sad to hear that. I felt that I was in such a bad condition only because I was beautiful."*

When she was rescued from the brothel, Durga arrived in Tirupati and decided to "devote her life in the service of God." She got her head-shaven and started working in a temple as a maid in lieu of daily meals, shelter and Rs 600 per month. She did not socialise much and preferred to stay in her allotted room in her free time. Later, she met a flower supplier in the premises of the temple and got married to him. After marriage, she moved in with her husband and helped in his flower-shop business. Her mother-in-law taught her to pick fresh flowers and make garlands. After a few years, Durga's husband died and she took charge of her family's flower shop. She now supports her old mother-in-law and her two children, one son and one daughter. Durga is keen to see her son study and become an officer. As she says: "*I work hard all day so that my family can eat. But I do not want my son to sit in this shop. He goes to school and wants to become an officer. I work all day to pay his fees. Today, this shop is our only source of money but some day my son will start earning and I will relax at home."*

At about 38 years of age, Durga is now content with her life. As a victim, she used to blame herself for her good looks which led her into sex-work. But now she realises that it was not her fault. As she says: *"I was not able to know what was happening to me and I was not able to do anything about it. I was so young and feared them (traffickers and brothel owners). I did whatever they asked me to do because everyone was doing the same thing. But I did not do anything with my heart."*

According to her, she "*washed away her sins when she cut her hair and served in the temple of God.*" Although she misses her husband yet she knows that she would have to pass her life without him. Despite her terrible past and loss of her husband, Durga believes that God is kind to her because she is, no longer doing the dirty job," and at least have a family now. She also believes that she was lucky to have a family after what had happened (to her)."

Durga was victimized and exploited for a good length of time, that is, about 10 years in a brothel. She used to hate herself because she believed that her good looks were the main reason to lead her into trafficking and eventually in a brothel. She was put to constant physical exploitation and emotional stress. During her stay in the brothel, Durga might have developed a lower self-esteem which is reflected in her passive submission, fear of brothel owners and self-abuse. On rescue, her act of offering her hair to God and turning indifferent, rather repulsive towards her grooming exhibits her strong desire to de-glamorise herself and thus, getting rid of her terrible past life as a glamorised sex-worker and memories associated with it. However, she found some solace in the company of her husband who married her for her good nature and not for her looks, and his companionship revoked her self-esteem and strengthened her faith in God. Today, she seems to overcome her fears and trauma as a victim. She now successfully runs her small flower shop and believes in hard-work for her living.

Case 6- Asha Lata

Asha Lata is a 26 years old housemaid in one of lesser known quarters in Khammam. She was trafficked at the age of 14 years by a person who pretended to be her lover. She eloped with him and ended up in a brothel. She spent about four years in a brothel. She was rescued with the help of an NGO and in her case, her parents refused to take her back. She stayed in a shelter home for two years and learned some basic tailoring and stitching work. After receiving her grants from government, Asha Lata was released from shelter home and she was lost once again. In her words: "*I did not know where to go and what to do. I was safe there. I was not very happy, but I was safe.*"

Since Asha Lata was very young when she started out on her own, she was feeling very insecure in the society. She said "*I was alone, I was young and everybody looked at me as if they owned me.*" NGO staff tried to get her married, but she was not ready to *"be touched by any man again."* She had lost her faith in love and marriage. But at the same time, she could not live alone (unmarried) in a traditional small town like Khammam. After sometime, she came up with this solution: "*I will live as a widow and that way no one will bother about me.*" Now she leads life of a widow, dresses very simply, puts on no make-up etc. and devotes her free time to the prayers.

Case 7: Swathi

Swathi is about 23 years and seems very fashionable. She dresses up nicely and wants to look good. She comes across as a happy, well-settled woman but as she starts telling her story, we can see the other side. Swathi was trafficked at a young age of 15 years and spent three years in a brothel in Calcutta. After she was rescued, her parents refused to accept her back in family and asked her to go far away from their native village. Swathi came in Hyderabad in search of work, and started petty jobs. She worked in petty shops as a salesgirl and started living with other two salesgirls in a rented place. After some time, both her room mates left the job and eventually they left the rented room. This was a major issue for Swathi, as there were fewer rent options for a single woman like her. Either the locality was not good, or the rent money was too high for her. In order to save herself from all this trouble, Swathi moved to a less developed locality and there she started calling herself as a married woman. When questioned about her husband, she will say to neighbours "*he works in Mumbai meets me only during long holidays like Duseera.*"

In order to protect her lies, Swathi goes to her village during long holidays and stays with her parents, who have now allowed her for short visits. The parents also tell their respective neighbours that Swathi is married and her husband is too busy to afford a long vacation. But is this arrangement safe for Swathi? She fears it is not. She feels that sooner or later someone will start questioning her about her husband, as why he is never seen around. She also fears that once she "grows older, the question of having children will also come up." But at this point of time, she has no answers for these questions and does not want to think too much about them.

Case 8: Renuka

Renuka is around 22 years and stays in Nellore. She has completed her graduation (after her rescue) and stays with her mother. Renuka was trafficked on the pre-text of economic work when she was 16 years and she was sold in a brothel. She was rescued after four years. When the NGO member tried to contact parents, they came to meet her in shelter home but expressed their inability to take her back with them. Renuka says "*They did not say it clearly, but I know I was like a black mark for them. I had let them down and they will not accept me as pure and clean.*"

However, Renuka continued to stay at Home and completed graduation by correspondence. At the same time, she received vocational training in tailoring and embroidery work. After some time, she re-located and started working as a piece-rate worker for a garment factory. Renuka did not get married but she missed her mother. She will secretly call her when her father was not at home and then cry all night after talking to her. As it turned out, her father died at a young age and her mother was left alone. Since Renuka is the only daughter, she felt responsible for her mother and urged her to be with her. Eventually her mother moved in with her. Now Renuka is the sole bread winner of her family. She keeps silent on issue of her marriage and it is not good to probe her further into this matter. But she also says "*I hope to be married some day. I am still young. But I will marry a boy who agrees to take care of my mother.*"

Case 9: Shaiza Fathima

Shazia is about 48 years old woman, she is married and lives in Warangal. She works as a housemaid and also earns some extra money by offering home-tailored clothes for small babies.

Shazia was trafficked when she was 20 years old. Her parents wanted her to get married but Shazia loved another boy and eloped with him. That lover turned out to be a sex-agent and he sold Shaiza in a brothel for just Rs 5000. When Shaiza was rescued, her parents did not wish to see her face. They flatly told NGO members that Shazia was dead for them. She felt sorry but she also blamed herself for this condition. She said *"I know what I did was wrong. I had hurt my parents. I let their name down. So it was right that they now hated me."*

Shazia got training in tailoring courses and with the help of NGO she started working in a local tailor shop. The owner of that shop was a widower whose wife died very young. He had no children. Gradually he developed interest in Shazia and proposed marriage to her. She told him everything about her past life and still he accepted her. She said "*He said it was not my fault. He said that Allah had already punished me for my bad sins and now I was pure for him.*" Once Shazia was married, her parents accepted her. After death of her father, her mother lives with Shazia and her husband supports her decision. They both work in the tailor shop where Shazia is actively involved and she does her best to pick and offer new designs for female customers.

She says: "*I am thankful to Allah for giving me such a loving and caring husband. Without his support, I would not be any good.*"

Case 10: Adii Lakshmi

Adii Lakshmi shyly tells us that this name is given to her by her husband. She does not remember her real name, because she was trafficked at a young age (below 10 years). The madam in brothel gave her a new name "Ruby." For next 10 years, Ruby suffered in silence, everyday as she entertained customers, and if she failed to do so, madam would beat her with out mercy and stop her food and water. Adii Lakshmi does not want to talk about her experiences in the brothel. She offered "*What is there to know about that place (brothel). It is same everywhere. Only our names and faces change. All of us live in hell there.*"

But Adii Lakshmi is equally excited to talk about her present life. She got married with the intervention of NGO and her husband knows all about her past life. However, her in-laws and relatives are not aware of her previous life as a sex-worker. She has two children, one boy and one girl and she takes pride in having a small and happy family. But Adii Lakshmi is also carrying a dark secret, as she says "*My husband and I have decided to keep my past a secret and not to tell even my children about it. They come running to me and say that I look like Goddess to them, and my heart weeps. I am not as pure and good as a mother must be. I only pray to Goddess that my secret goes with me.*"

Case 11: Alpa Mani

Alpa Mani works as a construction site labour in Warangal. She is a widow. Her life is full of sadness. First she was trafficked for sex work when she was still in school. She pitied herself everyday and prayed to God to save her life. In the brothel, she was denied any decent clothes and food. Since her brothel was a low-status brothel where usually high-way truck drivers and petty vendors came as customers, she was exploited for Rs 200 per session and she just got a pittance out of this.

Alpa Mani was rescued during a police raid, and she stayed in shelter home for nearly six months. Her parents took her back under pressure of NGO and police, but they soon "got rid of her" by marrying her off to a construction site labour in Warangal. She also started working at the construction site. In their haste to get rid of their daughter, the parents did not foresee what was coming. Her husband was suffering from TB and died within eight months of her wedding. Alpa Mani decided not to return to her parents and continue her work as a construction labour.

She pulls a flat face, lits a Beedi and says *"Only if my parents had taken some more time. They should have keept me for some more time and searched for a better match. At least then I will be still married and may be staying at home while my husband will go out and labour for money."* She laughs at the thought of sitting ideally at home and waiting for her husband, but one can see the pain, hurt and anger as she says these words.

Case 12: Marisa Amma

Marisa Amma is a 30 years old, divorced woman. She was trafficked on the pre-text of earning money through housemaid work in a big city. She was sold in a brothel and stayed there for more than 10 years. Marisa Amma was tortured every night but she was still hopeful that one day her sufferings will end. Marisa does not want to recollect details of her days as a sex worker. She tells us, " *I hate to even think of those days because it was something I did not choose for myself. It was something I was forced into. I used to think that this was God's way to punish me. But I never understood why he wanted to punish me like that."*

After her rescue, she got married to a person who was aware of her past. Marisa was thankful that her husband knows about her and still accepted her. But after sometime she started feeling guilty and self-conscious when he was near. In her words, "*It is not his fault. He was very nice and kind. But all times he talked and behaved in a way that I felt suffocated. I wanted him to behave normally, but he always showed me that he is caring for me because I have suffered a lot. I wanted to get out of it and he was pushing me more in bad memories. He will not let me watch movies or song where anything towards rape or prostitution was filmed. He will not let me go out alone. I know he was doing it because he wanted to protect me; but I was feeling more guilty and uneasy."* Finally Marisa could not bear it anymore and she took divorce from her husband. She is not keeping in touch with him anymore. She works as an attendant in a girls' Inter College and stays in staff quarters.

Case 13: Nazia

Nazia comes from a small village near Vikarabad. She works in a tailor's shop and she is known for her neat work. The customers at tailor's shop demand that their clothes are stitched and embroidered by Nazia only. Sometimes her friends and customers also ask her to go to big cities like Hyderabad and try her luck there. But Nazia gets uncomfortable at the very thought of leaving her small village home. Nazia was a young girl when she was forcefully taken to a brothel in Mumbai. She is not able to recall correctly if she was kidnapped or her parents allowed the trafficker to take her. But going by her faith in parents, she believes the former situation. Sadly for her, her parents are dead and this remains an unanswered question in her heart.

But what remains more is her fear of dark and moving away from home (familiar settings). It could be attributed to her childhood event and the terror and trauma she may have suffered due to this. Nazia was kept in a dark room, with no windows and only a narrow door for entry. She was kept there for many days and every day one man or other would come and have sex with her. After few days she lost count of how many men came in a day. The fear of dark is clubbed with fear of exploitation in her mind.

As a self-constructed rule, Nazia does not stay back in shop after dark, she will rather take her work home and finish it. She does not visit any clients' house to take orders, because she fears stepping into strangers' houses as well. Nazia is constantly living in fear. As she says, "*I cannot sleep in dark. I will always leave a light bulb open. If there is a power cut, I burn candles all night. I want to go out, especially in late night wedding parties, but I know I just cannot. I visit them in the morning of wedding day and give my wishes. But I feel safer when I am inside my home."* Nazia received some counselling at Shelter home, but it did not help much to remove her deeply embedded fears and she knows she will have to live this fear as long as she is alive.

Case 14: Lalitha

Lalitha was trafficked at the tender age of 14 years. She was a student then and had a boyfriend. Her boyfriend was at least five to six years older than her and used to bring lots of gifts for her, including purse, artificial jewels, and treats. She was fascinated by his money and lifestyle and therefore when he proposed marriage to her, she did not think twice. She says: *"I was jumping with joy when he asked me to marry him. I was seeing a good future for us where there were no money problems. I was very much in love with him and could do anything for him. When he asked me to run away with him, I did not think of my family. I was only thinking of him and my life in Mumbai."*

But like other classic cases of duping and dumping, Lalitha's dreams were broken when she ended up in a brothel. Her so-called lover had sold her for Rs 20,000. She felt cheated and cried for help but no one listened to her woes. She did not see her lover next and there was no way she could even contact her parents. After spending six long years of suffering and sexual exploitation in the brothel, she was rescued by the Police. Now Lalitha works in a factory and earns enough money to support herself. She got married but confessed that she could not really love her husband. She has three children and she feels only a sense of duty for them. Lalitha says, *"All feelings of love died when I saw myself in that place (brothel). Now all I have is some feeling for my husband and children because they are my family. But I am not sure how much I love them. I do not know if I really love them. I feel like a dead person inside."*

Case 15: Anupa

Anupa's story echoes the fate of many young poor girls in Andhra Pradesh. Like many young girls, Anupa was trapped into trafficking mainly because of her poverty and ignorance. She came from a large family, where her grandparents and parents lived with her six siblings. With limited means of income, her parents were not able to send her to school and rather saw her and her siblings as a means to earn more money. Under the pre-text of earning money for her family and more importantly for her dowry, Anupa was send away by her parents. She recalls: *"My mother told me that I was going away to make money for my own wedding. She also said that if I earned more, I would be able to help in my sisters' marriage and my brother's education. Now this was important for all of us."*

Anupa was thinking about getting work in a factory, as she and her parents were promised. But instead, she was taken to a brothel and forced to do sex-work. She stayed in the brothel for 12 years. Later on, she learned tailoring in shelter home and now works in a local garment factory. Anupa's words sum up the feelings of many girls like her: "*When we were young, money was the most important thing. But when we get into this (prostitution), we feel we were better off as poor for we were safe then. And know for sure that whatever we earn, even this money is not in our hands. Madam takes all money in the name of giving us food, clothes, make up and safety."*

Case 16: Shabana

Shabana's story highlights the plight of many girl-brides whose life is crumpled like a used piece of paper and thrown away in a dust bin. Shabana comes from a Muslim middle class family in the city and she had five siblings. Her parents settled her match with a man almost double her age when she was just 16 years old. The husband used to beat her often and exploit her sexually. One day, Shabana ran away from her husband's home and returned to her parents. Her parents feared her husband and so they asked "a known person" to get Shabana some job outside in the city where her husband will not be able to trace her. This known person was a familiar face in neighbourhood who claimed to be an agent for Gulf-country visa and work permits. Building upon this, the so-called help/ agents arranged for Shabana's work permit in Gulf country and send her off. Before she could realise it, Shabana was on board with few Bengali and Nepali girls on the way to Gulf. She was trafficked, as she says: *"I was trying to get away from my husband who used to beat me and use me against my wishes. But see, my fate brought me to another hell where any man can come and use me like he wanted to. I used to keep telling myself that God has punished me for I could not bear one man and ran away due to his beatings and using me and now I had to have sex with so many men".*

Shabana was rescued during an international sex-racket busting operation and sent back to her home town. But she did not want to return to her husband, who had re-married after she left him. She is willing to go back to her parents, but they are not too keen to take her back. Still struggling with her deep emotions, Shabana is currently living in a working women's hostel in the city. She works as an office assistant. On the issue of her personal life, all she can manage to say is this,*"I was not hoping for a queen's life or like they show in films. I was only hoping for a nice, decent home and a good husband. Did I not deserve it? I am still not able to understand why this happened to me? I have no hopes for future. May be I will live alone all my life and I will die all alone."*

Case 17: Cristie

Cristie is 26 years old, simple looking Christian woman. But her personality is more complex. In her case, Cristie's parents had sold her to traffickers for some money. She learnt the same from her trafficker. As she recalls: "*He said that my parents did not love me. I am a burden on them. Therefore, they got rid of me.*" With this bitter truth, Cristie started her journey in a brothel. She was among the youngest and most beautiful in-mates in her brothel. This made her one of the most-sought after girl too. The customers came in regularly and they demanded more and more from her. She was feeling weak and wasted but there was no rescue. At the same time, she wanted to forget the bitter fact that her own parents pushed her into this dirty work.

Cristie was rescued after nine long years in brothel. When she was rescued, she had already lost her looks, her zeal to live and her feelings. As the NGO member recalls, she was like a log of wood when she came in. But eventually with the counselling and the company of other in-mates in the shelter home, she found solace, and devoted herself to the service of God. One turning point in her life was when she decided to convert to Christianity and thus started seeing her as "reborn." As she said, *"No matter what I did, I was not happy. I was restless all the time. One day NGO madam (name hidden on request) took me into prayers and I started feeling calmness inside. I wanted to convert because I started believing that with a change in my name, I will be re-born."* And it seems to have worked in her case. According to NGO member, who is still keeping a tab on Cristie and looks after her, she is now on her way to lead a normal life. She is willing to be associated with the said NGO in future and help in her own little ways to bring peace to other women who have suffered in life.

Case 18: Balamani

Balamani was approached with the help of a senior police officer, whose wife is associated with a local NGO. She played a key role in getting Balamani the said job and place to live. Balamani was trafficked when she was just 18 years old. Like many other ill-fated girls of her sect, Balamani too was deceived and duped into sex-work. But what was different in her case was the fact that Balamani's husband, her lawfully wedded husband pushed her into sex-trade. Balamani got married when she was just above 15 years. Her husband was a labourer and also a drunkard by habit. He used to press her for money and often sent her to her parent's home (in the same village) to fetch more money. When she refused, he used to beat her. He sold her to a brothel owner for few thousand rupees. He told Balamani that they will go to Bangalore and find some new job there. And he left her in a hotel room and did not return. Later on, a middle aged woman (brothel owner) approached her, claiming that she was her husband's aunty and she took Balamani with her. This is how she reached a brothel.

Balamani stayed in brothel for about seven years. After she was rescued, she did not want to return to her husband and on the other hand, her parents refused to take her back, saying that she was not their responsibility anymore. Now at 45 years, Balamani works as a housemaid in a gated community and lives in a tiny servant quarter provided to her by community association. She passes time by watching colony's children playing in the lawns and sings songs for them. She is an integral part of that colony's common functions, weddings and birthdays etc, as she willingly helps them out. She is fondly called "Amma" and people only know that her husband died in an accident. She too believes that her husband is dead and does not even want to think of him or go back to him.

Case 19: Roma : A Success Story

By and large all the victims of trafficking that we met lived on with a negative self-image and low self-esteem. But we found one woman, Roma who had faith in herself and started all over from the scratch. Meeting her and talking to her we realised that here was one woman who did not give into all her sufferings and tortures but took it as a challenge. As a result, she now has a name and status in the society and has overcome her fears of the past. Roma (name changed on request), is now 42, and is a working woman. She was trafficked when she was 17 years of age. She was trafficked on the pretext of earning more money for her family. As she recalls, *"The woman (traffickers) told me that they had good contacts in the city. They told my parents that if I go with them, I would be able to send more money back at home."*

At 17, while she was studying in high school, Roma was pulled out of college and sent along with her trafficker to get a good job in the neighbouring state. She travelled with the so-called Aunty and three other girls from her place. They were kept together for two weeks and then all of them were separated. As Roma points out, *"Each of us will go to a different brothel. They (traffickers) planned it very carefully, they never let a group of girls from same place be in one brothel. Because, if many girls from same place are spotted in one area, it will be dangerous for the traffickers."*

In the brothel, Roma did not easily give in. She protested a lot and in turn got her skin and tongue burnt with cigarettes, she was even raped by two of the goons of the brothel owners. She was kept without food and water for many days, until she gave in crying out of hunger, pain and helplessness. Roma was in the brothel for five years and in that duration she was exploited almost every day. But some hope was still alive in her heart. As Roma says, *"I have always believed in God. Each day when I was going through this punishment, I was praying silently to God that this one would be my last one. Somehow I also believed that this ordeal was only temporarily and God will bring this to an end. It was very difficult to keep up the faith at times and I went into depression and cursed my life but somehow I did continue to have faith."*

Roma was rescued by the Police. Her parents showed sympathy for her but they did not want to take her back in the house. With a broken heart, Roma continued to live in the shelter home and in the meantime, she completed her 12th and graduation 1st year exams. She started taking interest in the work of the NGO. She was also helping the NGO staff in counselling as she felt for all other victims of trafficking and other women in difficult circumstances. As she says *"Whenever a new girl was brought to the Home, usually madam ji asked me to look after her. I always shared room with such new girls, because I could handle their crying and even shouting at times. I used to tell them my own story and tell them that life does not end there and there is always something new to look forward to".*

During her stay in Home, Roma came into contact with another NGO volunteer who had lost his wife and children in a natural disaster. He was devoting his free time and resources to education of deserted young girls. Roma fell in love with him and they got married in a simple ceremony. He is very much aware of Roma's dreadful past but they do not talk about it. Soon Roma became a mother of a daughter. All this while, Roma also continued her graduation degree. When her daughter turned four years, Roma took up a job in a school. Her daughter goes to same school where she teaches now. In her free time, Roma and her husband still visit the NGO and Home and try to help other victims to the best of their capabilities. Roma wanted to share her story, but at the same time, she did not want her daughter to find out about her past. She agreed to share her story because, as she told us, "*she wanted that this dirty practice should stop. It kills many girls, emotionally.. Physically also, they are so exploited that there is no life left inside.*"

Case 20: Nisha

Nisha is a lively lady, always smiling and telling a joke. At the time of her interview, she said that she would not answer any questions about her past. The only information we gather about her is that she was trafficked when she was a teenager and she stayed in a brothel for about 10 years. She was subject to physical as well as verbal abuse everyday and once tried to commit suicide. But what makes Nisha stand out now is the fact that she is fighting back the criminals. She was physically bruised and emotionally hurt when she was rescued. She did not make eye contacts with NGO/ Shelter home staff for many days, and one day she just broke into tears. She started taking part in counselling sessions and her wounds healed. Then one day she volunteered to help the NGO. Seeing her zest and her potential, NGO trained her and retained her as an active member. Nisha now serves as a key agent and informer for NGO. She has helped in busting couple of sex rackets in the City. The police department also acknowledges her work. Nisha feels for young girls who are trapped into trafficking. She says: *"I know how they will be feeling. I have gone through the same phase myself. Whenever I hear about a gang, my blood boils, I want these people (traffickers) to die. It is only because of them so many girls are punished for nothing."* Nisha feels satisfied with her role. She says, "*I will keep doing this work as long as I live. I feel that even if I am able to bring in a smile in one girls face or some happiness into the lives of one of these girls, I will feel that I have done something positive in my life.*"

Case 21: Mona

Mona is a sex-worker. Mona has studied up to 10th and she can speak in Hindi, English and Telugu languages. When approached initially, she was not willing to talk. But after pursuing her for many days, she agreed to speak about her life. Mona was betrayed by her so-called lover who sold her to a brothel. She was about 16 years when she was trafficked. She used to cry a lot in the beginning but it was of no use. Everyone in the brothel used to tell her that she was better off in brothel and the outside world is cruel and bad. It is not good for a young lonely girl like her. She was rescued after five years and she made an attempt to live a decent life. With what little education and training she got, she tried her luck in petty shops like tailoring shops and as a salesgirl. But luck did not favour her. She was always running out of money and sometimes she did not have enough to eat. At that point of time, Mona decided to go back into sex-trade. But she does not offer details on exactly how and when she resumed prostitution. When asked about how she feels, she changes the topic, saying that *"It does not matter. I am paid to look happy and beautiful. And to tell you the truth, I enjoy it sometimes. I enjoy the attention I get from all men."*

Apparently, Mona made her choice. But was it really her choice? In a moment of introspection, she says. *"No one really wants to do this (sex work). But once you are into it, it is not easy to get out. Even when you are really out of it (referring to rescue), it is still attached to you like a shadow. I always felt the fear that someone will recognise me and I will die of shame. I felt the fear that one day or other I will go back there (brothel). Sometimes you also start liking the false world and all the things. Sometimes I feel I should not be here. I should not be doing this. But the next moment, I ask myself, what else can you do?"* And the life moves on. But is that all she wants to tell? But is that really how she feels or does not she feel at all? That question remains hanging in the air and we find no answers.

Case 22: Laila

Laila is Mona's roommate. She is also a sex worker like Mona. She does not talk much, but Mona insisted her to share her story as well. Laila's mother passed away when she was six years. Her father remarried a widow with two children of her own. As the luck would turn out, her father soon passed away, leaving Laila into the custody of her step-mother. She sold Laila to a trafficker for few thousands of rupees when she was 15 years old. She was rescued and sent to a shelter home. Laila confessed to be missing all the glamour and fancy of the red light areas. She obviously had withdrawal symptoms, but as she said, she was constantly put on alcohol and sometimes on drugs, so that she will not make a scene when a customer came. Laila was rescued and she refused to provide details of her family for re-contact, that is her step-mother. She declared herself to be an orphan. In turn, she got some training on tailoring in the Shelter home. She did not see her life as a tailor. So when Laila left shelter home, she turned back to flesh trade. Unlike Mona, she did not even try alternate mode of living. Laila also worked with some phone-sex clubs.

Mona and Laila go silent on how they met each other and how they ended up living together. Mona just says *"we were meant to be together, so we are.*" Laila adds to it that, "*they are like sisters, because there is no one else to share their happiness and sadness.*" They have joined a college as students, in order to avoid trouble from neighbours and society. At the time of interview, Mona and Laila were planning to move into a new town and take up some job. When asked if the new job will be that of a sex-worker or are they thinking of leaving it – they just laugh and let it drop. Mona and Laila were approached through a journalist who is currently working on a documentary on sex-workers. Mona and Laila agreed to meet us in a food shop of a shopping centre. They did not wish to share any personal details and did not want to be re-approached again. They gave us an interview on this condition only and we agreed.

Case 23: Padma

Padma is one of the youngest in-mates in her shelter home. She was trafficked when she was 14 years and stayed in the brothel for about one year. Currently she is staying in the shelter home and continuing her education. She is an average student, but she has a strong desire to learn and do something on her own. Considering her tender age and the fact that she was recently rescued, a direct interaction/ interview with her was not permitted (by shelter home in-charge). But what is remarkable to note that Padma is trying hard to gather broken pieces of her life. She is a quiet and friendly girl. She wants to finish her college education and do B. Ed. too. She wishes to become a teacher. According to the in-charge, Padma occasionally breaks into tears or goes into a silent, distant mode. But considering the fact that her emotional-wounds are still fresh and hurting, it will take some more time before she is healed completely from inside.

Case 24: Sarla

Sarla is about 50 years of age. She was trafficked when she was about 12 years. She does not clearly remember her parents/ family members and details of her native place because it was the last time she saw them. All she remembers is that her father was a farmer and her mother used to take her to fields with her when she used to deliver lunch to father. She believes her village to be somewhere near Krishna river, but cannot exactly recall its name or location. Sarla had suffered for a long time in a brothel and she had lost all hope to live. But when she was rescued and brought to the shelter home, she found a new family. She is very much inspired by the chief officer of the shelter home and always is full of praise for her. Sarla is currently working in the same shelter home as a cook and lives in nearby quarters.

Sarla never married but she longs to have kids of her own. In a way, she sees and treats young victims/ young girls who are brought in the shelter home as her own children. She is always making them comfortable and giving them counselling and a shoulder to cry upon. Sarla lets young in-mates steal from her kitchen sometimes and also takes part in their jokes. Sarla is like their foster mother who sometimes saves them from the scolding of other staff members. Sarla is keen to remain associated with the shelter home and is willing to contribute to the well-being of other victims and in-mates to the best of her capacities.

Case 25: Usha Rani, Voice of Suffering or the Loss of it

Victims of trafficking often deal with physical abuse. But more than that, they also undergo tremendous mental trauma and stress. In trafficked conditions, every day is like a burning hell to them and rarely do they have an outlet for their feelings. The impact of trafficking is far beyond the physical and emotional exploitation. Sometimes, rather most of the times, it consumes the person in question.

Usha Rani is one such ill-fated victim of trafficking. She is mentally disturbed and does not want to admit that she was once forced into sex-trade. Since prostitution is seen as lowly and demeaning for women in our society, she is not able to confess the same about her. Neither is she able to absorb the fact that she too can live a life of dignity (post her rehab and treatments). She has a low opinion of herself and though she talks about being forced in a bad situation, she never clearly admits that the so-called bad situation was sex-trade. Usha Rani lives in a world of fantasy and has many versions of her story to tell us how she ended up in a shelter home. Sometimes she claims that her parents left her there, sometimes she will weave a story around her less affectionate brother and sister-in-law who did not want to carry her burden. On the other hand, she would be heard telling others that she herself ran away from home and the police handed her over to shelter home. But according to the official records, she was rescued in an anti-trafficking operation and was then a sex-worker. Her present mental condition may be seen as an escape from reality, or a conscious or rather unconscious attempt to hide her past life from inmates and staff members in shelter homes. But little does she know about official records.

Usha Rani is the depiction of how young girls suffer as victims of trafficking; particularly those trafficked for sex-work. Her shame, guilt and negative self-esteem put her in a critical spot- sometimes in a tight spot beyond any point of recovery. Some victims are reported to overcome the fears and impacts of trafficking (with proper counselling and aid), but there are also victims like Usha Rani who lose everything and suffer all along.

Chapter 8

Summing up

The present study is focused on trafficking for sex trade with data from the two states of Telangana and Andhra Pradesh. Sex trafficking is a serious concern in contemporary times as its incidence is found to be increasing rapidly in these two states. It is also called as modern slavery. Human trafficking generally involves extra-economic coercion, whereby individuals trafficked is not free to choose their occupation and lose their freedom to move out of the occupation they are forced into. Thus, human trafficking is a violation of basic human rights. Roots of sex trafficking can be traced from the preexistent 'slavery' practices which continues even in the present era. It has taken a massive shape in the contemporary society. Women and children forced into this trade are brutally treated, victimised, tortured, oppressed physically and mentally in order to gain huge amount of capital. In most of the cases, trafficking of women and children takes place from rural and backward areas where women have subservient positions and have been deprived of their rights. Researches and studies done in this area shows that, trafficking of women and children often happens as a consequence of poverty, gender discrimination, low education, caste and class discrimination, corruption in administration, globalisation, and ineffective law and policies.

Victims of sex trafficking are trapped by traffickers into sex work, through abduction, false promises of marriage, job opportunities, lucrative and safe work in sex industry, job training, or educational opportunities. They identify them mostly through interpersonal or social networks of family, friends, relatives and other social groupings. Further, they are subjected to physical abuse and undergo psychological trauma. Intermediaries, brothel owners, and customers inflict physical abuse in the form of beatings, rape, burning of breasts, genital areas with cigarettes, and even murder (victims in case of disobedience). These torn, tormented, and tortured victims undergo extreme psychological abuse like threatening their families, social disrepute, and denial of food. Indeed exploitation inflicted on victims is a violation of human rights.

Debates centering sex trafficking argue of false identification of sex work and sex trafficking. This overlapping works negatively for sex workers as the laws against sex trafficking criminalises women who are into sex work. Thereby, it thus, denies agency of women and reduces them to offenders or victims who need moral policing, care and protection. The tendency of overlapping the two, fails to recognise the wider scope of human trafficking and neglects the complexities involved in sex trafficking. Further, the debate of migration and its association with sex trafficking denies agency to women as the laws framed for combating trafficking control the mobility of women which in turn rejects their agency to move and victimizes them. Women essentially have the right to choose the source of her preferred economic activity and therefore such a flawed understanding would necessarily stand as an impediment in their attempt.

Trafficking of human beings especially that of women and children, is an organised crime that violates basic human rights. As per the UN Protocol to Prevent, Suppress and Punish Trafficking in Persons, especially Women and Children, trafficking is defined as any activity leading to recruitment, transportation, harbouring or receipt of persons, by means of threat or use of force or a position of vulnerability. As an organised crime, human trafficking, has been rapidly growing all over the globe, and the cases are being reported in a significant numbers particularly post-globalisation. Since 1980s, coinciding with the development and growth of social and economic globalisation, there has been a steady increase in the frequency and incidences of trafficking.

Human trafficking has been identied as the third largest source of profit for organised crime, following arms and drug trafficking, generating billions of dollars worldwide which are again re-invested in illegal criminal activities. Thus, the money generated from trafficking is directed back to the criminal activities, such purchase of more drugs, arms and human victims to fulfill the ever-increasing demand for cheap labour and prostitution, and the vicious cycle of trafficking goes on. Trafficking takes places for various purposes such as forced cheap labour, prostitution, begging, organ trade, drug couriers, arms smuggling etc. Often these three cited forms of trafficking, that is, trafficking of humans, drugs and arms are interrelated and overlap with one another. Moreover, the roots of the origin and operations of these organised criminal activities can be traced to a singular source and/or a network of close-knit sources. It is also seen that while the methods used for trafficking such as coercion, duping, luring, abducting, kidnapping, threats to physical violence such as killing, and mental torture etc. are commonly cited, it is the social and economic constraints of the victims that not only leads them to this situation in the first place but also make them most vulnerable and helpless in the network of trafficking. This holds true for Asia where women and young girls are already at the bottom of gender-hierarchy, highly vulnerable, and subject to violence, suppression and oppression in various forms.

In India, vulnerability of women due to their subordinate position in gender-relations is coupled with their low socio-economic and political status. Over the years, India has emerged as a potential source, destination and transit point for trafficking, mainly for prostitution and labour. It is difficult to estimate the exact number of trafficked persons, owing to the secrecy and organised nature of the trafficking networks. However, according to the official government reports, such as Ministry of Women and Child Development, there are nearly three million prostitutes in India and about 40 per cent of these are minor children, and majority of them induced into prostitution through trafficking.

Over a time, Indian states have recorded large incidences of trafficking, particularly that of women and young girls. In this connection, Andhra Pradesh has a long and rich history of trafficking. Andhra Pradesh serves as a main source, destination and transit point in the country and the patterns vary according to the nature and occurrence of crime in a given region within the state. The underprivileged areas of coastal Andhra Pradesh are main source points, whereas the metropolitan cities emerge as main destination point, besides facilitating cross-border trafficking to other Indian states and in some cases, to other nations. Traditionally, trafficking of women and girls in Andhra Pradesh was largely confined within state and neighbouring states of Karnaka, Odisha and Tamil Nadu and it was mainly aimed at forced marriages, prostitution and labour purposes. However, some new trends in trafficking in the state are noted recently, these are trafficking for sex-tourism in tourist destinations (these include pilgrim places also), and increase in cross-border trafficking.

Major Observations

There were various limitations in our study. The scope of our study was limited to those victims who consented to have interactions and give interviews. In few cases, those victims who were identified for interaction did not respond or walked out on the day of interview. Some brothels and spa centres where trafficked victims were suspected to be currently working refused to participate in the study. In this study, victims were identified and approached with the intervention of police or NGOs or both. In such cases, interactions and interviews with trafficked victims were indirectly controlled and monitored by

NGO/ police personnel up to some extent. They were also present at the time of interview and they reserved the rights to stop any interaction/ interview in the middle in case they suspected the victims were getting stressed or if they showed any signs of discomfort, re-trauma, and uneasiness. Police and NGO members did not share their personal and socio-demographic details. They cited personal confidentiality and safety as the main reasons for this as they are actively involved with rescue operations and often deal with critical situations. In case of victims, they did not confess their "once-trafficked" status quite openly. They could not be probed further into this. In the course of study, few NGOs, shelter homes and re-habilitation centres were identified and contacted. These centred have some trafficked victims (as per information released by police authority), but when contacted, these specific centres refused to participate in the study.

One interesting finding to note was that the younger victims were relatively shy/ reserved in their responses. Same is the case with unmarried young victims (who were under 30 years at the time of interview). This shows a departure from the assumption that the younger generations would be more open and expressive in comparison with their older counterparts, owing to their greater exposure to and closer proximity with modern means of communication (mobile etc.) in comparison with their older counterparts. One reason for this reserved attitude of younger lot can be attributed to the fact that they still look for an opportunity to marry, have children and settle down. In this regard, an exposure to their "terrible past life," may adversely affect their future plans. Therefore, they are cautious about sharing the information/details pertaining to their life as victims of trafficking.

On the other hand, the older victims (particularly those in the age group on 45-60) were more open in their expressions. Again, this observation indicates a departure from the earlier assumption that the older generations are more reserved and speaking of sexual violence is still a taboo for them. During the field work, one such victim remarked "*...there is nothing to lose now. Nothing to be scared of.*" She was ready to share her story to the minute details. The same person also allowed us to take her picture. Based on the same observation, one reason for the openness of older victims can be attributed to their outlook towards life and the fact that they have "nothing more to lose."

In some cases, the victims quizzed us if they would be receiving some money in return of their interviews. Nearly in all cases, the interviews were completed in one to three sitting. On the other hand in some cases, the interview process was interrupted due to victims' emotional outbursts (crying). However, with the help of NGO personnel, the victims were consoled and interviews resumed and completed. But in such cases, further probing of a particular questions (which might have initiated discomfort/ uneasiness or even sobbing) was not done.

We were able to carry out this study due to the support of the NGO's. In most cases, NGO/ activists were willing to help and provided relevant information on trafficking data and cases (victims). In practice, almost all NGO/ activists insisted that the interviews should be held in their presence, preferably in their office room only. In nearly all cases, we were not given the permission to visit the NGO and/or see the victims unless the concerned NGO person was also present and available for the entire duration of the interaction/ interviews. In this way, we can conclude that the interview sessions were monitored constantly by the NGO personnel in most cases. The fact that most of the victims, particularly the younger ones, were occasionally looking up to the NGO personnel during the course of interview might lead to a conclusion that their responses were approved/ rehearsed in advance. This was particularly noted during questions on life in shelter homes, amenities and services and financial aid.

Sometimes the trafficked victims keep shuttling between different shelter homes and rehabilitation centres due to their special conditions. These include victims with HIV-AIDS positive cases, TB patients, minor girls, emotionally unstable etc. For instance, the Swadhar and Ujjawala schemes of Government of India also bring out the differences in identification and separate treatment of such victims. While this provision may look neat on paper but in practice, it adds to a victim's suffering and dejection. This can be prevented by giving special attention to victims of trafficking and their needs and requirements. Considering their physical and emotional vulnerability, their transfers between different shelter homes should be minimised.

During fieldwork it was noted that some of the shelter homes had discontinued their schemes and provisions for trafficked victims. In majority of cases, such NGOs and shelter homes operated in their respective areas for less than 10 years. Lack of continuous funds, security issues for in-mates and no renewal or cancellation of their shelter home status are main reasons why some shelter homes and NGOs discontinue their services. In a situation like this, the existing in-mates of shelter homes are transferred to another home, which is emotionally disturbing for them.

The police personnel were cooperative and talked at length about their experiences with cases of trafficking. Interactions with Police centred around Police officer's perception on Human trafficking and their first-hand experiences with cases of trafficking. In majority, the police personnel viewed their department/ police force in positive lights and affirmed that they all were knowledgeable and trained enough to deal with such cases. They confirmed the active-participative role of police in rescue and rehabilitation of victims.

The biggest hurdles in the process of interviewing police personnel are obtaining an interview appointment and the intermittent interruptions during the interview (phone calls, staff calls, random exit in order to attend some other issues etc). In case of Police, data on personal information is denied due to security reasons. Since Police officers and their team are dealing with sensitive cases and at times they have to deal with armed traffickers, therefore their identity is a major security concern.

The NGO/ activists could provide information about and accessibility of only those victims who were either rescued recently or were in regular touch with their rescuers. For instance, an activist in Karim Nagar (requested for anonymity) said that he has dealt with 83 cases of trafficking (including men/ women/ children) so far (since 2006 when he started volunteering for the first time) and prevented 16 cases of trafficking in the last 6-7 months (as told in March 2013), yet he is not able to keep tab on everyone he rescued/ helped. At present, he was in touch with only eight victims, all in his own vicinity. According to him, most of the victims do not wish to keep in touch and they are not traceable after they are released from NGOs/ shelter homes. However, going by this observation, we can possibly explore the missing links between influx and outflow of victims from the shelter homes and the unavailability of data on their whereabouts after rehabilitation.

One prominent theme that emerged from field work was the recurrence of shame and silence on the part of victims. Most of the times, the victims would either avoid a question and when probed further, they would offered a monosyllabic answer. For example, in response to a question on "how they felt as a victim of trafficking," many of them responded in one word answers like they felt "sorry," "guilty," "ashamed of themselves," "shameful," "helpless," etc. In regard with this study, we need to look at the connecting dots between forced victimisation (as prevalent in the case of trafficking) and the notions of guilt, shame and silence.

Most of the victims reported to be "happy" or "satisfied" with their present life. But at the same time, they also felt "insecure," and "unsure" about their future life. This is despite the fact that many of them are at present financially engaged, in gainful employment (although their earnings are low, between Rs three to five thousand per month in most of the cases).

In continuation with the pervious observation, it was noted that the "insecurity" and "uncertainty" about life pertained both to victims' personal and work spheres, but somehow it was more pronounced in their personal lives. In case of still-unmarried victims, they admitted to be living under "an everyday fear that (their) past will be exposed," and that "it will destroy any chances of their getting married and having children (in the future)." On the other hand, in the case of married women (those who got married after being rehabilitated), their fear was rooted in the fact that "(their) life will be destroyed once the husband and in-laws find out about the past life." These women lived under a constant fear and also suffered from guilt for not able to tell the truth and pretend to be/ act normal. One such married woman stated that she broke down every time she recalled her past as a prostitute and the sufferings she had to go through, yet she could never tell her loving husband as why she is weeping. She always covered her true feelings under the pre-texts that she was tired, or having a bad headache or simply missing her parents.

Subsequently, in case of young victims, the data reveals a trend of "disguising the past," as in hiding their past experience and sexual torture as a victim of trafficking. This trend can be linked with the victims desire to settle down in future in terms of marriage and children. In some cases, where the victims were rescued and sent back to their parents, and most of them in the age groups of 15-25, their parents also forced them to remain silent, often relocated their residence and/or married off the victims to distance places, and to less-suitable persons, such as persons double the age of victims, widowers with children from first wife and the like. The victims also consented to such "arranged marriages" and reported to have "compromised with their situation." One such victim remarked that "*It was better to get married (to an elderly person) and have a family life than to remain single and always under the questioning eyes of people.*" In case of victims, who got married in the same way, which is by hiding their past lives, often reported to be living with a constant feeling of guilt, fear and insecurity least their past be revealed and they fear the consequences as well, yet they cannot bring themselves to tell the truth to their husbands, in-laws, and in some cases, to their children. These victims agreed to talk about their past life and their present sufferings and fears only on the promise of anonymity.

In continuation with the victims' disguise of their past lives, a couple of victims also admitted that they were pretending to live as "widowed/ divorced" women in order to avoid any social objections/ probing questions on their single (unmarried) status. At the time of their decision to disguise themselves as "once married," these women were above marriageable age (30-35 years and above) and had no hope to marry and settle down in real terms. This act of disguise indicates to the prevalence and significance of marriage and family life for Indian women and the notion of their honour/ shame in association/ absence of the same.

Another interesting pattern to note is the ignorance of AIDS and STDs among the victims, given the fact that many of them were involved in sexual work and most of them were living rescued from brothels. A majority of victims either expressed ignorance about AIDS or if they were aware, they denied having any tests done for AIDS/ STDs.

It was also noted that the victims adapted to their "new" environment (the new environment refers to the place/ destination of trafficking), based upon how and where they were trafficked. For example, it was noted that those victims who were trafficked internally (within the state of Andhra Pradesh and Telangana), remained Telugu-speaking and on the other hand, those victims who were trafficked outside the state of Andhra Pradesh could understand and speak other languages, such as Hindi, Marathi, Bengali and in few cases English words and phrases.

It was also noted that the victims trafficked for the purpose of sex-work were more fluent in languages other than Telugu as they stayed in Hindi/ Marathi/ Bengali- speaking areas for 5-10 years. Ironically, a victim who was trafficked at the age of five years stated that she had completely forgotten her native language (Telugu) and learned Marathi/ Mumbai-based Hindi in the brothel. On her return in Andhra Pradesh, she still feels like "an outsider" and has not yet become fluent in the language (Telugu) which is her mother tongue. In yet another case, a victim was forced to speak only Hindi and English to her "clients" in her Mumbai-based brothel and was severely beaten if she tried to speak/ communicate with other Telugu girls in their native language who were brought to the brothel from time-to-time.

In most of the cases, the victims were trafficked at a young age, below 14 to 18 years and some of them were trafficked when they were just five or six years old. This indicates to the patterns of traffickers' preferences of victims' age and vulnerability. Interactions with NGO and police also confirm the fact that young girls are the most easy and most vulnerable targets of trafficking.

Similarly, a majority of the victims were unmarried at the time of trafficking. Many of them were trafficked on the pre-text of love and marriage and later betrayed by their so-called "lover" (trafficker). This indicates to the deception-based method of traffickers. On the other hand, many victims were also trafficked on the pre-text of earning for their own dowries and help their families. This indicates to the poverty-based cause of trafficking.

The first issue was the problems in marriage. Victims who had been trafficked were very much afraid that they could get back into their married life. Others who were not married were not sure if they will be accepted in future once their past is known to the family. There were many safety concerns, especially in case of those victims who are deserted by family members and are forced to live on their own. Many of these victims had gone through a lot of trauma. Hence they needed emotional stability and proper counselling.

There was a need to provide proper training and employment opportunities. Health check up, partculary for HIV AIDS and STDs Late/ adult education programmes should aim to include such victims also or Proof ID – provisions for ID proof should be made. Easiness to open bank accounts, getting loans for employment and houses etc, also give some relaxation in ID and other document requirements.

Many of the NGO activists told us that more than 50 per cent of rescued victims fall prey to re-trafficking because they lack proper education, employment, housing and finance to support themselves. If these victims are provided adequate means to support themselves/ family, then their chances of falling into re-trafficking cycle are minimised. Hence they felt that there is a need to put special focus on children of women victims of trafficking and make provisions for their health, education and social security.

Since trafficking of women and girls and sex-trade is closely linked, investigation of this link needs to be given proper attention. According to an activist, there are more than 500 Kothas or brothel operating in Andhra Pradesh alone, and most of their in-mates are victims of trafficking.

Another issue of concern is the attitude of family and community members towards victims. In most of cases, they do not readily accept the victims and continue to see them as low and degraded human beings. Change in attitude towards victims of trafficking is required to ensure their successful re-integration in family and society.

Alcohol and drug addiction in victims is another burning issue. Most of the victims are drugged or given sedatives and alcohol so that they do not protest to traffickers/ pimps/ brothel owners. But when they are rescued, they also face withdrawal symptoms and need special treatment and therapy.

Another important observation is that the victims suffered from a "loss of self" and "loss of identity." Some of them were trafficked at a very young age; they do not recall their maiden names, their parents and even the name and location of their village. In addition, almost all victims were given new names in brothel, mostly to hide their past identity and also to glamorize their names. Most of them were named after popular female celebrities and actresses. The gravity of this issue can be understood with the fact that even after rescue and re-integration, most of the victims address themselves by their fictitious names.

The research found that victims of trafficking in Andhra and Telangana were mostly transported to bigger cities like Mumbai, Chennai, Goa, Kolkata, Pune and Delhi. Women are enticed by many lucrative opportunities in bigger cities. Therefore, apart from marriage and love proposals, the common tactic that the study found is the offer of job opportunities by traffickers and victims were traded with false promises of jobs. Many of the respondent's victims knew traffickers. Most of them were found to be neighbours or related to the victim and were of the same village. Our study also found gross economic exploitation of victims in brothels. They report working for long hours, that is around 12 to 15 hours a day and the payment received was meager. Moreover, victims reveal of being under inflated debt-bondage. Thereby it has been found to be one of the important mechanisms, which creates profit for brothel owners and traffickers.

This study also focused on the rescue and rehabilitation of the trafficked victims and the ideologies that guide such measures. Post rescue experiences of victims reveal instances of re-victimisation. They are subjected to exploitation and marginalisation in shelter homes. The authorities deny agency to inmates and seek to exert control over survivors of trafficking. They seek to cleanse anti-moral tendencies 'present' within trafficked victims. Thereby the study observed a similarity between shelter homes and brothels. It finds that victims like in brothels are exploited of their rights and choices in shelter homes. Moreover, the study notes of instances of physical and mental violence of victims in shelter homes, which however is a common instance prevalent in brothels. Therefore, the study found a contradiction in the objectives and ideologies of rescue and rehabilitation organisations of victims of trafficking. Though the principles of the organisations are formed for the wellbeing of victims, the actual practice works negatively for them as it negates agency and authority of trafficked women over their lives.

We found that trafficking of women and children in Andhra Pradesh and Telangana has upsurge over the time. The chief cause has been identified as lack of options in the economic sector and gender discrimination prevalent in the social structure. Women from the tribal communities are found to be an easy prey to traffickers. Thus, it could be inferred that being on the periphery is leading to victimisation of women in this region.

Suggestions and strategies

During our interactions with victims, police, CBO's and NGO's in Telangana and Andhra Pradesh, following suggestions and strategies emerged. These issues require immediate attention and action in order to assist the victims in their life.

- It is necessary to sensitise vulnerable regions of trafficking through information/education and communication activities. It is important to incorporate human trafficking information into professional associations' conferences, trainings, manuals, and other materials as relevant.
- There is a need to encourage local schools to partner with Police, NGO's and CBO's and include the issue of modern day slavery in their curriculum. As a parent, educator, or school administrator it is necessary to be aware of how traffickers target school-aged children.

- There is a need to encourage local newspapers and television stations to cover stories about trafficking. In this way the community can get involved.
- There should be attempts to negotiate, collaborate and partner with all sectors of the society in its victim rehabilitation ventures.
- Anonymity is of vital importance where the survivors are concerned. They are looked down upon and stigmatised. If their past history is known, their survival in the workplace or the society may become impossible. It is important to bring in experts in the concerned industry to train the survivors. Apart from the fact that they are technically skilled in their particular profession, their very presence lends legitimacy to the profession in the eyes of the survivors. There is a need for upholding 'agency' of survivors of trafficking.
- There is a need to focus on the infrastructure. It is essential to reduce the existing gender discrimination in the society. And it is indispensable to initiate the development of the social capital. It is vital to reduce poverty.
- There is a need for forming active and vigilant Anti-trafficking teams. Countries attempting to combat trafficking should create anti-slavery inspection forces.
- There should be a proper scrutiny and monitoring of shelter homes.
- Further, awareness on HIV/AIDS is required to break the myth- sex with virgin girls will cure AIDS.
- Most of the CBO's and NGO's that are involved with anti trafficking programmes do not address structural barriers—such as poverty and vulnerability in source sites, police violence, and criminalisation of sex work and present a nuanced understanding of the issue. Most of them have a welfare approach that they are rescuing these girls and encouraging them to lead

dignified lives. Therefore, their approach does not employ an expansive understanding of sex worker engagement beyond the limited realm of the red-light district.

- One needs to recognise the fact that trafficking is linked to the larger issue of poverty, underdevelopment and the region and sadly this is not the issue that is addressed by any institution and there is a urgent need to focus on this.

Bibliography

Books

Amarasinghe, V. 2008. *Female Sex Trafficking in Asia: The Resilience of Patriarchy in a Changing World.* Routledge International Studies of Women and Place, Routledge.

Agustin, Laura Maria, 1988. *Sex at the Margins: Migration, Labour Markets and the Rescue Industry,* Zed Books, London.

Andrijasevic, Rutvica, 2010. *Migration, Agency and Citizenship in Sex Trafficking.* Palgrave Macmillan, London.

Banerjee, S. 1998. *Dangerous Outcasts: The Prostitute in Nineteenth Century Bengal.* Seagull Books: Calcutta.

Baruah, S. 2009. *Beyond Counter-Insurgency: Breaking the Impasse in Northeast India.* New Delhi: Oxford University Press.

Banerjee, Sumanta. 1990. *Under the Raj: Prostitution in Colonial Bengal.* New York: Monthly Review Press.

Barry, Kathleen. 1979. *Female Sexual Slavery.* New York University Press.

Barry, Kathleen. 1995. *The Prostitution of Sexuality.* New York University Press.

Batliwala S. 2010. *The feminist and the sex worker: Lessons from the Indian experience.* Himal Southasian, August.

Bell, S. 1994. *Reading, Writing and Rewriting the Prostitute Body.* Indiana University Press: Bloomington and Indianapolis.

Bell, Laurie (ed). 1987. *Good Girls/Bad girls: Sex Trade Workers and Feminists Face to Face.* CIC Women's Studies Preservation Project. Women's Press.

Bener ìýa, Lourdes. 2003. *Gender, Development, and Globalisation: Economics as If All People Mattered.* Routledge.

Beotra, B.R., and Singh, Devinder. 1981. *Beotra's The Suppression of Immoral Traffic in Women and Girls Act, 1956, with State Rules.* Law Book Company.

Bhaumik, S. 2009. *Troubled Periphery: Crisis of India's North - East (Sage Studies on India's North-East).* New Delhi: Sage Publications.

Bhatia, Manjeet, Deepali Bhanot and Nirmalya Samanta 2008. *Gender Concerns in South Asia: Some Perspectives.* Rawat, New Delhi.

Biswas, P., and Suklabaidya, C. 2008. *Ethnic Life-Worlds in North-East India: An Analysis.* New Delhi: Sage Publications India Pvt Ltd.

Bose, M. 1979. *Historical and Constitutional Documents of the North-Eastern India (1824 - 1973).* Delhi: Concept Publishing House.

Brown, Louise. 2000. *Sex Slaves: The Trafficking of Women in Asia.* London: Virago Press.

Castells, Manuel. 2000. *The Rise of the Network Society: Economy, Society and Culture*, Blackwell Publishing.

Channa, S.M. 1998 *Sexuality and Culture.* New Delhi: Cosmo Publications.

Crawford, Mary. 2010. *Sex Trafficking in South Asia: Telling Maya's Story.* London: Routledge.

Crawford, Mary. 2010: *Sex Trafficking in South Asia: Telling Maya's Story.* New York: Routledge.

Crawford, Mary, Michelle R. Kaufman, and Alka Gurung. 2007. Women and Children Last: The Effects of the Maoist Insurgency on Gender-based Violence, in Mahendra,

Lawoti (ed.), *Contentious Politics and Democratisation in Nepal*, pp. 95-119. New Delhi: Sage Publications.

Davidson, Julia O'Connell. 1998. Prostitution, power and freedom. Cambridge:Polity Press.

Dalla, Rochelle L., John DeFrain and Lynda M. Baker. 2011. *Global Perspectives on Prostitution and Sex Trafficking: Africa, Asia, Middle East, and Oceania*. Rowman & Littlefield, London.

Enloe, Cynthia. 2000. *Bananas, Beaches and Bases: Making Feminist Sense of International Politics,* University of California Press.

Farr, Kathryn. 2005. *Sex Trafficking: The Global Market in Women and Children.* New York: Worth Publisher.

Farley, Melissa. 2003, *Prostitution, Trafficking and Traumatic Stress.* New York: Routlege.

Flowers, R. Barri. 2011. Prostitution in the Digital Age: Selling Sex from the Suite to the Street. New York: Praeger.

Goonesekere, Savitri. 2004. *Violence, law and women's rights in South Asia*, New Delhi: Sage Publications.

Gupta, A., and Ferguson, J. 2001. Beyond "Culture": Space, Identity and the Politics of Differencw. In J. X. Rosalda, *The Anthropology of Globalisation.* USA: Blackwell.

Gupta, C. 2001. *Sexuality, Obscenity and Community: Women, Muslims and the Hindu Public in Colonial India*, Permanent Black, India.

Jeffreys, Sheila. 2009. *The Idea of Prostitution.* Spinifex Press.

Joshi, Madhu D. 1997. *Women and Children in Prostitution: Human Rights Perspectives,* New Delhi: Uppal Publishing House.

Kara, Siddharth. 2010. *Sex Trafficking: Inside the Business of Modern Slavery.* New York: Columbia University Press.

Kempadoo, Kamala and Jo Doezema (eds). 1998. *Global Sex Workers: Rights, Resistance and Redefinition,* Routledge: New York.

Kotiswaran, Prabha. 2012. *Dangerous Sex, Invisible Labor: Sex Work and the Law in India,* Oxford University Press.

Kumar, Radha. 1993. *The History of Doing: An Illustrated Account of Movements for Women's Rights and Feminism in India* 1800-1990, Kali for Women.

Lerner, Gerda. 1986. *The Creation of Patriarchy.* Oxford University Press.

Malarek, Victor. 2003. *The Natashas: The Horrific Inside Story of Slavery, Rape, and Murder in the Global Sex Trade* . New York: Arcade Publishing.

McCabe, Kimberly. 2008. *The Trafficking of Persons: National and International Responses.* New York: Peter Lang.

Mukherji, Santosh Kumar. 1986. *Prostitution in India.* New Delhi: Inter-India Publications.

Nair, P.M. 2010. *Human Trafficking: Dimensions, Challenges and Responses.* New Delhi: Konark Publishers.

Nicholson, Linda J. 1997. *The Second Wave: A Reader in Feminist Theory.* Routledge.

Nussbaum, Martha Craven. 1999. *Sex and Social Justice,* Oxford University Press.

Outshoorn, Joyce. 2004. *The Politics of Prostitution: Women's Movements, Democratic States and the Globalisation of Sex Commerce.* London: Cambridge.

Rajan, R.S. 2003. *The Scandal of the State: Women, Law, and Citizenship in Postcolonial India.* Next Wave, Duke University Press.

Rajan, S. I. 2010. *Migration, Identity and Conflict.* New Delhi: Routledge Publications.

Sagar, Rajiv. 2011. *Violence, law and women's rights in South Asia,* New Delhi: Cyber Tech Publication.

Samarasinghe, Vidyamali. 2009. *Female sex trafficking in Asia: The resilience of patriarchy in a changing world.* New York: Routledge.

Sanders, Teela, Maggie O'Neill, and Jane Pitcher 2009. *prostitution: Sex Work, Policy and Politics.* New Delhi: Sage Publications.

Sen, Sankar. 2005. *Trafficking in Women and Children in India.* Hyderabad, Orient Longman.

Sachs, Jeffrey, D. 2005. *The End of Poverty*, London: Penguin Books.

Sheper-Hughes, Nancy. 2002. *Commodifying Bodies.* New York: Sage Publications.

Shelley, Louise, 2010. *Human Trafficking: A Global Perspective.* London: Cambridge University Press.

Sithannan, V. 2007. *Immoral Trafficking: Prostitution in India.* Chennai: Jeywin Publication.

Walkowitz, Judith R. 1992. *City of Dreadful Delight: Narratives of Sexual Danger in Late Victorian London.* Chicago: University of Chicago Press.

Zheng, Tiantian, 2010. *Sex Trafficking, Human Rights and Social Justice.* New York: Routledge.

Articles in Books

Bhattacharya, S. 2004. 'Brothels and Brothel Clients in Pune City,' in Ravi K. Verma, P.J. Pelto, S. Schensul and Archana Joshi (eds), *Sexuality in the Time of AIDS*, Sage Publications: New Delhi.

Doezema J. 1998. Forced to choose: Beyond the voluntary vs. forced prostitution dichotomy. In Kempadoo K & Doezma J (Eds.), *Global sex workers: rights,resistance and redefinition.* New York: Routledge, pp. 34-50.

Gorman, Daniel. 2007. "Empire, Internationalism, and the Campaign against the Traffic in Women and Children in the 1920s". *Twentieth Century British History,* Oxford University Press.

Pande, Rekha, 2014, "Human Security, Globalisation, and Trafficking of Women and Children in South Asia", in, *Globalisation, Development and Security in Asia*, (ed) Zhquin Zhu, Foreign Policy and Security in an Asian

Century: Threats, strategies and Policy choices, Vol. 1, (ed), Benny The Cheng Guan, World Scientific. Hackensack, N.J. U.S.A. pp. 277-296.

Pande, Rekha, 2013. Female Foeticide in India: Its Socio-Cultural Context, in Swain, B.K. Meshram, Pradeep, Borkar, Ashok (ed), *Female Foeticide in India: A Moving Trend,* Dattasons, Nagpur, pp. 3-11.

Pande, Rekha, 2010. Gender issues in South Asia, with special reference to India, Challenges in the new Millennium, in *Family in Development, Hopes and Challenges,* (Eds), Simon Polinder, Evert Jan Brouwer and Hank Jochesen, Just development Series, Prisma, Shaker Publishing, Netherlands, pp. 47-58.

Pande, Rekha, 2008. "Ritualised Prostitution: Devdasis to Jogins- A few case studies", in *Prostitution and Beyond, An analysis of sex work in India* (eds), Rohini Sahni, V. Kalya Shnkar and Hemant Apte, Sage Publications, New Delhi, pp.101-117.

Seshu, Saraswathi, Meena. 2008. Surfacing voices from the underground, in Sahni, Rohini, Shankar, V. Kalyan & Apte, Hemant (eds) *Prostitution and Beyond: An analysis of sex work in India,* New Delhi, Sage Publication.

Articles in Journals

Alary, M, Jayachandran AA, Lowndes CM, et al. 2010. Ecological analysis of the association between high-risk population parameters and HIV prevalence among pregnant women enrolled in sentinel surveillance in four southern India states. *Sex Transm Infect* 86(Suppl 1):10-16.

Augustin, LM. 2002. Challenging place: Leaving home for sex. *Development* 45(1):110-117.

Avahan, 2009. *Managing HIV Prevention from the Ground Up: Avahan's Experiencein Peer Led Outreach at scale.* New Delhi: Bill and Melinda Gates Foundation.

Anderson, Bridget and Andrijasevic, Rutvica. 2008. "Sex, slaves and citizens: the politics of anti-trafficking". Soundings, 40,

The Open University's repository of research publications No., pp. 135-145.

Andrijasevic, Rutvica. 2007. "Beautiful Dead Bodies: Gender, Migration and Representation in Anti- trafficking Campaigns". *Feminist Review*, 86, Palgrave Macmilan, pp. 24-44.

Bandopadhayay, Nandinee. 2008. 'Streetwalkers show the way: Reframing the global debate on trafficking from sex workers' perspectives', *Report 309*, Institute of Development Studies.

Balk, Deborah and Subrata Lahiri. 1997. "Awareness and Knowledge of AIDS among Indian Women: evidence from 13 states". Health Transition Review, Vol. 7, pp. 421-465.

Biemann, Ursula. 2002. "Remotely Sensed: A Topography of the Global Sex Trade". Feminist Review, No.70, Palgrave Macmillan Journals, pp. 75-88.

Beyrer, Chris and Julie Stachowiak. 2003. "Health Consequences of Trafficking of Women and Girls in Southeast Asia', *Brown Journal of World Affairs,* Summer / Fall X(1) 105-117.

Busza, Joanna. 2004. Sex Work and Migration: The Dangers of Oversimplification- A Case Study of Vietnamese Women in Cambodia. *Health and Human Rights*, 7(2)231-249.

K. Butcher, 2003. "Confusion Between Prostitution and Sex Trafficking,` Lancet 361 : p. 1983.

Button, Misty. 2007. 'Combating Human Trafficking in India: How the United States can Serve as Catalyst for Change', *ECON* 827: Seminar in Economics. Winter/Fall.

Cabrera, Marion Bernadette G. 2007. The Role of Cyberspace in Marriage Migration in Asia: Claiming Spaces for Intervention. *Women in Action,* Vol. 3, pp. 51-56.

Chakravarti, Sudeep. 2012. *Highway* 39, Harper Collins.

Chandrasekaran P, Dallabetta G, Loo V, et al. 2006. Containing HIV/AIDS in India: the unfinished agenda. *Lancet Infectious Diseases* 6: 508-21.

Chapkis, Wendy. 2003. Trafficking, Migration, and the Law: Protecting Innocents, Punishing Immigrants. *Gender and Society,* Vol. 17 (6), pp. 923-937.

Crawford, Mary and Michelle R. Kaufman. 2008. 'Sex trafficking in Nepal: Survivor characteristics and long-term outcomes', *Violence against women* 2008; 14 (8): 905-917.

Dandona, R, Dandona L, Kumar GA, et al. 2006. Demography and sex work characteristics of female sex workers in India. *BMC International Health and Human Rights* 6(5):1-10.

Davidson, Julia O' Connell. 2006. "Will the Real Sex Slave Please Stand up?" *Feminist Review,* No.83, Sexual Mortalities, Macmillan, pp. 4-22.

Ditmore, M, Wijers M. 2003. The negotiations on the UN Protocol on Trafficking in Persons. *Nemesis* 4:79-88.

Doezema, Jo. 2001. "Ouch!: Western Feminists' 'Wounded Attachment' to the 'Third World Prostitute'". *Feminist Review,* No. 67, Sex Work Reassessed (Spring), Palgrave Macmillan, pp.16-38.

Elabour-Idemudia, Patience. 2003. Migration, Trafficking and the African Woman. *African Feminisms Three,* Agenda No. 58, pp. 101-116.

Farley, Melissa. 2009. Theory versus reality: Commentary on four articles about trafficking for prostitution. *Women's Studies International Forum,* Vol. 32, pp. 311-315.

Gallagher, Anne T. 2009. "Human Rights and Human Trafficking: Quagmire or Firm Ground? A Response to James Hathaway". *Virginia Journal of International Law Association,* Vol. 50, No 1, pp. 789-846.

Ganguly, Ruchira. 2003, "Paradoxes of Globalisation, Liberalisation, and Gender Equality: The World Views of the Lower Middle Class in West Bengal, India". *Gender and Society,* Vol.17, No. 4 (August), Sage, pp. 544-566.

George, Annie, U Vindhya, and Sawmya Ray. 2010. Sex Trafficking and Sex Work: Definitions, Debates, and

Dynamics- A Review of Literature. *Economic & Political Weekly,* Vol. XLV (17), pp. 64-74.

Gidwani, Vinay and K. Sivaramakrishnan. 2003. "Circular Migration and the Spaces of Cultural Assertion". Annals of the Association of American Geographers, Vol.93, No.1 (March) Taylor & Francis, pp.186-213.

Ghosh, Biswajit. 2009. Trafficking in Women and Children in India: Nature, Dimension and Strategies or Prevention, *The International Journal of Human Rights,* Vol. 13, No. 5, December, 716-738.

Goodey, Jo. 2004. "Sex Trafficking in Women from Central and East European Countries: Promoting a Victim-centered Approach to Criminal Justice Intervention". *Feminist Review,* No.76, Post-communism: Women's Lives in Transition, Palgrave Macmillan, pp. 26-45.

Granik, lisa and Eileen Shields.1989. "The First U.S. Conference on Trafficking in Women Internationally". *Off Our Backs,* Vol.19, No.1 (January) pp.1-3.

Gupta, Jhumka, Elizabeth Reed, Trace Kershaw *et.al.,* 2011. History of sex trafficking, recent experiences of violence, and HIV vulnerability among female sex workers in coastal Andhra Pradesh, India. *International Journal of Gynecology and Obstetrics,,* pp. 1-5.

Handrahan, Lori. 2004. Hunting for Women: Bride-Kidnapping in Kyrgyzstan. *International Feminist Journal of Politics,* Vol.6 (2), pp. 207-233.

Halli, Shiva S., James Blanchard, Dayanand G. Satihal, Stephen Moses. 2007. "Migration and HIV Transmission in South India: An Ethnographic Study". *Culture, Health and Sexuality.* Vol. 9, No.1 (January-February), pp. 85-94.

Hawthrone, Susan. 2004. Wild Politics: Beyond Globalisation. *Women Studies International Forum,* Vol. 27, pp. 243-259.

Hearn, Jeff 2006. The Implication of Information and Communication Technologies for Sexualities and Sexualised Violences: Contradictions of Sexual Citizenships. *Political Geography,* Vol. 25, pp. 944-963.

Huda, S. 2006. Sex trafficking in South Asia. *International Journal of Gynecology and Obstetrics,* Vol. 94, pp. 374-381.

Jana, Samarjit, Nandinee Bandoyopadhyay, M.K. Dutta, et al. 2002. A Tale of Two Cities: shifting the paradigm of anti-trafficking programmes. *Gender and Development,* Vol. 10 (1), pp. 69-79.

Jeffreys, Sheila. 2009. Prostitution, trafficking and feminism: An update on the debate. *Women's Studies International Forum,* Vol. 32, pp. 316-320.

Jha, Vikas. 2005. "Migration of Orissa's Tribal Women: A New Story of Exploitation". Economic and Political Weekly, Vol. 40, No. 15 (April 9-15), pp. 1495-1496.

Kim, Eunyoung, Minwoo Yun, Mirang Park, *et.al.,* 2009. Cross border North Korean women Trafficking and victimisation between North Korea and China: An ethnographic case study. *International Journal of Law, Crime and Justice,* Vol. 37, pp. 154-169.

Limoncelli, Stephanie A. 2009. The trouble with trafficking: Conceptualizing women's sexual labour and economic human rights. *Women's Studies International Forum,* Vol. 32, pp. 261-269.

Maltzahn, Kathleen. 2006. Digital Dangers: Information and Communication Technologies and Trafficking in Women. *APC WNSP and AWID "Issue Papers",* pp. 1-12.

Masci, David. 2004. Human Trafficking and Slavery. *CQ Researcher,* Vol.14 (12), pp. 273-296.

Macklin, Audrey. 2003. "Dancing across Borders: 'Exotic Dancers', Trafficking, and Canadian Immigration Policy". *International Review,* Vol. 37, No. 2 (Summer) pp. 464-500.

Magar, Veronica. 2012. "Rescue and Rehabilitation: A Critical Analysis of Sex Workers' Anti-trafficking Response in India". *Signs,* Vol. 37, No. 3 (Spring), pp. 619-644.

Melissa Ditmore and Marjan Wijer, 2003. The negotiations on the UN Protocol on Trafficking in Persons, *Nemesis,* pp.79-88, http://www.bayswan.org/traffick/NEMESIS_Ditmore. PDF accessed, 29th March, 2015.

Neves, Ana Sofia Antunes das. 2011. "Women Trafficking for Sexual Exploitation in Portugal: Life narratives." *International Journal of Humanities and Social Science.* Vol. 1 No. 17, The Special Issue on Humanities and Behavioral Science, Centre for Promoting Ideas, USA (Special Issue – November), pp.186-192.

Onyejekwe, Chineze J. 2005. "Influences of Global Human Trafficking Issues on Nigeria: A Gender Perspective". *Journal of International Women's Studies*, Vol. 7, No. 2 (November), pp. 141-151.

O'Connell Davidson, Julia. 2006. Will the Real Sex Slave Please Stand up? *Feminist Review,* No. 83, pp. 4-22.

Okonofua, F.E. S.M. Ogbomwan, A.N. Alutu, et al. 2004. Knowledge, attitudes and experiences of sex trafficking by young women in Benin City, South-South Nigeria. *Social Science & Medicine,* Vol. 59, pp. 1315 – 1327.

Pal, B. 1999. Against legalisation. Women's activists in Pune are strongly opposed to the legalisation of Prostitution. *Human space:* 28-31.

Pande, Rekha, 2006. Globalisation and trafficking of women and Children, *Samyukta, A Journal of Women's Studies,* Vol. VI, No. 2, pp. 31-47.

Pyle, Jean L. 2001. "Sex, Maids, and Export Processing Risks and Reasons for Gendered Global Production Networks". *International Journal of Politics, Culture, and Society.* Vol.15, No.1, (September), Springer, pp. 55-76.

Saggurti, Niranjan, Shagun Sabarwal, Ravi K. Verma, Shiva S. Halli and Anrudh K. Jain. 2011. "Harsh realities: Reasons for women's involvement in sex work in India". Journal of AIDS and HIV Research, Vol. 3, No. 9, (September), pp. 172-179.

Samarasinghe, Vidyamali and Barbara Burton. 2007. "Strategizing Prevention: A Critical Review of Local Initiatives to

Prevent Female Sex Trafficking". *Development in Practice,* Vol.17, No.1 (February), Taylor & Francis, pp. 51-64.

Schauer, Edward J. and Elizabeth M. Wheaton. 2006, "Sex Trafficking into the United States: A Literature Review". *Criminal Justice Review*, Vol. 31, No. 1 Georgia State University Research Foundation, Inc, pp.1-24.

Sharma, Nandita. 2005. "Anti-Trafficking Rhetoric and the Making of a Global Apartheid". *NWSA Journal*, Vol.17, No. 3, States of Insecurity and the Gendered Politics of Fear (Autumn), Johns Hopkins University Press, pp. 88-111.

Soderland, Gnetchen. 2005. "Running from the Rescuers: New U.S. Crusades against Sex Trafficking and the Rhetoric of Abolition". *NWSA Journals,* Vol. 17, No.3, States of Insecurity and the Gendered Politics of Fear, (Autumn), pp. 64-87.

Srikantiah, Jayashri. 2007. "Perfect Victims and Real Survivors: The Iconic Victim in Domestic Human Trafficking Law". *Boston University Law Review*, Vol. 87, No.1, (February) pp.157-209.

Srinivas, M. N. 1977. "The Changing Position of Indian Women". *Man,* New Series, Vol. 12, No. 2 (August), Royal Anthropological Institute of Great Britain and Ireland, pp. 221-238.

Tambe, Ashwini. 2005. "The Elusive Ingénue: A Transnational Feminist Analysis of European Prostitution in Colonial Bombay". Gender and Society, Vol.19, No. 2, Gender-Sexuality-State-Nation: Transnational Feminist Analysis, (April), Sage, pp.160-179.

Tiefenbrun, Susan and Christie J. Edwards. 2008. "Gendercide and the Cultural Context of Sex Trafficking in China". Fordham International Law Journal, Vol. 32, No. 3, (August), pp.730-780.

Tzvetkova, Marina. 2002. "NGO Responses to Trafficking in Women". Gender and Development, Vo.10, No.1, Trafficking and Slavery (March), Taylor & Francis, pp. 60-68.

Sengupta, Chandan. 2001. Conceptualising Globalisation : Issues and Implications. *Economic and Political Weekly,* Vol. 36 (33), pp. 3137-3143.

Silverman, J.G., M.R. Decker, J. Gupta, *et.al.,* 2007. Experiences of sex trafficking victims in Mumbai, India. *International Journal of Gynecology and Obstetrics,* Vol. 97, pp. 221-226.

Sullivan, Barbara. 2003. Trafficking in Women: Feminism and New International Law. *International Feminist Journal of Politics,* Vol. 5 (1), pp. 67-91.

Vindhya, U. and V. Swathi Dev. 2011. Survivors of Sex Trafficking in Andhra Pradesh: Evidence and Testimony. *Indian Journal of Gender Studies,* 18(2), pp. 129-165.

Wang, Yi. 2005. Anti-Human Trafficking Program in Vietnam. *Oxfam Quebec, Hanoi,* pp. 1-29.

Walkowitz, Judith R. 1980. "The Politics of Prostitution". *Chicago Journals,* Vol. 6, No. 1, Women: Sex and Sexuality, Part 2 (Autumn, 1980), pp. 123-135.

Reports and Working papers

A Report on Trafficking in Women and Children in India 2002-2003. National Human Rights Commission (NHRC), Institute of Social Sciences (ISS), UNIFEM.

Acts and Laws,Government of India, The Immoral Traffic Prevention Act (1956).

Action Aid, Andhra Pradesh. *Intervention: Women in prostitution, trafficked persons and commercial sex workers.* Unpublished report.

Andhra Pradesh State AIDS Control Organisation. 2005. *HIV/AIDS in Andhra Pradesh: Situation and response – A report 2005.* Hyderabad: APSACS.

Asian Development Bank. 2003. *Combating trafficking of women and children in south Asia: Regional synthesis paper for Bangladesh, India, and Nepal.* Manila:Asian Development Bank.

Aengst, Jennifer. 2001. Litigation Report: Girl Trafficking in Nepa. *Human Rights Advocacy Clinic.*

Bickford, Donna M. Stories of Sex Trafficking: Rescue, Victimisation, and Silence. First Annual Interdisciplinary Conference on Human Trafficking, University of Nebraska, Lincoln, 2009.

Beyond Borders: Exploring Links Between Trafficking and Gender. Working Papers Series 2010, Global Alliance Against Traffick in Women (GAATW).

Broderick, Patrice M. Identifying Factors in Human Trafficking. Boca Raton, Florida Metropolitan University, USA, 2005.

Bruckert, Christine. Trafficking In Human Beings and Organised Crime: A Literature Review. Criminology Department University of Ottawa, Research and Evaluation Branch Community, Contract and Aboriginal Policing Services Directorate Royal Canadian Mounted Police, 2002.

Coomaraswamy, Radhika. 2000. Report of the Special Rapporteur on violence against women,its causes and consequences: on trafficking in women, women's migration and violence against women, submitted in accordance with Commission on Human Rights resolution.

Coomaraswamy, Radhika (former Special Rapporteur on Violence Against Women). 2001. *Report of the Special Rapporteur on Violence Against Women, its Causes and Consequences: Mission to Bangladesh, Nepal and India on the Issue of Trafficking of Women and Girls (28 October–15 November 2000).* United Nations, Geneva, (E/CN.4/2001/73/Add.2).

Consideration of the Issue of Trafficking. Background Paper. New Delhi: 11-12 November 2002.

David, Fiona. Labour Trafficking. AIC Reports, Research and Public Policy Series 108.

Eleni, Themeli. Trafficking in women for sexual exploitation: A major health and human rights issue. National and Kapodistrian University of Athens, School of Medicine, 2011.

Ending Violence against Women and Girls: Protecting Human Rights. Strenghthening Women's Rights, Planning and Development Department Governance and Democracy, Federal Minisrty for Economic Corporation and Development.

Female Temporary Circular Migration and Rights Protection in the Strawberry Seetar in Huelva, Spain. Global Alliance Against Trafficking in Women (GAATW).

Galiana, Carmen. Trafficking in Women. Civil Liberties Series LIBE 109 EN, The European Parliament, B-1047 Brussels, March 2000.

Gender and Migration: Negotiating Rights A Women's Movement Perspective. Centre for Women's Development Studies, 2012.

Government of India. 2008. India *Country Report to Prevent and Combat Trafficking and Commercial Sexual Exploitation of Children and Women.* Ministry of Women and Child Development.

Gozdziak, Elzbieta M. and Micah N. Bump. Data and Research on Human Trafficking: Bibliography of Research-Based Literature. Institute for the Study of International Migration, Walsh School of Foreign Service, Georgetown University, Georgetown University, Washington DC, 2008.

Harrison, Deborah L. Victims of Human Trafficking or Victims of Research? Ethical Considerations in Research with Females Trafficked for the Purposes of Sexual Exploitation. University of East Anglia, 2006.

Human Trafficking: A Brief Overview. Social Development Notes: Conflict, Crime and Violence, No.122, 2009.

Human Trafficking: A Crime that Shames us all. India South Asia Regional Conference: Responding to Trafficking for Sexual Exploitation in South Asia. United Nations Office on Drugs and Crime(UNODC), United Nations Global Initiative to Fight Human Trafficking (UN.GIFT), 2007.

Human Trafficking, Sex Work Safety and the 2010 Games: Assessments and recommendations. Sex Industry Worker Safety Action Group (SIWSAG) 2009.

Human Trafficking in India: Dynamics, Current Efforts, and Intervention for the Asia Foundation. Stanford University, USA, 2010.

Human Trafficking in Nigeria: Root Causes and Recommendations. UNESCO, Policy Paper Poverty Series no. 14.2 (E) Paris 2006.

Human Trafficking into and within the United States: A Review of the Literature. U.S. Department of Health and Human Services,

Human Trafficking, Sex Work Safety and the 2010 Games: Assessments and Recommendations. Sex Industry Workers Safety Action Group, 2009.

ILO CONFERENCE. 2001. STOPPING FORCED LABOUR: *Global Report under the Follow-up to the ILO Declaration on Fundamental Principles and Rights at Work,* 89th Session.

International Labour Organisation. 2007. Forced Labour Statistic Factsheet.

Irregular Migration, Migrant Smuggling and Human Rights: Towards Coherence. International Council of Human Rights Policy, 2010.

Kofi Annan. Address to the House of Parliament. London. 8 May 2007.

Kelly. Liz and Linda Regan. Stopping Traffic: Exploring the extent of, and responses to, trafficking in women for sexual exploitation in the UK. The Police Research Series, Paper 125, 2000.

Literature Review and Analysis Related to Human Trafficking in Post-Conflict Situations. United States Agency for International Development, 2004.

Literature review of trafficking in persons and gender-based violence. US Aid: For the American People, 2009.

Literature Review of Trafficking in Persons in Latin America and the Caribbean. United States Agency for International Development, 2004.

Literature Review: Trafficking in Humanitarian Emergencies. US AID: From the American People, 2006.

Manohar, Sujata. 2002. 'Trafficking in women and girls', Justice Focal Point on Trafficking in Human Beings, National Human Rights Commission, (India) (Consultant) Expert Group Meeting on "Trafficking in women and girls", 18-22 November, Glen Cove, New York, USA.

Ministry of Women and Child Development: Government of India, *Draft National Integrated Plan of Action to Prevent and Combat Human Trafficking with Special Focus on Children and Women,* 2006.

Mukherjee KK, Mukherjee S. 2004. *Girls/Women in Prostitution in India. A National Study.* Ghaziabad: Gram Niyojan Kendra. Supported by Department of Women and Child Welfare, Government of India, New Delhi.

Nair, P. M. Trafficking Women and Children for Sexual Exploitation: Handbook for Law Enforcement Agencies in India.UNIFEM, New Delhi: 2007.

Nationwide Survey: Trafficking in Women as a Social Problem in Ukrainian Society. Social Monitoring Center, Ukrainian Institute of Social Studies, Winrock International, US Agency for International Development, 2001.

National Crime Records Bureau 2008. Crime in India. Ministry of Home Affairs, New Delhi.

NATSAP 2007. *Trafficking in Andhra Pradesh. Network Against Trafficking and Sexual Exploitation in Andhra Pradesh.* HELP: Ongole, Andhra Pradesh.

Pandey B, Jena D, Mohanty S, 2003. *Trafficking in women in Orissa – An exploratory study.* Institute for Socio-Economic Development in collabouration with UNIFEM (South Asia Regional Anti-Trafficking Programme, supported by USAID, Bhubaneshwar.

Patrick Basler. 2005. Forced Labour and Human Trafficking: Estimating the Profits. Working Paper. Geneva: International Labour Office.

Pearson E. 2000. *Human rights and trafficking in persons: A handbook*. GAATW, Bangkok.

Pearson E. 2004. *GAPS Analysis on intervention strategies against trafficking in women in Nepal*. Nepal: Kathmandu.

Population Council. 2008a. *Patterns of migration/mobility and HIV risk among female sex workers: Andhra Pradesh*. Population Council, New Delhi.

Population Council. 2008b. *Migration/Mobility and Vulnerability to HIV among Male Migrant Workers: Andhra Pradesh*. New Delhi: Population Council.

Project Parivartan. 2007. *Results of a cross-sectional survey of female sex workers in Rajahmundry, Andhra Pradesh: A summary report*. Center for Interdisciplinary Research on AIDS, Yale University: New Haven, Connecticut.

Prevention of Trafficking in Persons. Addressing the root causes of Trafficking. OSCE Action Plan to Combat Trafficking in Human Beings.

Rajya Sabha Secretariat. 2006. *Excerpts from Parliamentary Standing Committee on Human Resource Development – 182nd Report on the Immoral Traffic (Prevention) Amendment Bill, 2006*. New Delhi: Rajya Sabha Secretariat.

Report of the Task Force on Violence against Women. Government of Ireland 1997.

Resources and Contacts on Human Trafficking. The Initiative against Trafficking in Persons, Global Rights, Washington, 2005.

Roundtable on Using CEDAW to Protect the Rights of Women Migrant Workers and Trafficked Women in South and Southeast Asia. International Women's Rights Action Watch Asia Pacific (IWRAW) Global Alliance Against Traffic in Women (GAATW) Coordination of Action Research on AIDS and Mobility (CARAM Asia), 2009.

Sangroula, Yubaraj. Trafficking of Girls and Women in Nepal: Building a Community Surveillance System for Prevention. Kathmandu School of Law, Kathmandu, Nepal, 2001.

Sex Trafficking of Women in the United States. International and Domestic Trends, Coalition Against Trafficking in Women, 2001.

Shamir, Hila. Trafficking in Workers: The Human Rights Paradigm to Trafficking in Persons and the Challenge of Labour Rights. A Working Paper.

Sikri, R. 2004. Northeast India and India's Look East Policy. *Seminar Papers*.

The Asia Pacific Forum of National Human Rights Institutions (TAPFNHRI). 2002.

The Demand Side of Human Trafficking in Asia: Empirical Findings. International Labour Organisation, Regional Project on Combating Child Trafficking for Labour and Sexual Exploitation (TICSA-II), 2006.

The health risks and consequences of trafficking in women and adolescents: findings from a European study. London School of Hygiene & Tropical Medicine, La Strada Ukraine, Foundation Against Trafficking in Women (STV), University of Padua, Department of Sociology, Global Alliance Against Trafficking in Women, London Metropolitan University, Child and Women Abuse Studies Unit, 2003.

Thomas H. 2002. *Trafficking in India*. Manila: Asia Development Bank.

Thomas, Nerea Bilbatua. Female Temporary Circular Migration and Rights Protection in the Stawberry Sector in Huelva, Spain. The Global Alliance Against Traffic in Women (GAATW) 2009.

Touzenis, Kristina. Trafficking in Human Beings Human rights and transnational criminal law, developments in law and practices. UNESCO migration studies 3, 2010.

Trafficking-2012: January to December 2012. Human Rights Documentation Indian Social Institute, New Delhi.

United States Department of State, 2011. *Trafficking in Persons Report, India*, Washington DC, 27 June 2011; URL: http://www.unhcr.org/refworld/docid/4e12ee7427.html (online, accessed on 10 December 2012)

U.S. Department of State. 2005. Trafficking in Persons Report 2005. Washington DC. URL: ojp.usdoj.gov/ovc/ncvrw/2005/pg51/html, accessed on 12.01.2013.

U.S. Department of States. Trafficking in Persons Reports, various years. Washington DC: U. S. Department of State.

United Nations Office on Drugs and Crimes. 2006. Trafficking in Persons: Global Patterns. Vienna.

United Nations (UN). 2000. *Protocol to prevent, suppress and punish trafficking in persons, especially women and children, supplementing the United Nations Convention against transnational organised crime.* New York: United Nations.

USAID. 1999. Trafficking in persons: USAID's response. U.S. Agency for International Development, Washington.

United Nations. Convention on the Rights of the Child (2008).

Vidyamali Samarasinghe and Barbara Burton. 2007. Strategizing Prevention: a Critical Review of Local Initiatives to Prevent Female Sex Trafficking. Development in Practice, 17:1, 51-64.

International Organisation for Migration. 2007. Counter-Trafficking Database.

Who Ethical and Safety Recommendations for Interviewing Trafficked Women. World Health Organisation, London School of Hygiene & Tropical Medicine, Daphne Programme of the European Commission, 2003.

Encyclopaedia

Singh, Ram, Shankar. 2009. *Encyclopedia on Women and Children Trafficking,* Vols. I to III, New Delhi, Anmol Publications.

Newspapers and Magazines

The Times of India, Dash DK. 2010. 6.8 lakh sex workers in India, Delhi red-light capital. July 21, 2010, accessed on August 14, 2010.

The Times of India. "India is a Transit Hub for Trafficking." 22 June 2006.

The Hindu. 27 November 2011. My Minor Daughters Forced into Prostitution, Says Woman. accessed online, URL: http://www.thehindu.com/2008/11/27/stories/2008112759410500.htm, retrieved on 12.03.13.

The Hindu. 29 September 2003. Man Tries to Sell Daughter. Accessed online, URL: http://www.hindu.com/2003/09/29/stories/2003092903700400.htm, retrieved on 12.04.13.

The Siasat Daily. 11 July 2012. 5 Minor Girls Forced into Prostitution by Their Parents. Accessed online, URL: http://www.siasat.com/english/news/5-minor-girls-forced-prostitution-their-parents, retrieved on 25.03.13

Web Resources

A.D.B. Asian Development Bank. 2003. *Combating of Trafficking in Women and Children in South Asia: Regional Synthesis Paper for Bangladesh, India and Nepal. Bangkok,* http://adb.org/sites/default/files/pub/2003/combating-trafficking-south-asia-paper.pdf, accessed, 3rd February, 2016.

"Andhra Registered Maximum Cases of Women Trafficking in 2010," Zeenews.com, 11 March 2011 accessed online, URL: www.zeenews.com/2011/andhra-registerted-maximum-cases-of-women-trafficking-in-2010/html, retrieved on 12.02.13)

Bahuguna,N., 2004. November 4, HumanTrafficking Escalates., from http://www.boloji.com/wfs6/wfs1053.htm. Retrieved November4,2009.

Basler, Patrick, 2005. *Forced Labour and Human Trafficking: Estimating the Profits,* Working Paper. Geneva: International Labour Office. http://www.civilandhumanrights.org/

documents/Forced_Labor_and_Human_Trafficking_-_Estimating_the_Profits.pdf, accessed 20th March, 2015.

Charpenel, Yves, 2012. *Sexual Exploitation Prostitution and Organised Crime,* Paris. http://www.fondationscelles.org/pdf/rapport_mondial/sexual_exploitation_prostitution_Fondation_Scelles.pdf accessed, 2nd February, 2016.

Change, 2010. *Human Trafficking, HIV/AIDS, and the Sex Sector Human Rights for All,* Center for Health and Gender Equity (CHANGE) and Center for Human Rights and Humanitarian Law at American University Washington College of Law. http://www.genderhealth.org/files/uploads/change/publications/Human_Trafficking_HIVAIDS_and_the_Sex_Sector.pdf, accessed, 11th February, 2016.

Chetty, Priya, 2012. Project Guru, http://www.projectguru.in/publications/state-wise-details-of-aids-in-india/accessed, 3rd February, 2016.

CNN-IBN India. 18 June 2007. Sex Trade Expose Wakes Up NHRC. Accessed online, URL: http://content.ibnlive.in.com/article/01-Feb-2007india/sex-trade-expose-wakes-up-nhrc-32523-3.html, retrieved on15.03.13. Also see, IBN- Live India. 18 June 2007. Parents Turn Pimp, Sell Girls in AP, Accessed online, URL: http://ibnlive.in.com/news/parents-turn-pimps-sell-girls-in-ap/32204-3.html, retrieved on 15.03.13.

Deboleena Sengupta, Pallabi, Deka, Her body, her rights: In reference to women trafficking in North East India, https://www.academia.edu/9154140/HER_BODY_HER_RIGHTS_In_Reference_to_Women_Trafficking_in_North_East_India accessed, 13th February, 2016.

Gautum, Nishat, 2014. dna, *How India Inc can help combat human trafficking* http://www.dnaindia.com/analysis/standpoint-how-india-inc-can-help-combat-human-trafficking-1959083, accessed, 12th February, 2016.

Haq, Khadija, 2000. *Human Development in South Asia:* The *Gender Question,* Oxford University Press, http://

mhhdc.org/wp-content/themes/mhdc/reports/HDRSA%202000.pdf Accessed, 25th April, 2014.

International Organisation for Migration, 2007. *Counter-Trafficking Database,* http://www.iom.ch/jahia/webdav/shared/shared/mainsite/activities/ct/iom_ctm_database.pdf, accessed, 21st March, 2015.

International Convention 1933. http://ec.europa.eu/anti-trafficking/sites/antitrafficking/files/1933_international_convention_en_1.pdf, accessed 29th March, 2015.

Jena Manipadma, 2003. *Trafficking in Overdrive,* http://www.boloji.com/index.cfm?md=Mobile&sd=Articles&ArticleID=6351 accessed, 17th February, 2016.

Linda Baker, Marcie Campbell, 2013. *Information Communication Technologies and Trafficking in Persons,* The Learning Network Brief, Centre for Research and Education on Violence against Women and Children, London, Ontario. http://www.learningtoendabuse.ca/sites/default/files/Baker_Campbell_Trafficking_and_Technology.pdf accessed, 12th February, 2016.

Melissa Ditmore and Marjan Wijer, 2003. The negotiations on the UN Protocol on Trafficking in Persons, *Nemesis,* pp.79-88, http://www.bayswan.org/traffick/NEMESIS_Ditmore.PDF accessed, 29th March, 2015.

Maggie Black, 2007. *Women in Ritual Slavery, Devadasi, Jogini and Mathamma in Karnataka and Andhra Pradesh, Southern India, Anti-slavery International.* http://www.antislavery.org/includes/documents/cm_docs/2009/w/women_in_ritual_slavery2007.pdf, accessed on 21st March, 2015.

Mazumdar, Dibasri. "Human Trafficking in Assam." *Eastern Panorama,* http://www.easternpanorama.in/index.php?option=com_content&view=article&id=173:human-trafficking-in accessed, 23rd February, 2016.

National Network of Sex Workers — India, 2013. Statement. http://www.nswp.org/sites/nswp.org/files/Statement-national-network-of-sex-workers-India.pdf accessed, 12th February, 2016.

NDTV- India. 15 March 2013. Unable to Pay back Rs. 34000, Parents Give Away Daughters as Collateral. Accessed online, URL: http://www.ndtv.com/article/south/unable-to-pay-back-rs-34-000-parents-give-away-daughters-as-collateral-343060, Accessed 20.05.13 http://avoice4.org/blog/portfolio-post/a-voice-for-prostituted-women-and-men/ A Voice for Prostituted Women and Men.

Nedan Foundation, Trafficking & HIV/AIDS, North East report, http://nedan.in/reports-1/trafficking-and-hiv-north-east-report accessed, 13th February, 2016.

Polaris Project, Human Trafficking Trends in the United States: National Human Trafficking Resource Center 2007–2012, https://polarisproject.org/sites/default/files/Human%20Trafficking%20Trends%20in%20the%20US%2011-21-13.pdf accessed 2nd February, 2016.

Purohit, Bhumi, 2015. Morality vs. reality: examining intentionality in India's human trafficking policy, Malangs South Asia Essay. http://www.area-studies.ox.ac.uk/sites/sias/files/documents/Morality%20vs%20Reality-Examining%20Intentionality%20in%20India's%20Human%20Trafficking%20Policy.pdf accessed, 12th February 2016.

Report, Trafficking in Persons, 2005. U.S. Department of States. Office to monitor and combat trafficking in persons. http://www.state.gov/j/tip/rls/tiprpt/2005/46606.htm, accessed 2nd February, 2016.

Shakti Vahini, 2014. Anti trafficking in India and south Asia – national legal research desk – a Shakti Vahini research initiative https://traffickingnews.wordpress.com/tag/west-bengal/ accessed on 13th February, 2016.

UN Palermo Protocol, 2000. Also known as UN Protocol to Prevent, Suppress and Punish Trafficking in Persons, Especially Women and Children Article 3. http://www.ohchr.org/EN/ProfessionalInterest/Pages/ProtocolTraffickingInPersons.aspx, accessed, 28th March, 2015.

Appendix

Map of Telangana and Andhra Pradesh

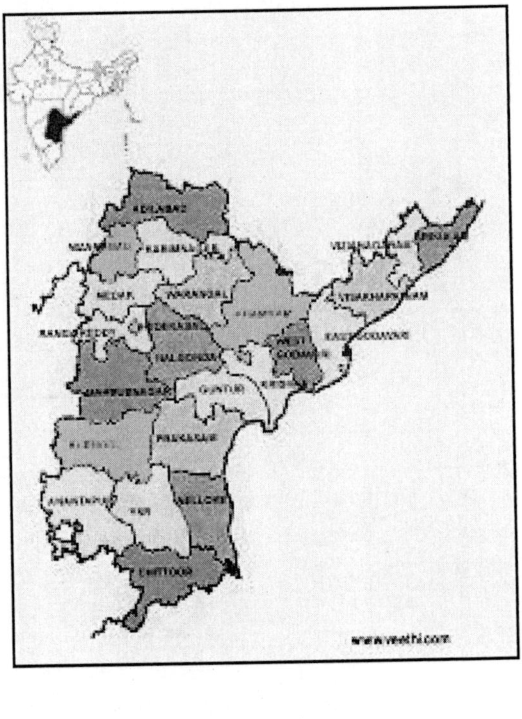

List of NGO/Shelter Homes

Source: http://wcdsc.ap.nic.in/index.php, As in February 2013

1. Swadhar homes – sanctioned by GOI

LIST OF SWADHAR SHELTER HOMES / HELP LINES SANCTIONED BY GOI

Sl. No.	*District*	*Name of the organisation & Contact Numbers*	*Location of the Project*	*No. of beneficiaries*
1.	**Anantapur**	**Praja Seva Samaj,** H. No. 1-364-6-4 A, Post Box No.10, R.S. Road, Kadiri, Anantapur Dist. -515591 **Ph.No. 08494-222833, 222453**	H No.1-1189-99, NGO, Glong, Kadiri, Anathapur Dist	50
2.		**Ambedkar Harijan Samajam, (AHS),** # D.NO. 5/532, Industrial Estate, Kummarivandlapalli, Kadiri, Ananthapur Dist. **Ph. No. 08494-2264166** **Cell No. 9440152829 / 9866687888**	Plot No.S-9, Near Telephone Exchange Industrial Estate, K.Kummaravonadala Palli, Kadiri-515594 Ananthapur	50 + Helpline

(*Contd...*)

3.	**Kadapa**	**Bharat Ratna Mahila Mandali,** 4/369 – J, Vivekananda Nagar, Cuddapah – 516001 ***Ph.No. 091-8562-243117*** ***Cell No. 9849050422***	H. No. 4/369 J to L Vivekananda Nagar, Near Hero Honda Show Room, Kadapa Dist AP	50
4.		**Rayalaseema Harijana Backward Minorities Seva Sangam,** Pothkurupalli Cross Roads, Near Anjaneya Temple, Kadapa Main Road, Rayachoti, Kadapa. ***Ph: 9848061373 (Mr. Ratnam)*** ***Mail ID: rhgbmssrso@gmail.com***	Masapet, Raichoti Municipality and Mandal Kadapa Dist.	50
5.	**Kurnool**	**Shanti Educational Society,** H. No. 15/81, Shareen Nagar, Kurnool Dist. -518002 ***Ph. No. 235983*** ***Cell No. 9849190019***	No. 11/126, at Venkatadri Nagar Near, Sharoor Nagar, Kurnool-518002	50
6.	**Chittoor**	**Rashtriya Seva Samithi,** #9, Old Huzur Office Building, Thirpathi, Chittoor –517501 ***Ph. No. 0877-2242404*** ***Mail ID: rass_org@rediffmail.com***	R.S.S, ARKVA Anjaneyapuram, Kara kambadi (Vil) Renigunta Mandal, Chittoor Dist.	50 + Helpline

(*Contd...*)

7.	**East Godavari**	**Sree Harsha Educational Society,** D. No.1-226, Vedireswaram Road, Ravulapalem Mandal, East Godavari Dist. ***Ph. No.08855-257646 (O)***	Plot No. 8-556 and Plot No. 8-288-9/11, Mian Road of NH-5 of Ravulapalem, East Godavari Dist.	50 + Helpline
8.		**Sri Kandukuri Veereshalingam Educational and Welfare Society,** 29/1-7, Lepakshi Handi Crafts Emporium, Upstairs GNT Road, Rajahmundry, East Godavari Dist. ***Ph. No. 2447016 / 2448016 / 5655655***	D.No.73-3-9/2 & Narayanapuram, Rajahmundry, East Godavari Dist.	50
9.	**West Godavari**	Annie Owe Memorial Orphanage, D.No. 181, Near Vijaya Lakhsmi Mini Theatre, Benarjeepeta, Eluru, West Godavari Dist. ***Ph. No. 0881-2249282 9908320943*** And #13-99, Vidyanagar, Eluru-534007 ***MailID: aomosuseela@yahoo.com***	D. No 10-120 & 10-121, Chantaparru Road, Eluru, Benerjepeta, WG Dist.	50 + Helpline
10.	**Krishna**	**Vasavya Mahila Mandali,** D. NO. 40-9/1-16, Vasavya Nagar, Benz Circle, Vijayawada, Krishna Dist. ***Ph.No. 0866 – 2812232***	Vemavaram K Tadepalli Gram Panchayat, Vijayawada Rural Mandal, Krishna Dist.-520012	100
11.		**Gram Vikas,** Sainagar, Krishna ***Fax – 08761-281566*** ***Mail ID: gramvikas_mgo@yahoo.com***	125, Nuzvid, Krishna Dist	50 + Helpline

12.	**Nellore**	**Community Association for Rural Development (CARD),** Mannapolur, Sullurpet Mandal, Nellore Dist. –524121 ***Ph. No.9440496765/0862-2341613*** ***Mail ID: nathcard1@rediffmail.com***	S. No.102B, Mannarpolur Village, Sullurpet Mandal, Nellore Dist.	50 + Helpline
13.		**Vasantha Lakshmi Charitable Trust and Research Centre,** 16-11/131, Kasturidevi Nagar, Pogathota, Nellore Dist. –524001 ***Ph. No. 0861 2326228, 2347276*** ***Fax: 0861-2347277*** ***Mail ID: Vasanthalakshmi_vlct@yahoo.com***	D. No.5-492, Osmansahebpeta, Nellore Town-1, Nellore Dist.	50
14.	**Prakasam**	**Dasari Adivaiah Memorial Ele. School Committee,** Uluvapadu, Prakasam Dist.523292 ***Ph. No. 08599- 234376/9010790965***	Ulavapadu Vil & Mandal, Prakasham Dist. NH-5	50 + Helpline
15.	**Guntur**	**JMJ Social Service Society,** Nallapadu, Guntur Dist. ***Ph. No. 08644 –236137 / 222458*** ***Cell No. 9848073836/9441394798*** ***jmjtelanl@rediffmail.com***	D. No.58-3, 58-4, At Angala-Kudutu Panchayat and D.No. 58-3D, 58-4B at Angala-Kuduru, Opp of J.M.J College for Women, Tenali, Guntur, AP	100

(Contd...)

16.		**BARK Educational Society,** Akbar Pete, Bapatla, Guntur Dist.–522101 ***Ph. No. 08943-220660*** ***Cell No. 9440434310***	H.No.4-8-43 &4-8-35/A, Bapatla, Akbarpet, Guntur Dist.	50 + Helpline
17.		**Kothapet Mahila Mandali,** Pothuraju Vari Chowk, Kothapet, Guntur Dist.– 522001 ***Ph. No.0863-2212382*** ***Mail ID: kmm_csw_gnt@yahoo.com***	Venkatadripet, Nehru Nagar, 2nd Line, Guntur Dist.	50
18.	**Visakhapatnam**	**Society for Education and Environment Development (SEED),** D. No.45-52-5/2, Aravind Apartments, Abid Nagar, Akkayyapalam, Visakhapatnam Dist.	14-70 Simhadri Nagar, Near RTC Depot, Gopalapatnam, Vizag Dist.	50
19.		Priyadarshini Service Organization, D. No. 45-56-9,Narasimhanagar, Akkayapalem, Visakhapatnam ***Ph:9848193466/9848275928*** ***Mail ID: pso.csw.vskp@yahoo.co.in***	D. No.45-56-6/1, Narshimhanagar, Akkayyapalem, Visakhapatnam Dist.	50 + Helpline
20.	**Vizianagaram**	**Chaitanyabharathi,** Plot No. 754, Gouthaminagarvuda Colony, Near Phase-III, Junction, Contonment (PO), Vizianagaram Dist. ***Ph. No. 08922-231704*** ***Cell No. 9440343498***	S. No.36, Ward No.35, Ambedkar Colony Cantonment, Vizianagaram	100 + Helpline

21.	**Karimnagar**	**Prakriti Environmental Society,** H.No. 5-3-182, Ashok Nagar, Karimnagar ***Ph.No.0878-2240840*** ***Fax – 040-23772776***	H.No.6-4-288, Bomma Kisthaiah nagar, Bommakal Road, Karimnagar Dist.	50
22.	**Khammam**	**Gram Vikas (GV),** Hyderpet, Sathupally, Near B.C. Hostel, Khammam Dist.–507303 ***Cell.No. 9393511537***	Plot No.122, H.No.3-138, Sathupalli, Khammam	100 + Helpline
23.		**Chaitanya Mahila Mandali,** Mamillagudem, Khammam Dist. ***Ph:9848183006***	No.10-2-36 Mamillagudem, Khammam Dist.	50 + Helpline
24.	**Warangal**	**Pragathi Seva Samithi,** # 2-5-578, KLN Reddy , Subedari, Hanumakonda, Warangal Dist. ***Ph.No. 0870 –2550659, 2540851*** ***Fax – 0870-2540979*** ***Mail ID: info@pragathisevasamithi.org***	2-5-279 Nakkalagunta, Hanumakonda, Warangal Dist.	50 + Helpline
25.	**Adilabad**	**Society for Urban and Rural Enlightenment (SURE),** Pulenagar, Bhainsa, Adilabad Dist. ***Ph.No. 08752-230056*** ***Cell No. 9849013297***	H.No.3-4-61/62#, Pulenagar Bhainsa, Adilabad Dist.	50

26.	**Ranga Reddy**	**Development Organization for Village Environment (DOVE),** Adm. Office 1-92/2/A, Prabhath Nagar Colony, Chaitanyapuri, Dilsukhnagar, Hyderabad ***Ph.No. 24057624*** ***Cell No. 9440418424***	4-7-2515, Manjara Pipeline Road, NGO colony, Ranga Reddy Dist.	50
27.		Kasturba Gandhi National Memorial Trust, Mahila and Vikasa Kendra, Hydershakote, Via Langerhouse, Hyderabad –8 ***Ph.No. 040-27140986 / 27801688*** ***Cell No. 9391011282*** ***Mail ID: kgnmthyd@yahoo.com***	Kasturba Gandhi National Memorial Trust, Hydershahkote Langarhouse, Hyderabad	50 + Helpline
28.		***Human Resource Development Society (HRDS)***, 8-7-96/61, Plot No. 61, PRTU Colony, Vysalinagar, B.N. Reddy Nagar, Sagar Road, Hyderabad, Ranga Reddy Dist. ***Ph.No. 040-23754367***	Plot No.58, PRTU Colony Vaisali Nagar, B.N. Reddy Nagar, Hyderabad-500079 (consisting of 2 Floors)	50
29.		Hyderabad City Women's Welfare Council, H.No. 7-140 / /2, S.S. Nagar, Street No. 8, Habsiguda, Ranga Reddy Dist. **Ph.No. 23754367, 23045774**	H.No.3-16-203/c/12, Venkat Reddy Nagar, Ramanthapur, Hyderabad-500013 AP	50 + Helpline
30.		Run by Government of Andhra Pradesh **Location of project at Kukatpally**	Kukatpally, Hyderabad Dist.	200 + 40 children

31.	**Hyderabad**	**Mahila Dakshata Samiti,** H.No. 8-3-430 / 1/ 21, NSC, Employees Society, Yellareddyguda, Ameerpet, Hyderabad ***Ph. No. 040-23732366*** ***(Anuradha- 9246214934)***	H.No.8-3-430/1/2 Yellareddyguda, Ammeerpet, Hyderabad AP	50
32.	**Nizamabad**	**Rural Infrastructure Development Organisation (RIDO),** Jadi Jamalpoor, Bodhan, Nizamabad Dist. ***Ph. No. 08467-2208864*** ***Cell No. 9440477017***	R.I.D.O, Plot No.157, Near Satyanarayana Swamy Temple Road, Boregam (P) Nizamabad Dist.	50
33.	**Mahaboob Nagar**	**Navodaya Seva Sangam,** 10-107, Netaji Road, Jadcherla, Mahaboobnagar ***Ph. No. 08542-202200***	Plot No. 104-105 and S.No. 74A, 74B, Balanagar, Mahabubnagar Dist.	50 + Helpline
34	**Nalgonda**	**Krushi Seva Samastha** Nalgonda ***Ph: 08683-237443***	Hauzar Nagar Mandal, Nalgonda Dist.	50

List of NGOs without Govt aids

List of NGOs working in the field of women in the state without receiving grants from Women Development and Child Welfare Department

S. No.	*District*	*Name of the Organisation*	*Address*	*Contact Details*
1.	**Ananthapur**	Rural and Environment Development Society (REDS)	#1-1160-1E, M.P, Ramachandra Reddy Building, M.P. Street, Kadiri-515591, Ananthapur District	Ms. C. Bhanuja - PresidentPh: 08494 - 223622Cell: 9440017188e-mail: bhanureds@yahoomail.com
2.		Society to Help Rural Empowerment and Education (STHREE)	Yerradoddi (Village & Post) Kadiri Mandal - 51592 Ananthapur District	Ms. Hema BediPh: 08494 - 200599 Cell: 9849866494 e-mail: sthree.india@rediffmail.com, hemabedi_pkd@yahoo.co.in Website: www.shtreeindia.org
3.	**Ranga Reddy**	Ashiritha	Plot No. 59, Jayanagar, New Bowenpally, Rangareddy District.	Ms. Pushpa Rani -President Cell: 9440011553
		Operation Mercy Charitable Company	Logos Bhavan Medchal Road, Jeedimetla Village Secunderabad, Andhra Pradesh 500 055	Phone: (+91) 40-2786-2786 Email: ceo@omccindia.org Visit: www.omccindia.org
4.		People Environmental & Action for Community Education (PEACE)	H.No. 2-29, Kachavani singaram, Ghatkesar Mandal, Ranga Reddy district.	Ms. G.V.L. Anuradha - Secretary, Ph: 040 - 27202977

5.	**Hyderabad**	Prajwala	# 20-4-34, III floor, Behind Charminar Bus stand, Hyderabad - 500 002.	Dr. Sunita Krishnan Ph: 040 - 24510290 Fax: 040 - 24410813 e-mail: praj_2010@yahoo.com Website: www.prajwalaindia.com
6.		Ankuram (Women & Child Development Society)	12-13-309, St.NO.19, Tarnaka,	Ms. M. Sumitra Ph: 040 - 27017446 Secendrabad– 500017 Fax: 040 - 27017447 e-mail: ankuram@yahoo.com Website: www.ankuram.org.in
7.		Tharuni	H.No. 27, Nagarjuna Colony, Near Champapet Cross Roads, Nagarjuna Sagar Road, Hyderabad - 500079	Dr. Mamata Raghuveer - Director Ph: 040 - 24072038 Cell: 9848145819 e-mail: tharuni@lycos.com, tharunisandhya@yahoo.com Website: www.tharuni.tripod.com
8.		Hyderabad Council of Human Welfare (HCHW)	12-2-790/56, Ayodhya Nagar Colony, Mehadipatnam, Hyderabd	Dr. Mahmad Rafiuddin - Director Ph: 040 - 23526554 / 55505827 Fax: 040 - 23526674 e-mail: hchw_in@hotmail.com
9.		Divya Disha	H.No.9-1-103/A, Tatachari Compound, Secendrabad - 500025	Mr. Philips Ph: 040 - 2700113 Fax: 040 - 27700113 e-mail: divyadisha@gmail.com Website: divyadisha.org
10.		MV Foundation	Flat No. 201, Narayan Apartments, West Maredupally, Secendrabad	Ms. Santha Sinha Ph: 040 - 27801320 / 27710150 / 27700290 Fax: 040 - 27808808 / 27701656 e-mail: mvfindia@gmail.com
11.		Human Action for Rural Development (HARD)	1-1-199/A/1, Chikkadapally, Alahabad Bank Opp. Lane, Hyderabad.	Mr. A. Jagannada Rao Ph: 040 – 27635264 Cell: 9849555356

12.		Sangamitra	Vasanthkunj, Plot No: 3 & 4A Bank colony, Jedimetla, Hyderabad.	Rev. Fr. John Vatamattam Ph: 040 – 23176353 / 2317654, Cell: 9894453732 / 9963024567
13.	**Chittoor**	Sree Sakthi Sanghatana - SSS	10-177, Navajeevan Colony, Opp. Viswam High School, Jeevakona, Tirupathi – 517507 Chittoor District.	Ms. T.Suseela (PCO) Ph: 0877 - 2282157 e-mail: ssstpt@inida.com
14.	**East Godavari**	Sravanthi Association	86-3-15/1, Shirdi Sai Marg, J.N.Road, Manthena Gardens, Rajahmundry, East Godavari District.	Ms. P.Annapurna - Exe. Secretary Ph: 0883 - 6557755 Fax: 0883 - 2461139 e-mail: sravanthi1992@yahoo.com
15.		Samata Vidya Vyavasaya Sankshema Sangham (SVASS)	Secretary SVAS, Alamuru, East Godavari.	Mr. G. Yesudas Ph: 08855 – 278993 Cell: 9866030171
16.	**Medak**	Society for Women Awareness and Rural Development (SWARD)	H.No.11-4-82/1/1, Opp. Area Govt. Hospital, Siddipet - 502103, Medak district.	Ph: 08457 - 231437 / 230605 Fax: 08547 - 228391 e-mail: sward_2k@rediffmail.com
17.	**Guntur**	Social Educational and Economic Development Society (SEEDS)	# 4-16-25/3, Bandlamudi Complex,Near Andhra Bank, Amaravathi complex, Guntur - 522002	Mr. Roshan Kumar - Secretary Ph: 0863 - 2351631/ 2238230 e-mail: seedsorg@yahoo.com
18.	**Prakasham**	Society for Help Entire Lower & Rural People (HELP)	2nd Lane, Sujatha Nagar, Lawyerpet Extn., Ongole - 520002	Mr. Rama Mohan - Secretary, Ph: 08592-221209 / 281738 / 270664 e-mail: helpap2002@yahoo.com Website: www.helpap.org, www.traffickingap.org
19.		Society for National Integration through Rural Development (SNIRD)	Railpet, Post Box - 24, Ongole -523001 Prakasham District	Mr. Jawahar Ph: 08592 - 2320008 e-mail: snird_org@yahoo.com

20.		Society Activities for Rural Development Society (SARDS)	Janachaitanya Nilayam,Kondapi road, Tangutur, Prakasham District.	Mr. R. Suneel Kumar Ph: 08592 – 242867 / 242342 Cell: 9912340222
21.		Chaitanya Development Society	Akbarpet, Bapatla, Prakasham District.	Mr. K. Siva Varaprasad Ph: 08594 – 248203Cell: 9849690657
22.	**Warangal**	Lodi Multipurpose Social Service Soceity (Lodi MSSS	Fathima nagar, Warangal - 506004	Fr. B. Leeno Reddy Ph: 0870 - 2459405 e-mail: lodimsss@redifffmail.com
23.	**Vizianagaram**	Community Development Centre	Chandana Street, Ramabhdrapuram, Vizianagaram.	Mr. S. Venkateswara Rao Ph: 08964 – 250036 Cell: 9866409596.
24.	**Nellore**	Jagruthi	27-1-1039, 11th Cross road, Puttavedhi centre, Balaji Nagar, Nellore.	Mr.T.Badrinarayana Ph: 0861- 2328171 Cell: 9849983749
25.	**Krishna**	Guide	74-24-17, Ashoknagar, Yarlagadda Apparao street, Vijayawada.	Mr. B. Venkateswara Rao Ph: 0866 – 6537391 Cell: 9849709394
26.	**West Godavari**	Action for Development	2-6-25, Ramaraopet, Tadepalligudem, West Godavari.	Mr. J. Suresh Kumar Ph: 08818 – 225396, 221241 Cell: 9848494333
27.		Shruthi	19-16-53 (A), Aravari Street, Near SBI colony, Bhimavaram, West Godavari.	Mr. A. Nageswara Rao Ph: 08816 – 232207 Cell: 9440539174
28.		Janakalyan Welfare Society	8-99, Durganagar, 2nd Street, Mallaipeta, Rajahmundry, W.G. Dist.	Mr. B. Nageswara Rao Ph: 0883 – 2442293 Cell: 9848320500

29.	**Visakhapatnam**	Rural Energy for Environment Development Society (REEDS)	27-99, Gandhinagar, Yelamanchili, Visakhapatnam.	Mr. O. Vidya Sagar Ph: 08931 – 231293 Cell: 9849946797
30.		Visakha Jilla Nava Nirman Samiti (VJNSS)	Sivaram Nilayam, Behind RTC Bus stop, Narsipatnam, Visakhapatnam.	Mr. Sri Raghuram Ph: 08924–235285 Cell: 9849594616
31.		Association for Rural Development & Action Research (ARDAR)	Flat No. G-10, 6-20-20/5, Sri Varshini Enclav - 1, Behind K.D.P.M. High School, East Point colony, Visakhapatnam - 530017	Dr. V.V.Ramana - Secretary Cell: 9440019036 e-mail: ardar_vvr@yahoo.com
32.		Centre for Environment and Development	Godicharla Post, Via Payakaraopet, Visakhapatnam.	Ms. G. Vijayalakshmi Ph: 9866187934 Cell: 934795364
33.		Grama Swarajya Samiti (GSS)	Guntapalli colony, Opp. Z.P. Guest House road, Payakaraopet, Visakhapatnam.	Mr. B. Ram Ph: 08854 – 645167 Cell: 9989016699
34.		Green Vision	# 31-31-22, Sai Baba Street, Dabagardens, Visakhapatnam - 530020	Dr. G. Prabhakar - Medical Director Ph: 0891 - 2559429 e-mail: greenvision@sify.com

Research Questionnaires

Interview Schedule I

(Victims of Trafficking)

Schedule No.:
Date:
Place:

Part A: Socio-demographic Profile

1. Name:
2. Age:
3. Marital Status (current):
   a. Unmarried
   b. Married
   c. Widowed
   d. Divorced
   e. Separated
   f. Any other (specify)
4. Status of children (current)
   a. Do you have any children? Yes/ No
   b. If yes, how many children do you have?
5. Religion:
   a. Hindu
   b. Muslim
   c. Christian
   d. Any other (specify)

6. Caste:
   a. General Category
   b. Scheduled Castes (SC)
   c. Scheduled Tribes (ST)
   d. Other Backward Classes (OBC)
   e. Any other (specify)
7. Details of Current Residence:
   a. Village
   b. Town/City
   c. Mandal
   d. District
   e. State
8. Educational Qualification:
   a. Illiterate
   b. Below 10th Standard
   c. Intermediate
   d. Graduate
   e. Post-Graduate
   f. Any other (specify)
9. Current occupation:
   a. Unemployed
   b. Student (specify)
   c. In training (specify)
   d. Salaried job (specify)
   e. Daily wage earner (specify)
   f. Self-employed (specify)
   g. Any other (specify)
10. If currently employed, what is your monthly earning (in Rupees)?

Part B: Life and Experiences as a Victim of Trafficking

11. What was your age at the time of trafficking:
12. What was your marital status?
    a. Unmarried
    b. Married
    c. Widowed
    d. Divorced

e. Separated

f. Any other (specify)

13. Did you have any children at the time of trafficking?
Yes/ No
14. If yes, how many children did you have at the time of trafficking?
15. What was the reason that led you into this situation (trafficking)?
    a. Personal reason
    b. Economic reason
    c. Wish to support family
    d. Don't know/ Cannot recall
    e. Cannot disclose
    f. Any other (specify)
16. How did you get in this situation?
    a. Through false promises of making money
    b. By deception (other than making money)
    c. By force
    d. Don't know/ Cannot recall
    e. Cannot disclose
    f. Any other (specify)
17. Did you know the person(s) who led you into this situation?
Yes/ No/ Cannot say
If yes, how did you know the person(s)?
18. What methods did the traffickers use to:
    a. Control your life, mobility and earnings
    b. Recruit you further to work for themselves/ others
    c. Any other form of exploitation (specify)
19. At the time of trafficking, were you aware of the kind of work you were going to do? Yes/ No/ Cannot say
If yes, was the nature of work the same as you were told earlier?
Yes/ No/ Cannot say
20. What was the nature of you work? (multiple choices)
    a. Economic- domestic (maid etc)
    b. Economic- industrial (labour work etc)
    c. Sexual (prostitution)
    d. Any other (specify)

    Please indicate whether your work included only economic work/ only sexual work/ both.

21. How long have you been in this situation (in years)?
22. How did you feel in this situation? Give some details.

    Please indicate if you ever feel any of the following:

    a. Your life is controlled by others- physically and psychologically. Yes/ No/ Cannot say
    b. You are abused- physically and psychologically. Yes/ No/ Cannot say
    c. You have no control on your earnings/ money. Yes/ No/ Cannot say
    d. Your health is in a poor condition. Yes/ No/ Cannot say
    e. You feel fear, depression and hopelessness. Yes/ No/ Cannot say
    f. You always feel in custody of others. Yes/ No/ Cannot say
    g. You feel unable to move freely (control on mobility). Yes/No/ Cannot say
    h. You worked in pitiable working conditions. Yes/ No/ Cannot say
    i. You worked against your wish. Yes/ No/ Cannot say
    j. You feel cheated/ deceived. Yes/ No/ Cannot say
    k. You feel exploited. Yes/ No/ Cannot say
    l. Any other feelings (specify)
23. Did you ever get an opportunity to meet your family members? Yes/ No/ Cannot say

    If yes, did you tell them about your situation? Yes/No

    If yes, what was their response?

Part C: Life and Experiences of Re-integration and Rehabilitation

24. At what age were you rescued?
25. Who rescued you:
    a. Self
    b. Police
    c. NGO
    d. Both police and NGO
    e. Individual social/ media activist
    f. Any other (specify)

26. Life at the shelter home:
    - a. Are you still living in the shelter home? Yes/ No

    If no, then how long did you stay in the residential shelter home?
    - b. Were/ are your daily basic needs provided in the shelter home? Yes/ No

    Also indicate separately for the following:
    - i. Food Yes/ No
    - ii. Clothing Yes/ No
    - iii. Bedding Yes/No
    - iv. Toiletries Yes/ No
    - v. Hygiene Yes/ No
    - vi. Medical facilities Yes/ No
    - vii. Safety Yes/ No
    - viii. Recreational activities Yes/No
    - ix. Any other (specify).
27. How was/ is your relationship with inmates?
    - i. Feel comfortable with others
    - ii. Feel uncomfortable with others
    - iii. Feel isolated/ alienated from others
    - iv. Feel indifferent towards others
    - v. Cannot say
    - vi. Any other (specify)

      Give some more details on your relationship with inmates, in terms of cordial terms, fights, care-giving etc.
28. Skills and training:
    - a. Have you received any vocational skills and training at shelter home? Yes/ No
    - b. If yes, what skills did you learn? Specify.
    - c. If yes, do you think that learning of these skills is/ will be useful to you? Yes/ No
    - d. Are you satisfied with your skill training? Yes/ No/ Cannot say
    - e. Are you using your skills to earn some money? Or in case if you are still learning it, do you intend to use your skills to earn money in the future? Yes/ No/ Cannot say

29. Counselling, Financial Aid and Other Forms of Assistance:
    a. Have you received any counselling, financial aid and assistance in any form? Yes/ No/ Cannot say
30. If yes, please specify the forms of assistance that you have received:
    a. Psychological counselling
    b. Financial aid
    c. Medical aid
    d. Assistance in vocational training
    e. Assistance in employment
    f. Any other (specify)
31. What are the sources of your assistance? (multiple choices)
    a. Government
    b. NGO
    c. Community members
    d. Any other (specify)
32. How have you used your aids and assistance? Give details.
    a. Are you satisfied with the aids and assistance that you have received? Yes/ No/ Cannot say
33. Are you aware of any governmental aid for trafficked women? Yes/ No/ Cannot say

    If yes, have you availed this aid? Yes/ No

    If yes, can you disclose how much aid did you receive? Yes/ No

    Give amount (in Rupees)
34. Awareness of HIV-AIDS :
    a. Are you aware of HIV-AIDS? Yes/ No/ Cannot say

    If yes, have you ever got yourself tested for HIV/ AIDS? Yes/ No

    If yes, what was the outcome of your test for HIV-AIDS?

    b. Are you aware of STDs? Yes/ No/ Cannot say

    If yes, have you ever got yourself tested for STDs? Yes/No

    If yes, what was the outcome of your test for STDs?
35. Health and medical aid and facilities:
    a. Do you get health check-ups and/ or treatments on a regular basis? Yes/ No

36. Who helps in your health check-ups and/or treatments?
    a. NGO
    b. Police
    c. State/ Government
    d. Any other (specify)
37. In what ways do you receive help:
    a. Medical aid Yes/ No
    b. Health counselling Yes/ No
    c. Medications Yes/ No
    d. Any other (specify)
38. Re-integration with family and community:
    a. How do you feel about being re-integrated with your family and community?
    b. Comfortable
    c. Un-comfortable
    d. Isolated/ alienated
    e. Indifferent
    f. Cannot say
    g. Any other (specify)
39. Do you ever feel any constrains and problems due to the fact that you have been a victim of trafficking? Yes/ No/ Cannot say

    If yes, explain some major constrains and problems that you face.

    What do you do to overcome these constrains and problems?
40. Do you feel any particular constrains due to the fact that you are a woman? Yes/ No/ Cannot say

    If yes, explain some major constrains.

    What do you do to overcome these constrains?
41. Do following people around you know that you were a victim of trafficking?
    a. Family members Yes/ No/ Cannot say
    b. Neighbours Yes/ No/ Cannot say
    c. Friends Yes/ No/ Cannot say
    d. Community members Yes/ No/ Cannot say
    e. Fellow workers (in case of employment) Yes/ No/ Cannot say
    f. Any other (specify) Yes/No/ Cannot say

42. How is the general attitude of people towards you?
    a. Friendly
    b. Unfriendly
    c. Helping
    d. Non-helping
    e. Any other (specify)
43. How is your general attitude towards people around you?
    a. Friendly
    b. Unfriendly
    c. Helping
    d. Non-helping
    e. Any other (specify)
44. Do you think that the following can assist in the process of re-integration of the victims? Comment for each of them separately.
    a. Community members Yes/ No
    b. Police Yes/ No
    c. NGO Yes/ No
    d. Media Yes/ No
    e. Legal system Yes/ No
45. Overall, do you feel satisfied with your life at present?
    Yes/ No/ Cannot say

    Give reasons for any of your answers and your overall experience as a victim of human trafficking and life after re-integration in general.

Interview Schedule II

The Police

Schedule No.:
Date:
Place:

Part A: Socio-demographic Profile

1. Name:
2. Age:
3. Marital Status:
    g. Unmarried
    h. Married
    i. Widowed
    j. Divorced
    k. Separated
    l. Any other (specify)
4. Religion:
    e. Hindu
    f. Muslim
    g. Christian
    h. Any other (specify)
5. Caste:
    f. General Category
    g. Scheduled Castes (SC)
    h. Scheduled Tribes (ST)
    i. Other Backward Classes (OBC)
    j. Any other (specify)
6. Details of Current Residence:
    f. Village
    g. Town/ City
    h. Mandal
    i. District
    j. State

7. Educational Qualification:
   g. Illiterate
   h. Below 10th Standard
   i. Intermediate
   j. Graduate
   k. Post-Graduate
   l. Any other (specify)
8. Professional details:
   a. Name of your department:
   b. Year of joining:
   c. What is your specialisation?
   d. Total tenure of your service till date (in years)
   e. What is your current designation?
   f. How long have you been in the current designation (in years)?
   g. Monthly income (in Rupees):

Part B: Perception and Experience of the Police with cases of Human Trafficking

9. Experience with cases of human trafficking:
   a. Have you ever dealt with any cases of human trafficking? Yes/ No
   b. If yes:
   i. Are you dealing with any case of human trafficking at present? Yes/ No
   ii. How many cases of human trafficking have you dealt with so far?
   iii. Of these, how many cases were related to women trafficking alone?
   iv. Are all the victims from India? Yes/ No
   If no, how many victims are from other countries?
   How many women victims are from other countries?
10. Have you received any training on how to identify and respond to the cases of human trafficking?
   a. Training on cases of human trafficking in general? Yes/ No/ Cannot say
   b. Training on cases of women trafficking in particular? Yes/No/ Cannot say

c. Training on cases of children, including young girls, in particular? Yes/No/Cannot say

11. Your understanding of trafficking:
    a. Do you think that human trafficking is a violation of human rights?
    b. Are you aware of anti-trafficking laws such as SITA and ITPA in India? Comment.
    c. In what ways do you think human trafficking differs from drugs and arms smuggling?
    d. In what ways do you perceive trafficking of women (in terms of suffering, impact etc.)?
12. How can the Police department successfully address a case of human trafficking? Comment.
13. In what ways do you think that NGOs and community members can assist with a case of human trafficking? Comment.
    a. Role of NGOs
    b. Role of community members
14. Problem of human trafficking in your vicinity:
    a. How many cases of human trafficking were reported in your vicinity in the last one year?
    b. Of these, how many cases were reported on women trafficking alone?
    c. Have the police made any arrests involving agents human trafficking in your vicinity?

    If yes, how many arrests were made in the last one year?

    d. Have the police rescued any victims of human trafficking in your vicinity?

    If yes, how many victims were rescued in the last one year?

    Of these victims, how many women were rescued?

    e. Have the cases of human trafficking increased or decreased in past one year?
       Increased/ Decreased/ Cannot say
15. Addressing the issue of human trafficking:
    a. Do you think that the police in your vicinity is fairly aware of and concerned about cases of trafficking?
       Yes/ No/ Cannot say
    b. Do you think that the police in your vicinity deals with cases of trafficking in an efficient manner? Yes/ No/ Cannot say

c. Do you think that the police in your vicinity is adequately trained to deal with cases of trafficking?
Yes/ No/ Cannot say

d. Do you think that the police in your vicinity has adequate resources to identify cases of human trafficking?
Yes/ No/ Cannot say

e. Do you think that the police in your vicinity has adequate resources to investigate cases of human trafficking?
Yes/ No/ Cannot say

f. Do you think that the police in your vicinity has support and cooperation from the police in other places in dealing with the cases of human trafficking?
Yes/ No/ Cannot say

g. Do you think that the police enacts upon alerts from NGOs/ community leaders/ media and other possible sources on identification of human trafficking? Yes/ No/ Cannot say

Part C: Role of the Police in Re-integration and Rehabilitation of Trafficked Persons/ Women

16. Do you think that re-integration and rehabilitation of trafficked persons benefits them? Yes/ No/ Cannot say

17. Do you think that the police plays a key role in the re-integration of rescued victims of trafficking? Yes/ No/ Cannot say

    If yes, list some ways in which police assists in the re-integration process? Give examples.

18. Do you think that community members, NGO, media and legal system can assist in the process of re-integration of the victims? Comment for each of them separately.

    f. Community members Yes/ No
    g. NGO Yes/ No
    h. Media Yes/ No
    i. Legal system Yes/ No

19. Describe your overall experience with issue of human trafficking in general and women trafficking in particular.

Interview: Schedule III

NGO's (Non Government Organisations) Social Activists/ C.B.O.'s (Community Based Organisations)

Schedule No.:

Date:

Place:

Part A: Socio-demographic Profile

1. Name: Designation
2. Age:
3. Marital Status:
   - Unmarried
   - Married
   - Widowed
   - Divorced
   - Separated
   - Any other (specify)
4. Religion:
   - Hindu
   - Muslim
   - Christian
   - Any other (specify)
5. Caste:
   - General Category
   - Scheduled Castes (SC)
   - Scheduled Tribes (ST)
   - Other Backward Classes (OBC)
   - Any other (specify)
6. Details of Current Residence:
   - Village
   - Town/ City
   - Mandal
   - District
   - State

7. Educational Qualification:
   - Illiterate
   - Below 10th Standard
   - Intermediate
   - Graduate
   - Post-Graduate
   - Any other (specify)
8. Any training in social work (PG/ Diploma in social work; specify)
9. Organisation Profile:
   - Name of your NGO/ Organisation
   - Location
   - Year of establishment of NGO/ Organisation
   - Name of the current Head of NGO/ Organisation
   - Main thrust areas of NGO/ Organisation
10. Professional information:
11. Year of joining this NGO/ Organisation
12. How long have your been working with this NGO/ Organisation?
13. What is your current designation?
14. Monthly income (in Rupees)
15. Part B: Perception and Experience of Social Activists with cases of Human Trafficking
16. Experience with cases of human trafficking:
17. Have you ever dealt with any cases of human trafficking? Yes/ No
18. If yes:
19. Are you dealing with any case of human trafficking at present? Yes/ No
20. How many cases of human trafficking have you dealt with so far?
21. Of these, how many cases were related to women trafficking alone?
22. Are all the victims from India? Yes/ No
23. If no, how many victims are from other countries?
24. How many women victims are from other countries?
25. Your understanding of trafficking:
26. Do you think that human trafficking is a violation of human rights?

27. Are you aware of anti-trafficking laws such as SITA and ITPA in India? Comment.
28. In what ways do you think human trafficking differs from drugs and arms smuggling?
29. In what ways do you perceive trafficking of women (in terms of suffering/ impact etc)?
30. How can an NGO help to successfully build a human trafficking case? Comment.
31. In what ways do you think that police and community members can assist with a human trafficking case?
    - Role of police
    - Role of community members
32. Your interaction with victims of trafficking:
33. Do you interact with victims of trafficking on a regular basis? Yes/ No
34. Do you share a good rapport with these victims? Yes/ No
35. Do you face any difficulties during your interactions with victims? Yes/ No
36. If yes, can you list some major difficulties in your interactions with them?
37. Language barrier Yes/ No
38. Lack of time Yes/ No
39. Lack of privacy/ spatial issues Yes/ No
40. Shyness/ inhibitions on the part of the victims Yes/ No
41. Victims are not able to express themselves freely Yes/ No
42. Victims get re-traumatised during the course of interactions Yes/ No
43. Difficulty due to gender differences between the activist and the victims? Yes/No
44. Any other difficulty (specify)
45. What methods and interview techniques do you use in order to build trust and prevent re-traumatisation of a victim? Explain.
46. **Part C: Role of NGO/ Organisation in Re-integration and Rehabilitation of Trafficked Persons/ Women**
47. Do you think that re-integration and rehabilitation of trafficked persons benefits them?
    - Yes/ No/ Cannot say

48. Do you think that NGOs play a key role in the process of re-integration of trafficked persons? Yes/ No
49. If yes, list some ways how NGOs help in the re-integration process? Give example of your NGO.
50. Do you think that community members, police, media and legal system can assist in the process of re-integration of the victims? Comment for each of them separately.
    - Community members Yes/ No
    - Police Yes/ No
    - Media Yes/ No
    - Legal system Yes/ No
51. In your opinion, what are the major requirements of trafficked persons' re-integration and rehabilitation? Do women victims have special requirements? Comment.
52. How do NGOs assist in providing for victims' requirements in order to re-integrate them?
53. Do you think that NGOs play a vital role in providing for victims' health requirements?
    - Yes/ No/ Cannot say
54. If yes, list some of the ways in which NGOs provide for victims' health requirements.

    Describe your overall experience with issue of human trafficking in general and women trafficking in particular.

Index

Y